Allman Joy

MUSIC AND THE AMERICAN SOUTH

ALLMAN JOY

Keeping the Beat with Duane and Gregg Allman

Bill Connell

with John Lynskey

MERCER UNIVERSITY PRESS

Macon, Georgia

MUP/ P675

© 2023 by Mercer University Press
Published by Mercer University Press
1501 Mercer University Drive
Macon, Georgia 31207
All rights reserved

27 26 25 24 23   5 4 3 2 1

Books published by Mercer University Press are printed on acid-free paper
that meets the requirements of the American National Standard for
Information Sciences—Permanence of Paper for Printed Library Materials.

Printed and bound in the United States.

This book is set in Adobe Caslon Pro.

Cover/jacket design by Burt&Burt.

ISBN   978-0-88146-900-4
    Cataloging-in-Publication Data is available from the Library of Congress

This book is dedicated to my two loving sons:

Braxton Finlay Connell

Nathan William Connell

IN MEMORY OF:

Duane Allman

Gregg Allman

Bob Keller

Eddie Hinton

Tippy Armstrong

Johnny Sandlin

Roger Hawkins

Jimmy Johnson

Barry Beckett

Ray Honea

Joe Rudd

Pete Carr

Johnny Wyker

Rodney Davis

Scott Boyer

John D. Loudermilk

Chet Atkins

Glen Campbell

Roy Orbison

Charlie Daniels

CONTENTS

Jeff Craig was the co-author of two of my books; *Between Rock and a Home Place* and *Growing a Better America*, but soon became a close and dear friend. Jeff had an outstanding career as a journalist in Canada, first making a name for himself at the *Edmonton Sun*. He also was a true lover of music, and became a fine guitarist in his own right. Jeff was excited and pleased to be involved with telling Bill's story, and made great contributions to the early stages of *Allman Joy*, before a tragic accident took him from us way too soon. John and I appreciate all Jeff did to make this book a reality—he will be sorely missed.

—Chuck Leavell

Bill Connell and Chuck Leavell with the original manuscript
to *Allman Joy*. Tuscaloosa, Alabama, September 2022.

Courtesy Bill Connell; photo by Jackie Sullivan

FOREWORD

by
Chuck Leavell

Bill Connell was one of the few natural drummers I've ever heard. From the first touch of the skins that I heard him play, he blew me away. On top of that, he was only seventeen years old at the time, in 1966, not long after he had hooked up with Gregg and Duane Allman. I first saw him at the Fort Brandon Armory in Tuscaloosa, Alabama, with the Allman Joys. I was a thirteen-year-old fledgling musician in my own band, the Misfitz, and had heard of the Joys from some other musicians touting how good they were...and Lord, were they! Gregg and Duane were the front men, with Gregg playing a Vox Continental organ and singing with what even back then was a strong and unique blue-eyed, Southern soul voice, and Duane playing guitar like some kind of possessed angel. Both were amazing and I'd never heard anything quite like it. But as great as the two of them were, Bill's drumming was equally impressive. Plus they all looked *sooo* cool! They were all long-haired, skinny cats who wore very hip garb and just had "The Look" that the rest of us musicians aspired to. I didn't actually meet Bill until a year or so later and unfortunately never got to play with him. But I always admired his natural talent and, when I did get to know him, found him to be a fun and gracious soul.

In more recent times, Bill told me that he had written down some memories from those early days with Gregg and Duane and asked what I thought about him putting a book together. I jumped at the idea and was happy to assist him in making that happen. I suggested he send what he had to my friend J. Marshall "Jeff" Craig, who had helped me with two of my own books. Jeff did some good initial work with Bill on the project, but fairly early in the process, Jeff had a most unfortunate accident in a fall, which caused his demise. That created a pause in the effort and, as Jeff and Bill had become good friends, was a shock and heavy blow to all of us. But after a time, I encouraged Bill to continue and suggested he approach my friend John Lynskey, an excellent writer and historian of all things Allman for help.

John and Bill hit it off beautifully and the work continued. Along with Bill, Jeff, John, and me, some friends from the "old days" in Alabama—Jack Leigh, Jim Harrison, Rush Smith, Mark Harrelson, and Fred Styles—also supported the effort, financially as well as "spiritually." Together, and after quite a lot of work and back-and-forth on the script, the first draft of the manuscript was done. Our friends at Mercer University Press—Dr. Marc Jolley and Marsha Luttrell—read it and immediately signed on to publish it, realizing the importance of the history of those early days that eventually led to the forming of The Allman Brothers Band.

Then something totally unexpected and tragic happened. Bill suddenly passed away in his home before the book was finalized and released. It was another shock and very sad to all of us that he never got to see the finished product and know that his story was out in the world. But the good news is that he was able to hold the initial manuscript in his hands. He was so happy and excited about it.

This is Bill's story—a wonderful, fun, engaging, and interesting journey of a talented young man just out of high school who hooked up with some guys who would eventually become icons of the rock-music world. Bill's memory of events was strong and the experiences he recounted are colorful. While he eventually slid out of the music scene for other adventures, I am forever grateful for his friendship and for inspiring me to continue my own musical journey. The tales within these pages reflect a life well lived as a young and beautifully blessed talent. RIP, my friend...thanks for helping pave the way for so many of us.

1

Welcome to the Allman Joys

Okay, it's 5:00 in the morning, and I can't lie here any longer. That's what I did all night because I was too excited to sleep. I still find it unbelievable that Duane and Gregg Allman sent me the plane ticket, but they had promised it would be waiting after I graduated from high school, and it was. Last night's graduation took its sweet time coming, but now it was finally over. "You have a long day ahead of you, son," I told myself, "so get yourself up and get your butt in the shower...now!"

I keep relishing the continuing thought: "Who else in my graduating class is flying to New York City to play in the greatest rock and roll band ever? No one—nada más!"

Oh yeah—and now I don't ever have to listen to Principal Greer and my teachers badger me to get a haircut again—I can grow it down to my ass now. How can those people have the power to tell someone when to get their hair cut, anyway? Even though he never taught me, Mr. Patrick was the worst. Every day he would find me in the lunch line and try to put a bow in my hair.

In my other bands, I went to the gig, played the gig, and then went back home. But playing with these guys wouldn't be just another gig—it was a lifestyle! With the Allman Joys, I was going to be living with the band full time on the road, 24/7.

I put on my sharkskin, Sunday-go-to-meetin' suit after my shower. My folks thought that a suit would be the nice thing to wear for arriving in New York City for a new job. Pooh! I had already seen what was hip for a New York City band to wear, and my church suit wasn't it! My parents were a little upset that I was leaving, though, so I had to respect their opinion and humor them a little bit, you know? So I decided to wear the suit since I knew they were worried about their seventeen-year-old baby boy leaving home to work in the Big Apple.

The whole family—my mom, dad, brother, and grandparents—were there at the Tuscaloosa airport to see me off. They were looking rather sad at seeing me leave this laid-back community the morning after I graduated. We hugged, and I headed to the small two-prop Southern Airways plane. Hot damn! I'm going to be playing in New York City way before I thought I would, and I didn't have to read drum music. I'm living my dream of being a professional drummer who's going to be living and playing in NYC and other states—and maybe the world. I'm only seventeen...blow me over with a feather. This move to New York City is beyond exciting!

There must have been a visual glow around me while I was walking to the plane. I just might be the first teenager from West Alabama who would become famous without being a football star. All the glory around here is given to a few young athletes on the Alabama Crimson Tide football team. The team hadn't won a national title since 1941, and now they've won three in the last four years under Coach Paul "Bear" Bryant and with the leadership of star quarterback Joe Namath. Joe was heading to play for the New York Jets; Namath's life had sure turned around quickly in the last several years, and my life seemed to be doing the same thing.

It's kind of strange: Joe Namath had been recruited from his high school in the little town of Beaver Falls, Pennsylvania, to play for Alabama, and now he was moving to New York. Ironically, I was recruited from the small city of Tuscaloosa in Alabama to play with Duane and Gregg Allman in New York City. See ya in the Big Apple, Joe!

Now, the thing is, growing up, and even until my teens, I was one small, skinny dude. Soaking wet I might have weighed 110 pounds by the time I was in high school. Even if I'd begun to shoot up and fill out, I didn't relish getting brutalized playing football to get the attention of the ladies. So, fortunately, long before getting to high school, I took an interest in music and playing drums.

2

Most everyone who graduated last night with me was either going on to college or directly into the workforce. A great number of them would likely be landing a job at one of the larger businesses in Tuscaloosa, such as B. F. Goodrich Tire Company, Gulf States Paper Corporation, or the largest employer, the University of Alabama. Unfortunately, a few would be heading into the armed forces and probably over to Vietnam.

Tuscaloosa had been very good to me; I don't think my musical achievements could've been reached anywhere else. The University of Alabama brought in thousands of national and international students, all blessed with different talents, especially music. The large number of musicians made it possible for a couple of music stores to prosper.

The Lively Music Store was instrumental in giving me the start at playing drums. I progressed from simple drum lessons to playing in the Lively Music Store Swing Band. I was startled when the Lively Band's conductor slyly asked me to fill in for their drummer one weekend. He said that they could pay me twenty-five dollars...*twenty-five dollars*! Holy moly. It was my first paying gig. Their song list consisted of Dixieland and dance-band music, and after playing in the Lively Music Swing Band, I fit right in.

It wasn't long before I was vaulted into playing in a college rock and roll group called the Pacers. I couldn't have reached these achievements without the comradery among all my great musician friends. One friend, guitarist Tippy Armstrong, even calls Tuscaloosa a "Mecca for Musicians." So true; per capita, I bet there could be more good musicians in this small blip on the map than anywhere else on earth.

The Allman Joys' offer was wild: Duane and Gregg's promise to fly me to New York City—the day after my high school graduation—was serious as a heart attack. It was actually kind of mind-boggling. I'm going to be playing with a few of the only musicians that I've ever known who keep their promise and are generous, too. Damn; what other band would be paying for my flight to New York

City? The local musicians that I know would not have that amount of money, anyway. I couldn't wait to start playing with them.

As I sat on the plane waiting to take off, I flashed back on how I'd first met Duane and Gregg Allman...

It was the summer of 1965, and my band, the Nightcaps, had Sunday night off after playing the matinee show that afternoon at the Casino on Dauphin Island, Alabama. We'd all seen the posters plastered around announcing a huge R & B concert at the Mobile Auditorium that Sunday night. The show had Otis Redding, Sam and Dave, Joe Tex, Billy Stewart, and many other great R & B artists. Two other band members—Tippy Armstrong and John Townsend—decided to go with me, and when we came into the auditorium, the show had already started. Our first surprise was seeing that we were the only white people there—or so we thought!

Then it was like we spotted each other at the same time. Over across the auditorium were these other three young white guys, all with long hair—much, much longer than ours. They were looking over at us as if asking themselves the same question that we were: "Are those guys musicians and in a band, too?"

In 1963, the Beatles had exploded onto the pop-music scene with an incredible new style of rock music. Along with their huge hit records, they also introduced a revolutionary change in how men would wear their hair and how they would dress. There was no more grease—their hair was a lot longer and cleaner. This "pudding bowl" haircut hadn't quite caught on yet with men in the States, other than with some musicians. When you saw a man with clean, longer hair, we thought he was most likely a musician, and that was certainly the case here. We approached each other with big smiles, glad to see that we were not the only white guys who appreciated soul music. The guy with the long, reddish-blond hair spoke first: "Great show, huh? You dudes play?"

Johnny replied, "Yeah, we're playing down on Dauphin Island at the Casino."

The guy said, "Well, it's great to run into some other musicians. We're from Daytona Beach and have a gig here in Mobile at the

Stork Club. I'm Duane Allman; I play guitar. This is Bob Keller, our bass player, and our drummer, Maynard Portwood. My brother Gregg plays with us, too, but he drifted over to New Orleans to meet some gal."

Johnny said, "Alright then. I'm Johnny Townsend, and I'm the singer. This is Tippy Armstrong, our guitar player, and Bill Connell, our drummer. We're from Tuscaloosa, and our band's name is the Nightcaps."

Duane said, "Well, great to meet you, Nightcaps from Tuscaloosa. We call ourselves the Allman Joys. I'd like to catch your act. When do you play on Dauphin Island?"

I spoke up and said, "We play weekends: Friday and Saturday nights plus a Sunday afternoon matinee."

Duane replied, "We play every damn night but Sunday at the Stork Club. They have us playing six, maybe seven fuckin' sets a night."

Johnny said, "Shit! We just do four sets a night and then the Sunday matinee. Do y'all play Sunday afternoons?"

"Nope," Duane said.

Johnny asked, "Well, why don't you all come down next Sunday afternoon when we're playing?"

"Deal," was Duane's simple response.

We were all surprised; these were the first musician friends we'd made here, and this was also the first big R & B show for all of us. We soaked in the music and carried away some lessons learned.

The Nightcaps returned to Tuscaloosa the next day, and the following Friday night we were back playing Dauphin Island. We had told the other band members about meeting the Allman Joys. When we finished that Friday night, Doug Hogue, our bass player, said that he was going over to Mobile to scout around for some clubs and was planning to drop by the Stork Club to listen to a set of the Allman Joys.

It must have been about three in the morning when we heard Doug drive up. We were all still awake and shooting the breeze. He busted in the door and was ecstatic, with a big grin on his face. "The Allman Joys aren't your run-of-the-mill rock and roll band," he said. "These guys are as good as any of the new acts out there! Their harmony is the best I've ever heard. They do all kinds of material, and every song is perfect. They do them better than the original artists and dress in top-of-the-line Beatle-style suits. I'm taking you guys to see them after we finish tomorrow night. They play real late, so we have plenty of time to catch them. Be ready for the surprise of your life."

After finishing Saturday night, our entire band headed straight to the Stork Club. When we entered the door of the club, we were hit by the greatest sounding four-piece rock band that we'd ever heard. Doug was right—this band was very hot! I mean *very hot*!

The club was packed, so we made our way to the back and stood because there was not one chair available—it was standing-room only. Our understanding was that Duane's brother, Gregg, would be singing and playing rhythm guitar. We hadn't met Gregg yet, but we quickly saw that he was also sporting long hair that was ultra-blond. Doug told us to expect them to be wearing suits like the Beatles, and they were. Their suits were well tailored and impressive and must have cost them a chunk of change.

Although Gregg was singing most of the lead vocals, each one of the four could sing lead, and together they all sang superior harmony. Their repertoire included tunes by the Four Tops, the Temptations, Little Anthony and the Imperials, and other rhythm and blues artists. They also jumped into songs by the Beatles, the Rolling Stones, and several other British groups. Doug was right: they played all these songs better than the records—it didn't matter if it was R & B or British rock.

Duane's guitar work sounded as seasoned as a professional guitarist twice his age—it was astonishing for a nineteen-year-old. Bob, the bass player, was a real showman. He was always smiling, moving, and dancing while playing and singing. He inspired their audience, like James Brown would say, to get on up. The drummer, Maynard, was right in the pocket and jumped in on vocals, which really enhanced their great four-part harmony, while Gregg's lead singing was as seasoned as Duane's guitar work. It was as if Gregg and Duane had been performing for decades yet they were still only in their teens. They both must have listened to hours of R & B and soul music. Gregg's voice had a certain distinction that stuck in my head long after hearing him that night.

While Gregg was the featured vocalist on most of the tunes, Duane and the others sang lead on a few. What a mindblower it was when Duane sang "Ol' Man River" by the Righteous Brothers. Here stands this very thin guy singing so low—it blew our minds! Duane also took front and center between songs and handled all the microphone work: he announced songs, recognized birthdays and anniversaries, took requests, and introduced the band members.

During the fifteen-minute set breaks, we all got together and shot the breeze, mostly about music. Our band couldn't say enough about how knocked out we were with their band. We complimented them on everything—the songs they had chosen to perform, their great arrangements, four-part harmony, right down to the clothes they were wearing. Both of our group's musical mentors were similar, but boy, did they ever have a huge leap over us for replicating records. We discussed various rhythm and blues artists and their songs, the recent introduction of British rock, and the current American evolution of rock and roll.

Gregg and Duane had somewhat different personalities. Offstage, Duane was much like he was onstage—talkative, always smiling, super positive, and clearly the spokesman for the band. Duane was a born leader. Onstage, Gregg held the audience in the palm of his hand with his fantastic vocals, but offstage he was shy, not nearly as talkative as his brother. Gregg kept to himself, but both were humble about their God-given talents.

Those two brothers loved music more than any other musicians I had ever met, and each was eager to talk about anything to do with it. If I hadn't known them offstage, I could see why some in their audience might think they were stuck-up and standoffish, but that was not the case. Hell, they were much friendlier than most of the musicians in other bands that I knew. As a musician, being around them was refreshing and inspiring; I wanted to have their enduring love to play music and the desire to make it fun to hear.

The Vietnam War was escalating, so we all actively voiced concern over our uncertain futures regarding the draft. Since Duane's and Gregg's father had been murdered after World War II, their understanding was that one of them would be exempt from the draft. Duane emphasized that if one of them had to go, he would be the one to volunteer. He loved Gregg so much that he was all the more willing to take the fall—now that's real brotherly love.

The following Sunday, as we were playing the afternoon matinee, who popped up but Gregg and Duane, as they had promised. They watched and listened intently to our selection of R & B, blues, and rock, which we were grabbing from Muscle Shoals, Memphis, Philadelphia, and various Motown artists. We were doing songs from some of the same artists that they were drawing from.

After hearing the Allman Joys' harmonies the previous weekend, the Nightcaps were simply outgunned, but Duane and Gregg graciously clapped after each song we played. They were aware of how important it was for an audience to be supportive and courteous to a performing band, and their attentiveness and appreciation demonstrated that they were real gentlemen as well—mature Southern gentlemen. The thing is, I had no idea on that Sunday afternoon that I was actually being auditioned—not a clue!

The Allman Joys had one more job to play their last night in Mobile after completing their contract with the Stork Club. Their gig was playing for a large party at an apartment complex, after which they would be leaving for Daytona Beach. Wanting to hear them one more time, the Nightcaps drove to Mobile. Both bands had made some lasting friendships and knew that this might be the last time either group would see each other for a while.

...And this is how the Alabama Boys met the Daytona Beach Guys.

2

First Gig in New York

I didn't sleep on the small plane to Atlanta or on the jet up to New York, where the flight arrived exactly on time. Looking out the window, I saw not only Duane peering through the window of the gate, but also an entourage of ten or so of the most strangely dressed, long-haired people I had ever laid eyes on. Duane was right there as I stepped into the terminal, surrounded by his Greenwich Village friends.

"Billy!" he yelled. "I am *so* glad to see you!"

I was as thrilled as I was embarrassed. Somehow I had traveled from a world of conservative Southern dress and values to the land of blooming flower power in a matter of just a few hours. Back home, these folks would be arrested on sight—but now I was the one out of place.

"Damn!" Duane said, looking me over. "I'm taking you shopping in the morning to get you some new threads."

His entourage didn't seem to notice my lack of "cool "clothing. They welcomed me with big hugs and handshakes as if we'd known each other all our lives. I didn't see Gregg or Mike Alexander, the new bass player, but Duane said everyone else was anxiously waiting back at the hotel for my welcoming party.

I overheard one of the other passengers whispering to another, "Those are hippies! Look at them. You think they smell bad?"

Well, these hippies didn't! I noticed right off that they had several pleasant aromas about them. Later, I learned that one of their distinctive scents had become a favorite of Gregg's—patchouli oil. He'd buy it at head shops in the Village and dab it all over. It was a damned sight finer than the English Leather all the guys at home would wear under their button-down collars and khakis. Patchouli was to become the scent of the age, and thirty years later, Madonna insisted that her *Like a Prayer* album be scented with patchouli because she wanted it "to smell like the '60s."

I grabbed my bags and Duane asked about my drums. I told him they'd been shipped ahead and were at a freight storage place. We grabbed a cab and headed for my drums, which we barely managed to load into the trunk and most of the back seat.

The cabbie maneuvered through the city and entered Greenwich Village. After we were a few blocks in, I was hit suddenly by another strange odor, and this time it wasn't patchouli, and it wasn't the city's common foul smell of garbage or a strange food that I didn't recognize.

"What's that?" I asked.

Duane and the cabbie both let out a howl. "Somebody's smoking some herb, man."

I didn't get it. It wasn't any kind of herb that I smelled when my mom cooked back home. "What kind of herb?" I asked.

Duane had fun with this one. "It's weed, Novice. Pot...grass."

I had been almost disgustingly well-behaved all the way through high school, never having had an alcoholic drink or smoked a cigarette, much less "herb" to get high. In short order I learned what it was like to smoke to get high, and, as my quickly broadening mind learned, one of the reasons patchouli oil became so popular was because it helped hide the smell of weed.

The cab pulled in front of Trude Heller's, and suddenly Duane, the cabbie, my drums, and I all spilled out onto the sidewalk. All of us, cabbie included, entered the club.

To me, Maynard Portwood, the previous Allman Joys drummer, seemed to be a very likable dude and a good drummer. I felt a little bad about taking his job, but what was most on my mind was getting through this first night without getting fired. I had never even rehearsed with these guys.

Duane told me to set my drums up where Maynard's had been. "Then we'll head to the Albert," he said. "We don't have time for a practice."

Although Duane had consistently phoned during the last several months, giving me the tunes that I should learn, the reality of having to perform all those songs in just a few hours gave me an uneasy chill.

While setting up, I mentioned my nervousness, and Duane reassured me that the rest of the band would give me cues all the way along to help me with changes, accents, stops, and endings.

"Don't worry," he told me. "You've got a good idea of what we're playing. Just apply those great chops of yours, and you'll prevail."

Duane was right. I knew the tunes backwards and forwards. Sure, I'd been trying to keep my grades up to graduate, and I'd still been doing gigs with the Men-its, a local Tuscaloosa band, but every night, for months now, instead of going to sleep at night, I had been rehearsing for this moment, in my head.

The butterflies were floating away, but I was still rattled. Performing in front of a New York City audience was not going to be like playing in my hometown's Elks Club, the Sigma Nu house, or a high school prom. Then again, I was soon to learn that staying with a rock band in a Greenwich Village hotel was nothing like my hometown, either; as I entered the suite, three scantily clad hippie girls were laughing loudly and spraying shaving cream all over the room—walls and all!

Gregg was sitting in one of the living room chairs, calm but laughing just the same. Mike Alexander was prancing around the room and joking with the girls. He was the replacement for bassist Bob Keller, who had been let go a few months prior. Mike was an extremely talented musician and added a great deal onstage by being such a flamboyant showman. The guys told me, however, that offstage, Mike was a bit temperamental and unpredictable. At various times in the past he had gotten badly out of control, and Duane and Gregg said they found it difficult to forgive Mike or keep accepting his apologies.

I'd met Mike back in February in Tuscaloosa, but I'd never seen him play. He had a raspy voice and an earring in one ear—I'd never

11

seen a man with a pierced ear. He must be a good musician, I fig-ured, or else Duane wouldn't have hired him.

Gregg and Mike continued laughing at the girls going bonkers decorating the suite with shaving cream, but they soon saw the look on my face and realized my shock at the unexpected scene that I'd walked in on.

"Knock it off," Duane said, "so I can introduce you to our new drummer."

They instantly settled down after hearing Duane's tone. Duane was fun-loving and humorous, but he was always in charge. He used to slap Gregg upside the back of his head if he did something he didn't like; Gregg must have had calluses under all that hair because it happened so often. Gregg told me years later that just maybe he could have used a few more of those slaps over the years to come...

"This is Billy," Duane said. "Treat him with some saneness and respect. I mean, the most respect you can muster, or you'll all be outta here! You fuckin' hear me, damn it? Act right or you're outta here."

He sure as hell wasn't kidding. After few displays of bad man-ners and disrespect, Mike Alexander was fired a few months later. Duane brought Bob Keller back into the band, since the devil you know is better than the devil you don't know, right...?

Since I very obviously didn't have a thing to wear for my Green-wich Village rock and roll debut, everyone gathered around and be-gan sorting through the other band members' clothes for me. The band and girls tastefully dressed me in a white, blooming long-sleeved shirt and a pair of nice black bell-bottom pants, complete with a wide black mod belt.

Not having Beatle boots, as the others wore, I was forced to wear my Sunday-go-to-meeting shoes...just not cool. I kept re-minding myself that those ugly, horrible shoes wouldn't matter on-stage because my feet would be hidden behind the drums. That said, I was still kind of embarrassed. Beatle boots were a must if I wanted to blend in with the rest of the guys offstage, too.

Then I had one more "back home" chore to complete before showtime. Prior to getting on the plane, my parents had pleaded with me to call them once I arrived in New York. When things settled down and my stage clothes were set, I found a few spare minutes to call the long-distance operator, who finally got me through to my mom. She was relieved. We hung up, and I was on my way...

Duane had a policy for playing every night that I still carry today: "Watch and listen." He told me to watch the other band members and to really LISTEN to what they were playing. That lesson was absolutely invaluable. Duane was the most influential in pulling me through that first night, as well as the many nights and days ahead. Before each song was counted off, he set the tempo and reminded me how the song began, giving me cues for accents and stops and signaling when and how the tune was to end. He signaled with the neck of his guitar, his whole guitar, his head, and his feet and legs. His signaling while the band played may have been more entertaining than the Allman Joys stage show itself!

About the second or third set, I thought, "Damn, he's getting me through it!" Duane was not only an incredible guitar player, he was an amazing musical director, too. That first night confirmed the undisputed leader of the band was Duane Allman.

Now, all bands have songs that they can't conclude during a live performance like they sound on the album version. Some songs slowly fade out at the end, so musicians have to put a definite end on those tunes when they're playing them live. "Watch and listen, Novice!" Duane and Gregg were supportive all night, saying things like, "You're playing fine, everything's going great, don't be nervous, we'll get you through this." They just kept on giving comments of encouragement.

It worked. Mine was a debut to be proud of. This is not to say that my first performance with the Allman Joys was without shock value. One of the only things Duane hadn't told me about was that we were backing another entertainer on alternating forty-five-minute sets, a dude who called himself Monti Rock III. No amount of patchouli oil or, for that matter, weed could have prepared me for him. I think Duane didn't mention him because Monti was kind of beyond describing—for a seventeen-year-old from Alabama, anyway!

At first, he was just another guy who was obviously and proudly gay. Then he underwent a metamorphosis. He wore full makeup and outfitted himself in outlandish stage clothes, along with earrings, necklaces, rings, bracelets, and anything else that could adorn his body. As the band and I began to play the music to back his first set, Monti made a startling, over-the-top dramatic stage entrance...dancing, jumping, strutting, and bowing. A big ad at the front of the club featured an autographed professional photograph of him that was, just like Monti himself, larger than life and glossy. He was billed as a "must-see" showman and great singer. I can't say his voice was his strong suit, and I didn't have an inkling what his songs were or how to play them that first night, but I did my best.

Some people may remember Monti from his eighty-four appearances on *The Tonight Show Starring Johnny Carson* or, in later years, his appearances on his lifelong-fan Howard Stern's show. Monti's still going strong, fifty years later, with a career as an ordained minister who presides over weddings in Las Vegas. He's now the Very Reverend Monti Rock, but back then, he was the most openly gay and outlandish person I'd ever seen—not that I'd seen a lot of them in Tuscaloosa, Alabama, mind you. Nothing about Monti was in the closet. At the time, he was a celebrity hairdresser-turned-performer at his close friend Trude Heller's club, where he first caught the eye of Carson and later joined novelty acts like Tiny Tim, Mrs. Miller, and Charo on shows hosted by Mike Douglas and Merv Griffin. He ended up with a multimillion-selling disco hit, "Get Dancin'," and the role of the DJ in the blockbuster film *Saturday Night Fever*. Bless his big rainbow heart!

Trude Heller's was small, so small that numerous round tables had to be placed very close together in order to seat a maximum crowd. The club's size also forced the stage to be tiny, which left the band jammed together with absolutely no room to move. The club also was very dimly lit, with a bar at the back facing the stage.

The management liked both a good-spending crowd and one that turned over frequently. To run a club like this, most of the money was earned by selling a lot of booze followed by the collection of numerous cover charges. The music sets were arranged so that a customer could catch two different acts in two hours. Each set would last forty-five minutes, with a fifteen-minute break in between. During the break, the stage lights came down and background music was played, giving customers time to talk among themselves while ordering more drinks. The dressing room was a walk-in closet that the band squeezed into for our much-needed breaks.

After performing every night, we walked back to our hotel, first of all to save money, but also for a rehearsal of sorts without instruments because we continuously reviewed the songs and the sets we played.

That first night back at the hotel was the most alarming for me, however. The "Shaving Cream" girls were still there and would be spending the night, I was told. My bed assignment included a Shaving Cream girl.

Mine, as Duane and Gregg pointed out, had legs that were very large at the top and slim at the bottom. They kept whispering to me, "You have the one with 'the ice cream-cone legs.'" They just kept coming up, snickering, "You have the one with the ice cream-cone legs!"

A little while later, I got in bed next to this strange girl, and I couldn't have been more sexually dysfunctional if I tried. Hell, I was still a virgin, though of course I wasn't about to let the band or anyone else know that. From what I had overheard, they were all very sexually experienced. I was ultimately grateful that the "ice cream-cone lady" was not going to be my first—I would never have heard the end of it!

The next morning, Duane's first words to me were, "Billy, we're gonna go shopping. The band has chipped in $250 to spruce up your wardrobe, so let's go."

This was a lot of money in 1966—over a month's pay, if I was working a regular 9-to-5 job. They must have wanted me to play with them awful bad because they paid for my plane ticket up to New York and now were buying me new clothes after only one show. What's more, they told me I didn't have to pay them back one red cent for any of it. That was one generous band! Hell, my old bandmates would have made me pay them back if they had bought me a soft drink!

So, off we all went to the most out-of-sight clothing stores I'd ever seen. I bought blooming long-sleeved shirts, long-sleeved striped T-shirts, bell-bottomed jeans, bell-bottomed dress pants, and a couple of wide belts. Up here in the happening, mod, fashion scene, wearing long-sleeved shirts all year round was in style. I was living the dream, having all these new radical clothes—nothing like this could be purchased back home in Alabama. After I bought my high-heeled Beatle boots, Duane took me to a shop where he had the heels made even higher. He called them "stacked" heels. The new boots hurt my feet so much walking back to the hotel that I had to wear my sneakers to the club that night. When I got to the club, I changed into my new stacked heel boots to play, and the band got a real big hoot out of that.

"You're gonna get the hang of wearing your new boots shortly, Novice." Duane said. "Since you've never worn stacked heels, it's gonna take some time as a drummer to get adjusted to playing in them, too." He was right. Duane was pretty much always right.

During my second Allman Joys show, I had to make some feet-placement adjustments while working my bass drum and hi-hat pedal with such high heels. My feet would slide off the pedals occasionally during a song, so inconspicuously I had to be real creative to cover my mistakes when this happened. I became more and more confident very rapidly playing with those guys because of the caliber of their talent. Playing every day at rehearsals and for hours at night at the club gave me plenty enough time to continue developing my drumming chops. Rehearsals, especially with a band leader such as Duane Allman, were like going to advanced rock and roll and rhythm and blues dynamics classes. I was having so much fun that I couldn't wait for the next rehearsal and the next show. I was playing with the best rock and roll musicians I had ever known. They had the right stuff, and when you're musically challenged every day by "Best of," then you begin putting in every effort to play like a "Best of" too.

Musically, Duane inspired the band to stretch our boundaries tastefully, but he also insisted on "keeping the house in order," meaning to play the basic parts that we had rehearsed and keep the arrangement of each song intact. It was not acceptable to go off on some tangent and play parts that weren't meant to be in the song, but throwing in a small lick that improved and added to one of our arrangements was fine. One of Duane's codes was to "salute" someone for trying his best to improve a part, but to "help" them if the change didn't add anything complimentary to the song.

My playing soared—I didn't even get in a small rut. If I flubbed an accent or a stop, I'd ask to go over it at the next rehearsal and that would be it. Duane never got on to me for mistakes. For me, he knew, it was punishment enough just knowing I'd made a mistake.

When I first met them in Mobile, Duane captured my attention as being in charge. There was no doubt Duane and Gregg were a team, but Duane took care of the group's business. Once I was a member, early on I recognized that he took all the booking calls, negotiated payments for the gigs, accounted for the members' income and expenses, managed the band's accommodations, held the rehearsals together, stepped up to handle any complications that might arise, and maintained the group's day-to-day activities. He kept the band on course musically, but also logistically as well.

Gregg sometimes had a lot to say about everything we did, too, but his talent was truly in the selection of tunes and as the director of arrangements, since he had to sing almost all the lead vocals. It will not come as a surprise to anyone to hear that even back in the spring and summer of 1966, not one song we ever considered at rehearsals was beyond Gregg's capabilities. From where I sat behind the players, Gregg's vocals were always incredible and delivered with superior confidence. He did not even need a vocal monitor—he was a master.

I also never heard Gregg throw in the towel on a performance, or even a rehearsal, for that matter. He might complain that he was losing his voice, but he never quit. He would use all the tricks to soothe a tiring voice—lemon juice and soda water, honey, herbal tea—but he never gave up.

Occasionally, Duane would step in and give Gregg a break by singing lead on a song like "Ol Man River," which was a perfect song for Duane's lower voice. It was always remarkable to hear such a skinny guy singing so low.

My father was a major in the US Army Infantry during and after World War II, and in retirement, his military manner still dominated. Though Gregg and Duane had both attended military school at Castle Heights Military Academy in Lebanon, Tennessee, Duane stood out with many of the same qualities as my dad. What Duane directed was the undisputed way things were going to be, which was easy for the rest of us to accept, since his decisions were always well thought-out. He was a band leader who everyone re-spected—Gregg above all. He not only insisted on prompt arrivals at gigs and rehearsals, but that all the members' equipment be spit-shined clean before each gig. He made sure that our Chevy station wagon was cleaned before any trip and kept clean while we were on the road. He also insisted that all the band members' pants and shirts be cleaned and pressed weekly so we'd look our best onstage. It's funny—I can still see Duane going up to the counter at the cleaners and insisting on "a light starch" so we looked "clean, crisp, and professional" onstage.

In dealing with business, Duane handled himself and the band extremely well, and he also didn't take any crap off anyone—his brother included. And sometimes they behaved exactly like broth-ers. Duane saw right through people and made quick and accurate assessments as to whether he and the band were being taken ad-vantage of—he was the perfect band leader. Duane had that charisma and aura that commanded respect, and the band was compelled to follow his lead. You didn't have to actually see Duane walk into a room because when he did, the energy changed. That charisma and aura preceded him; Duane could literally suck the air right out of any room he entered.

Duane was an early riser, and I often found him in the lobby of a motel reading a newspaper first thing in the morning. He was very well read, and I often referred to him as a "Road Scholar." When the two of us drove together, our discussions would vary from current events to history to controversial topics. These ranged from disputed music history to analyzing the Kennedy assassination. Any stranger who had the pleasure of discussing issues with Duane would have thought that he had a doctoral degree. I guess he did have a PhD in guitar-nomics. For all of us who knew and worked with him, he might as well have been Dr. Duane Allman. His oratories were sometimes spectacular.

Being the older brother, Duane sometimes kept a tight a rein on Gregg, but he would also step in and stand up for him in a second. Of course, when the situation was reversed, Gregg would do the same for his brother. Duane and Gregg had an undeniable love for each other.

Duane sometimes lightly smacked the back of Gregg's head when he heard him mumbling, which Gregg was known to do. I must admit, sometimes I had to lean in to hear Gregg when he was talking to me. The two had been raised without a father, so Duane naturally took on that role. And not just for Gregg—for all of us.

He was the leader in every sense. Hell, he was even in charge of coming up with the nicknames. In the year since we'd met, Duane and Gregg had called me "Billy," but in my first eighteen hours as the Allman Joys' drummer, I'd left home in Alabama, flown to Atlanta and on to New York City, smelled weed for the first time, played my first gig in New York, and been introduced to the Shaving Cream Girls. Not to mention one Monti Rock III. From that night on, I was "Novice."

The last time I spoke with Gregg, in the days just before his death, he came on the phone and said, "Hey, Novice."

3

Rhythm Lad

Both my mother and grandmother played piano very well, but even with all their teaching and instructing, I just couldn't get the hang of it. This was a problem because I really wanted to play music. As time went by, I found myself consumed with tapping two pencils, one in each hand, on anything handy—a schoolbook, kitchen cabinet, pillow—anything. I was even patting my hands on my legs in school. Turning my radio up loud and tapping along with the songs all evening began to interfere with homework. Suddenly, one night an epiphany occurred. It hit me like a brick wall—I had rhythm! This epiphany would lead me down an adventurous road to my destiny of playing drums professionally with a great number of top musicians in the coming years.

My closest neighborhood friend when I was a child was Danny Fields, who lived at the bottom of the hill from my house. Danny had gained popularity for becoming Tuscaloosa's best young guitar player and singing talent. I truly admired his ability to perform so well on the local radio stations. I was probably his biggest fan, but I couldn't or wouldn't tell him—I guess I was embarrassed. So, I continued to be a fan of Danny's anonymously.

Not only was Danny a good guitarist and singer, but he also walked the walk by having that Everly Brothers' ducktail haircut. My mom loved Danny, but she disapproved of the hair. My folks' generation's idea of how a man should wear his hair went back to the haircuts of the War II era: short on top with "white sidewalls" around the ears and almost shaved in back, which was the haircut older men continued to sport. A "white sidewall" appeared when the barber finished your haircut by shaving around your ears, displaying a white area.

Dad was a military man. He was in the US Army and fought all the way across France to Germany in WWII. He eventually stayed in the Army Reserve for years until his retirement as a major. Playing a musical instrument was OK because he had been in a twenty-two-piece orchestra/dance band before the war interrupted his musical career; he played upright bass and violin. When I was eleven or twelve, the mention of longer hair would have been quickly brushed off. Matter of fact, barbershop haircuts were not a subject that could even be brought up.

Major Albert Braxton Connell cut both my and my brother's hair to save money. He had bought a set of haircutting tools, complete with shears, at our local Sears and Roebuck store. For a while, it was just a straight crew cut, but when the flattop came in style, he allowed me to have one because other men his age were beginning to wear a flattop. Also, I think he enjoyed the challenge of trying to get my flattop completely even or flat on the top, which it never was—never! Sometimes it was so embarrassing when my flattop leaned to the right real far, or to the left too far. I was always saying to myself, "Someday I'm gonna have my own money and be able to go down to Mr. Montgomery (the neighborhood barber) and get a professional flattop. One that's always straight, even, and perfectly flat on top." At that time in my life, however, it was my "duty" to get a haircut from my military dad.

I use the word "duty" because my grandmother, my dad's mother, had told me that my father was a war hero. He wouldn't talk about the war, but Nanny—that's what I called both of my grandmothers—said that my dad had landed at Normandy on D-Day while in command of an infantry company. Nanny told me, "When your dad's company got past the beach, only your father and one other soldier were still alive."

She also told me that my dad was wounded three times during the fight to Germany. He would be taken to a field hospital to be treated, recover, and then sent right back to the front to fight again.

At the end of the war, my father commanded a POW camp in Germany, which he actually did talk about. He would talk about the camp, his duty, and the prisoners, who he conveyed were very courteous and extremely smart. They did their best to make their confined living area a pleasant and even beautiful environment by cleverly remodeling their spaces and turning outdoor sections into attractive flower and vegetable gardens. They would also create fantastic pieces of furniture and art and play music on their homemade instruments.

The POWs even rounded up parts of various Allied and German vehicles which had either been blown up, damaged, or wrecked and built my dad a car. They actually built him a car! I sure would like to have a picture of that vehicle.

After hearing of my father's experiences during the war, I felt it was now my "duty" to mow the lawn, weed the flowerbeds, scrape and paint the house inside and out, and suffer the humiliation of his uneven flattop haircuts because he was a war hero, a REAL war hero.

Two streets over from my house, in the little Arlington Shopping Center, Mr. Montgomery had a two-chair barbershop, even though he was the only barber. The barbershop had one of those swirling red, white, and blue barber poles outside, so you knew that he was a real, professional barber. Next to his shop was a lady's beauty parlor where my mother had her hair done. Next to the beauty shop was a typical 1940s/50s drugstore with a soda fountain, complete with a jukebox. It was the neighborhood hangout, and it was where neighbors shared the latest news, which my mom called idle gossip.

Directly across from the little shopping center, on the opposite corner, was George's Grocery, with its own meat market and butcher. The butcher, Jimmy Herndon, and his family lived on Arlington Drive, which was my neighborhood. Catty-cornered from the drugstore and across the narrow two-lane Hargrove Road was a Phillips 66 gas station. Hargrove Road led downtown in one direction, and toward the Little League Baseball Park and Veterans Administration Hospital in the other. When a car pulled into the gas station, not only was gas pumped for you, which ranged from eighteen to twenty-six cents a gallon, but the attendant cleaned your windshield, checked the oil, and adjusted the air in the tires, performing other simple, rudimentary tasks that the driver might ask for—and all of this extra service was free.

During the summer in the 1950s and early 1960s, when school was out, all the neighborhood kids would take bicycle rides down to the little shopping area to buy candy and sodas or, with enough money, a hot fudge sundae. One of the boys' favorite treats was candy cigarettes, which we handled as if we were really smoking. Another favorite was bubble gum packaged with baseball cards. All the guys collected the cards that had a photo of a player on each. If you were fortunate enough to get something like a Mickey Mantle or Ted Williams card, you were the king cheese that day!

Occasionally, neighborhood moms would have their children go down and pick up an item they needed from George's Grocery. Most every mom was a homemaker who kept the house clean, did the laundry, and cooked the family's meals. Dinner, or supper, as we called it, was the day's biggest meal, and the family would all sit at the kitchen table and toss around the day's events. I really miss that era, when American families were as close as those portrayed in Norman Rockwell's paintings.

When kids needed a little spending money, we would collect empty drink bottles and take them to George's Grocery. The store gave two cents apiece for the returnable bottles, which the drink companies would then buy back from the grocery and reuse. Since most candy pieces, ice cream, and Cokes ranged from one to five cents, the money made from a few returnable bottles would go a long way. If a dozen bottles were collected, then an expensive hot fudge sundae or banana split could be sprung for, and that was high living to afford one of those! When my folks took me down to the soda fountain to buy me a sundae, there was always a catch. Payback was having to do all kinds of assigned chores the next week.

Whenever we kids were out riding our bikes, keeping an eye out for a flung empty drink bottle was business as usual. The area around road signs sometimes reaped several bottles because the teenage boys who had their drivers' licenses would try to hit the road signs as their cars did the speed limit...not any slower. A real pro could hurl one over the car from the driver's side and hit a sign on the right shoulder.

My mom would tell us, "Get on your bike and go down to the store and pick up the roast that I called Jimmy to cut for me." Jeanne Connell could be a taskmaster, and even though I was a boy, vacuuming, mopping, dusting, and washing dishes (considered "women's work" at the time) were just a few of my mother's assigned chores.

Dad was strict but somewhat quiet most of the time. He thought of my mother as an Annie Oakley type of woman, and she freely spoke her mind. Up until the last few years of her life, she cussed like a sailor and could drink like one, too—both while smoking a Winston cigarette. If you crossed her or anyone she loved, you were in for a serious tongue-lashing. "Kiss my ass" was just the beginning. My mother's mom, my other grandmother, or "Nother Nanny," would say, "Now, Jeanne, don't talk like that." I had always called her Nother Nanny because when I was very young, we lived with my father's mother, whom I called Nanny. So, in those years, when I was beginning to talk, I referred to my mother's mom as Nother Nanny, trying to say, "the other Nanny."

Mom was an attractive lady, which led to her having to yell out the car window when men would stare at her, "Take a damn picture—it'll last longer!" She provoked a million laughs with her countless one-liners like, "I'm so hungry I could eat the south end of a north-bound jackass." "I knew him when he didn't have a pot to piss in or a window to throw it out of." "That makes me so damn mad I could eat nails." "Well, he shit and fell back in it this time."

When I became older and was courting the ladies, there was this classic: "Remember, a few minutes of pleasure can give you a lifetime of pain." And, of course, all my guy friends loved this one: "Oh, hell, there's a zillion fish in the sea. Go out and get you another girl because when you turn them upside down, they all look the same."

25

Mom didn't shy away from work. She could get up in the morning and get more done in a day than most women could in a week. All the neighborhood kids loved her because she was a cutup. She was terribly funny and she loved young people. They never knew when she might break out into a dance like the funny 1920s Charleston or tell a joke that would split their sides. Like a late-night comedian TV host, she viewed anyone as fair game for one of her hilarious punch lines.

Mom was from the Houston family side of my lineage. We were descendants of Sam Houston's family. All those Houstons were somewhat like her—joking, laughing, clowning around, and pulling pranks. It must have come naturally; my great-grandmother, Ella Houston, whom everyone called "Granny," had said to me more than once, "It's common knowledge that Sam Houston was always drinking and running around with painted women." From the stories that I heard, he must have been one hell of a character.

Those Houstons sure were a handful. My mother's brother, Uncle Joe, was one of the funniest. He was always pulling your leg and was a real practical joker. My mom would say, "To this day, no one knows how your uncle and those other boys managed to get that huge horse-drawn wagon up on top of the railroad station one Halloween night in the 1930s." His life turned all too serious when he volunteered to be a fighter pilot during World War II. He flew in the Pacific, but he wouldn't talk about it, just as my father wouldn't. Uncle Joe never flew again once he was discharged; I can only imagine why.

Both of my parents had special and unusual backgrounds. I was named after my paternal grandfather; he was also called Billy Connell. He became a famous railroad engineer, and there was even a song written about him entitled "Billy Connell and the Sixty-Two," which was his locomotive number. He passed away before I was born, as did my grandfather on my mother's side.

My father's mother was raised on the Native American Reservation in Philadelphia, Mississippi. With some research, I discovered that my great-grandmother was a full-blooded Choctaw named

Apolona. I would listen intensely to any and all stories told about both sides of my family. I have an interesting heritage, yet there was something incredibly special about a few of my family members—music.

As mentioned earlier, not only did my mother play piano, but her mother, Lillie Kate Houston Malone, or Nother Nanny, did as well, and my father had assembled a twenty-two-piece orchestra/dance band in the 1930s called Al Connell's Rhythm Lads. I still have the megaphone they used as their public address system, which has painted on it Al Connell's Rhythm Lads, and one old music stand which displays the same band name. Unfortunately, his musical career was cut short due to World War II. The Wurlitzer baby grand piano that the Rhythm Lads used still sat in our living room, and my mom played it daily. To this day, all of my friends who are great pianists say that it was the best-sounding baby grand that they had ever played. My father told me that his band would take the legs off the piano so it could be loaded on the train when they traveled. They must have been "on the rails" instead of "on the road."

Although my mom read music, she also played wonderfully by ear and could play anything she heard or that you could hum. The list of her favorites included boogie-woogie, pop, blues, standards, and spirituals. When she played driving and pounding tunes with so much zest and vigor, her ass would continually come off the piano stool! She kept her radio on several stations, each playing songs by a varied array of recording artists like Frank Sinatra, Dean Martin, Patsy Cline, Brenda Lee, Floyd Cramer, and Tennessee Ernie Ford as well as spiritual quartets. A few years later, she became fond of listening to Aretha Franklin and Ray Charles. She had all these artists in her record collection.

I loved hearing Tennessee Ernie Ford's song "Sixteen Tons." It hit me later why I especially liked hearing the steel hammer hitting on an anvil rhythmically during that song: it was the rhythm in my bones already beginning to grow.

In the late 1950s, my mom also began tuning in a new station that played what was being referred to as bebop, or rock and roll—

she loved this new music. The station played tunes by Elvis Presley, Little Richard, Jerry Lee Lewis, Chuck Berry and Buddy Holly. In my room at night, I tuned in that station, too. I would tap my pencils along with these new and different rhythms, and these new artists became my renegade mentors. I would think, "Man...if I only had a drum with real drumsticks, I might even learn to play along with my guitar-playing buddy Danny."

Then one day, while thumbing through the ladies' lingerie section of the Sears and Roebuck catalog, I came across a page that had musical instruments. There it was—a red sparkle snare drum with a cymbal mounted on a device attached to the drum stand. The setup came complete with real drumsticks and a drum music book. That would work!

I hinted around the family that I sure would like to learn how to play this drum and cymbal combination that was in the Sears and Roebuck catalog. Miraculously, on my eleventh birthday, Nanny Connell, who my parents said spoiled me rotten, gave me, direct from the Sears and Roebuck catalog, that *red sparkle snare drum* with the cymbal, drumsticks, and drum music book. I had no idea at the time, but this gift marked the start of all my future music adventures.

All that fall, I studied and practiced the exercises in the drum music book over and over. By Christmas, I found myself pushed in front of my entire church congregation, playing along as the choir sang and my mother played the piano on "The Little Drummer Boy." My stomach was in my throat, and my knees were knocking, but I made it through the song without throwing up! I can't remember what I played on that old red sparkle snare drum that day in church because I really didn't know much about actual drum technique or rudiments. I just played what I tried to apply from studying the little drum music book; poorly self-taught was the drum de jour. It must have been a real mess, but everyone complimented me after the Christmas service. Strangely, no matter how much I improved over the years to come, I would still have some stage fright before every performance for the rest of my musical career. Ain't it interesting how a lot of accomplished musicians started out playing in church?

With that church performance I was no longer just a pencil-beating nobody. Now I was a performer like my buddy Danny! Now my goal was to play with those renegade musician mentors I'd been listening to on the radio.

During the next few months, I continued practicing on that snare drum and cymbal without getting any formal instruction. I quickly realized, though, that I wasn't going to be able to play with a group of proficient musicians until I had a real drum set like I had seen on TV and in movies. I should have been holding onto my pants because very soon I was in for the musical ride of my life!

One Saturday morning, I was sitting on the front porch, thinking, "Where do I go? What can I do about my obsession with playing drums?" I approached my father about it, and that led to a father/son trip to a local music store to find the answers. The Lively Music Store was in a small shopping area called Parkview Center that was located between my house and downtown Tuscaloosa, and only a short distance from the University of Alabama. Although there was another music store downtown named Newman's Music, my father thought Lively Music attracted a bigger pool of musicians. They catered to the schools and colleges in the area and to regional dance-band musicians. Lively also had music teachers, and Dad knew one of them, Cliff Hurter, who was also a full-time employee.

Cliff played in swing and dance bands at clubs my parents frequented, like the Elks Club and the Moose Lodge. Cliff's main instrument was trombone, but he had taught music at schools around the area and could play the basics on just about any instrument, from various horns to vibes and drums.

Lo and behold, when we drove up, there in the window sat this fabulous set of white drums. The set had a bass drum with a tom-tom mounted on it, a large tom-tom that had legs and sat on the floor, a cymbal on each side of the set, and this other thing that we found out later was called a sock cymbal or hi-hat. This was two cymbals rigged up to hit each other like the marching bands' cymbal players would do, except these were made to come together with a stand that was operated by your foot. One foot operated the bass drum pedal, and the other foot operated the sock of the hi-hat. It was a beautiful set that was displayed with overhead lights bouncing off the whole set and shiny cymbals. My heart raced until I saw the price—$450. That's a lot of empty drink bottles.

My dad and I thought that the store name came about because of the nice musical ring it had, Lively Music, but that was not the case. When we walked in, we were greeted by the owner. Mr. Lively said, "Nice to see y'all," as he introduced himself to us, and Dad returned the greeting.

My father said, "Bill and I came over to see if Cliff or anyone else could give us some information about drum sets and lessons."

Cliff Hurter was called over, and Mr. Lively clued him in on the reason for our visit. Cliff was shorter than my dad and had hair a little longer and parted. He began by answering questions about what we might be looking for and then directed us to the back counter, where he pulled out a William F. Ludwig Drum Catalog.

Cliff told me, "Bill, this is our top-selling brand of drums. We also carry another line of drums by Slingerland, but we sell more Ludwig drums for some reason. I don't know why. Maybe it's the tones, or maybe it's the colors." He then gave this big grin. I was going to become very familiar with his grin in the upcoming years. It was friendly but kind of sinister at the same time. I knew that I was going to like Cliff Hurter right off. He was how I imagined a dance-band musician would be—cool, real cool, but that grin gave him away as being a bit mischievous too. Interesting...

Cliff walked us through the catalog, pointing out the different price ranges and types of sets that were available. I was overwhelmed, but at the same time, I wanted one of the biggest sets right off.

Dad asked, "Cliff, what about lessons?"

Cliff replied, "Oh, yeah, man, we can give trap set lessons," with that Cheshire cat grin again! A trap set was what Cliff called a drum set, and I later noticed the great Buddy Rich's early stage name was "Baby Traps the Drum Wonder."

Cliff said, "Al, you and Bill take this catalog home with you and go through it. If you have any questions, give me a call. I'll be glad to help you any way I can. We could use a trap-set drummer around here. Oh, and by the way, if Bill did get a set of drums and decided to take lessons, we have a student dance band here that rehearses every Tuesday night together." Again with the grin, Cliff nodded at me as if I already had a drum set. All I thought was, "Too cool!"

Taking the catalog home that night, I pored over it page by page. There were so many colors of sets to choose from. I was familiar with red sparkle, but there in the catalog was blue sparkle and green sparkle, solid black and solid white (like in the Lively Music Store window), natural mahogany, blue with a silver strip around each drum, green with a gold strip around each drum, and also some real far-out finishes that were a mesh of several colors called oyster blue pearl and oyster white pearl and *more*!

It was too much, man! I could start off with a simple set that had a bass drum and a snare drum and one cymbal for $185, and add other drums and cymbals on down the road. I didn't have to put up $450 right then for the whole big kahuna. It was all too much, man, way too much! I could hardly hold back from yelling out loud. A few other things were really interesting. There wasn't just one size of drumstick, but dozens. There were skinny ones all the way up to big fat ones. Was it a different stick size for different songs or different stick sizes for different hands? I would have to ask Cool Cliff. There were also different sizes of snare drums, tom-toms, bass drums, and cymbals. There were all these decisions to be made, and I got confused just looking at the pictures. I fell off to sleep with the catalog still open in my hands.

One evening, as Dad was reading the paper, he asked, "What do you want for Christmas this year, Monkey?" He peered out over the Sunday paper.

Mom added, "Yeah, what do you want, honey?"

My father had called me Monkey from the get-go. He said that when he looked at me through the glass window at Northington Hospital's delivery room, his first comment was "he looks like a monkey."

It stuck. I never thought much of it when I was real young, but once I got older, being called Monkey was getting to be a little embarrassing around my friends. One day, Mom barked, "Damn it, Al! Don't call him Monkey anymore."

Under the paper, Dad just chuckled, snorted once, pulled out his handkerchief, and said, "Oh, Butch, he is a monkey," and then blew his nose. Dad also had a nickname for my mom: he called her Butch affectionately. No one ever asked where the name came from. Maybe nobody really wanted to know!

Mom yelled out, "He's getting too old for a damned name like Monkey." Mom then turned to me and asked again, "So, what do you want for Christmas, honey?"

I looked up sheepishly and said, "A trap set."

Dad replied, "A set of drums? Those things don't come cheap. Maybe next summer you can get some small jobs like mowing lawns and doing yard work, and save up for a drum set." He snorted again and put his handkerchief back in his back pocket. Then he said, "Your mother said that with a set of drums, the two of you could get up a band and that I could play upright bass with you all if I practiced up a little."

My mother began this strange dancing configuration and laughed loudly, but Dad said, "I've probably long since lost that talent."

Encouraging, but halfway begging, I said, "Oh, Dad, you can get it back!"

Christmas morning of 1960 came, and a huge, wrapped box was under the Christmas tree. *Huge*! It had a tag on it which read, "To: Bill, From: Santa." I knew who Santa was by then, but my parents continued with the charade. This was partly because my younger brother, Terry, was five years old and still believed in Santa Claus, and partly because they didn't want me to grow up so fast.

Tearing the paper off the box, the first thing I saw was the big bold letters—The William F. Ludwig Drum Company.

"This can't be real," I almost screamed. This was a dream. Pinch me, pinch me! It was real! I opened the box, and inside was a bass drum and a snare drum, both made of real solid wood, not plastic, like my old silver sparkle drum. Both new drums were blue with a silver ring around them. This was the color I had marked with a star in the catalog.

Along with the drums were a bass drum pedal, a real chrome snare drum stand, a cymbal stand that attached to the bass drum, and a real cymbal, not tin, like the one that was attached to my old plastic drum. This one was genuine brass!

Lighting his pipe, Dad said, "Wait—there's more."

"More?!" I couldn't believe it!

Mom chimed in, "Yeah." She stretched to reach another present for someone else, and then added, "Your daddy said that Cliff Hurter is gonna teach you how to play these, and that you'll end up playing with the Lively Music Dance Band on Tuesday nights."

Man, I was going to be learning to play a trap set with Mr. Cool Daddy himself. I chuckled and thought, "My guitar-playing neighborhood friend Danny Fields is gonna shit!" That's the way my mother would have put it.

On the first Monday of the new year, 1961, Dad took me over to Lively Music for my first lesson and told me he'd pick me up after I was finished. I entered the music store and was greeted by Mr. Cool himself, Cliff Hurter.

Cliff smiled and said, "Hey, Billy Connell, looks like you had a pretty good Christmas." He gave that big Cheshire cat grin while putting his hand on my shoulder, and then added, "Let me show you where we're gonna set up."

Cliff led me through a door behind the back counter and into the back room. Off to the right side were two small rooms with soundproofing tiles on the walls and a piano in each. He pointed out the second room. "Set your drums up in there," he told me, "and

I'll be right back." He then headed out into the store while I was thinking, "Man, this is a tight space!"

I spent the next several minutes arranging the drums in a way that both Cliff and I could fit into the room. Shortly, Cliff came back with a book in his hand and said, "This is what we're gonna start with these first few weeks."

He held out the book, which was titled "Swing Drumming." It had a picture of this smiling guy sitting behind a white set of drums with drumsticks in hand. At the bottom, it read "by Wm. F. Ludwig, Jr." "Alright, now we're getting to the big leagues," which made me realize I had to quit talking to myself! I couldn't be saying this kind of stuff out loud in front of Mr. Cheshire-Cat-Smile Cool Daddy Cliff.

Cliff put the music book on a stand he had placed to the side of my drum set. He then said, "Since you haven't had any formal training yet, we're gonna start where every great drummer starts, with the rudiments. There are twenty-six of them, so we'll take it slow. Nobody's in a hurry here." He gave me a different but reassuring grin this time.

Cliff told me, "We'll start with the single-stroke roll, which is particularly important in dance-band drumming." And from there we began. Cliff carried me through the rudiments, mixing them with pointers on a sitting position when playing, bass drum technique, bass drum and snare drum combination exercises, swing time for snare and bass drum, cut time, wire brushes technique on the snare drum, rim shots on the snare drum, cymbal technique, drum tuning, and on and on. I could not wait for the next lesson and especially Tuesday nights, when I could apply what I had learned by playing with the Lively Music Dance Band.

The dance band was made up of a potpourri of different instruments, from all types of horns to string instruments. Several different ages were represented, beginning at about ten years up through the mid-teens. Playing with the band was a blast because I was performing along with other musicians, but I wouldn't want to hear a recording of how we sounded!

Soon, I would be ready to add to my set by incorporating a hi-hat, or sock cymbal, as Cliff called it, and this would be a fine addition. By bringing two small cymbals together using a foot pedal, the effect would be a nice compliment to my other drum parts. I knew that to add a hi-hat, I was going to have to earn the money myself.

I had played Little League baseball just a mile or so down Hargrove Road from my house for the past three years, and my team won the championship two years running. I didn't want to play ball anymore, just play drums, but I had an idea. Coach Tarleton, the basketball coach at Tuscaloosa High School, ran the Little League park during the summer season. The coach knew me, and I knew he hired kids to help him with field maintenance and operating the concession stand each season.

I thought, "It's worth a try. I'll just go talk to Coach Tarleton about a job for the summer. If I get it, I'll have a hi-hat by the end of ball season." The next afternoon came around, and I went down to the baseball park to see him. Well, what do you know! Not only did Coach Tarleton give me a job, he also put me in charge of the concession stand. That was the best job with the most hours of any job I could have asked for. I'd have that hi-hat and maybe even a tom-tom to mount on my bass drum by the end of ball season. Working at the ballpark, I'd have to readjust my lessons and postpone my dance-band rehearsals until fall, but that was fine by me.

The summer came, and day after day, at about midday, except Sundays, I headed off on foot from my house on Arlington Drive and walked up two-lane Hargrove Road to the Little League park. I started my day helping to line the fields with lime, then I met with the vendors to stock the concession stand, and, finally, I opened, ran, and then closed the concession stand after the last game.

A highlight of each day was when Charlie Morris of the Coca-Cola Bottling Company delivered soft drinks. He was a distant cousin on my father's side and a card himself, always joking and joshing with me. This really was a fun job.

All the drinks had to be poured into cups that I filled with ice. I sold Cokes, Sprites, orange drinks, grape drinks, and root beer along with all kinds of candy bars and bubble gum, popcorn, peanuts, and hot dogs. There was always drink syrup everywhere—on the counter, on the drink cases, on the floor, and on me. Walking home each night, my shirt, pants, and shoes were so sticky with drink syrup that I was always wondering if the bats flying under the streetlights were going to attack me. Every night I was a sticky mess, but there were fringe benefits. I could have all the popcorn and drinks I wanted, and frequently a hot dog or two at the end of the night if there were some left over. I would even sneak my friends—and this one girl I liked—a little extra in their empty drink cups when the coach wasn't looking.

By the end of the Little League season, it was true: I had not only saved enough money to buy a hi-hat stand with cymbals, but also enough to purchase a tom-tom that matched my snare and bass drum. The new drum set purchases couldn't have happened at a better time because when I went in for my next lesson, Cliff had a surprise for me.

Cliff told me, "OK, now that you've got your hi-hat, we're going to work on that this week. I know that with some practice at home, you will have it down by the weekend. The reason that I'm saying this is...well, I've got a gig at the Moose Lodge this weekend." Hanging around the music store, I had already picked up that a gig was a playing job that paid money.

Cliff continued: "The band leader is Eddie Welch. He plays trumpet. Tut Yarborough is on upright bass. You know Tut—he works with your dad at the employment office. There's a piano player, and I will be on trombone and vibes. Our usual drummer has another gig. I know you're ready, so would you like to make some money Saturday night?"

Cliff gave me the biggest grin and continued, "I've already checked with your parents, and it's OK by them. The band will all help you with the tempos and rhythms, so just relax and have a lot of fun. It pays twenty-five dollars." Cliff looked at me for an answer.

I was thinking, "*Twenty-five dollars!* That's more than I make in a whole week at the Little League Park!" I instantly said, "Sure, but do you really think I'm ready?"

Cliff replied, "Yeah, man, you've been ready for a while. I just didn't have a job for you until now. I'll pick you up and carry you home. I know your folks want to come to see you play your first gig, but we need to get there early to set up, and they may not want to stay as late as we need to play. OK with you?"

I just nodded and smiled. I would never forget that day or that week for the rest of my life. I was going to get to play drums for money in front of an audience at twelve years old. First, a drum set for Christmas, then landing a job at the ballpark to add to my set, and now playing for big money at the Moose Lodge. *Dang*, what a year! I don't think my neighborhood buddy Danny Fields ever got paid when he played on the radio.

Cliff had already talked to my mom about what I was supposed to wear, which was a dark pair of pants and a white shirt with a dark tie. Cliff said that they had an extra matching sports coat that I could wear, but it would probably eat my little frame alive.

Cliff showed up at my house early that Saturday evening. We loaded my drums into his car and made our way down to the southside of Tuscaloosa, where the Moose Lodge was located on Greensboro Avenue. We unloaded my drums and Cliff's trombone and entered the club.

I had never been in a nightclub before, and my head was in slow motion as I entered. People were laughing and talking loudly at the bar, which was the brightest spot in the room other than the lights over the two pool tables. The only other light came from the beer and liquor signs and the jukebox. This early in the evening, all the tables were empty. There was this smell about the place. Was it cigarettes and beer? There was also a kind of perfume smell, too, like my mother would wear, only stronger.

WHAM! The jukebox started up and drowned out the talking at the bar. It was a song with a swing beat that I knew and would probably be playing tonight. The song was "Mack the Knife."

At the same time, up walks a tall, thin man with a big smile on his face: "Hi, Bill, I'm Eddie Welch." I recognized his name because he was the band leader and trumpet player. "Glad you could make it. I've got a jacket for you to try on, but I can see right now it's going to be too big for you." It *was* way too big! When I put it on, I couldn't see my hands.

Eddie said, "Well, I guess you're gonna have to play in just a shirt and tie, but that's alright," and he smiled.

Cliff and Eddie showed me where to set up, which was right beside this big set of vibes that Cliff would be playing, along with his trombone.

Vibes are an instrument with metal bars arranged in a keyboard configuration that are played with mallets, which look like drumsticks with large felt heads on the end. Vibes look like a large xylophone and are properly called vibraphones. I couldn't wait to hear Cliff play them because I'd never heard a set of vibes before.

Tut Yarborough, the bass player, walked up. He was a large, round man, and if you didn't know him and had to guess his instrument, you would immediately say the big bass fiddle; he looked like his instrument. I had seen him many times at my father's office in downtown Tuscaloosa. They both worked at the state employment office, where they interviewed prospective employees for various jobs that were available around the area.

Tut said, "Evening, Mr. Connell. We're gonna swing tonight," and he let out a big hearty bass laugh.

"I hope I'll play OK," I said.

"Oh, from what I hear from Cliff and your dad, you'll do better than that. Don't you worry about a thing. Let's just make some good music." Tut reassured me with that big hearty bass laugh again and then yelled to one of the waitresses, "Hey, Trudy, get me a Pabst please, ma'am! Wanna coke, Bill?"

"Yeah, that'd be great," I replied.

I was then introduced to the keyboard player while I set up my drums. She looked to be a little older than my mother, but she didn't look like the type of lady who might be playing the organ in church the next morning.

I finished setting up and then sat down at one of the side tables with the rest of the band. They were joking and laughing and having a lot of fun. I was so nervous that I was about to come out of my skin, but I laughed along with them.

The room started to fill up and get louder, but no one had to tell me when my Mama Jeanne arrived. The front door busted open, there was some loud laughter, a few damns and hells, a kick with her right foot to Cliff's ass, and there was no doubt that Jeanne Connell had entered the building!

"Well, you know you got the best damn drummer in town tonight, don't you?" She directed her statement to the band leader, Eddie. Eddie came back, "Yeah, Jeanne, we know we do, and we're glad to have him." Eddie was a quiet, refined man, but he knew what to expect from Jeanne Connell...anything goes!

"Glad you all got here in time for the first song. We're gonna kick it off in just a minute," Eddie politely said to my mother before he turned to the band and said, "Let's get on up there and play these nice people some music."

After we all got on our instruments, Cliff walked over to me and said, "Eddie wants to start off with a little Dixieland. He'll give you the tempo with his finger snaps. Just play the same Dixieland beat that we've been using in the music-store band—it'll be a piece of cake."

Cliff took a long draw off his cigarette, thumped it on the concrete floor, and then smashed it with his shoe. He put his trombone to his lips, blew a little air through it a couple of times, looked at Eddie, and nodded. Eddie snapped his fingers with a 1, 2, 3, and we were off and running.

About halfway through the first verse, Cliff looked back while still playing and nodded his head and trombone approvingly at me; it was going to be OK. I looked over at my parents' table. My mom was pointing at me and was just cutting up with the people at the tables around them. I could tell that she was bragging about me. I didn't have to read her lips—I could hear her over the band: "Hey, Juanita, that's our drummer boy Bill up there!" she screamed.

The night was going well and everybody was having a good time—both the band and the crowd. I made a few mistakes, but when I did, one of the other band members would look over and say something like, "That's OK," or "Don't worry about it, you're doing great." Occasionally, they would just look back, smile, and then keep on playing.

I relaxed as the night went on and I didn't want it to end, but suddenly we were playing one of the last songs of the night. The band was really swinging. Everybody was on their feet dancing, and Cliff was in the middle of a terrific solo. Just when you thought that he had run out of notes, he gave that slide on the trombone one more outward push. He used so much force to reach yet another note that the slide came out of the trombone and out of his hands and into the crowd! Cliff—along with what was left of his trombone—fell back into my drums and the vibes with a crash like the whole wall had fallen in!

What an end to a song! Cliff picked himself up, looked back at me with that grin, and proceeded to go out in the crowd and find his slide. "Hot damn, this is fun! This is what I want to do," I was saying to myself, and thinking all the time, "Twenty-five dollars. *Twenty-five dollars*! They're paying me? With all the fun I'm having, I should be paying them!"

Cliff told me, "I guess I had one too many and got a little too jazzy!" That phrase lives on today: "I was feeling just a little too jazzy."

I spent the next couple of months playing gigs with a rotating cast of swing and jazz musicians at various clubs and venues around the Tuscaloosa area. In addition to playing at the Moose Lodge, we played the Elks Club, the Veterans of Foreign Wars Club (or VFW), the Tuscaloosa Country Club, the Indian Hills Country Club, and so on and so on.

I became more confident playing fox trots, polkas, waltzes, swing, and Dixieland. I also got better at using brushes on ballads, but I was still struggling a bit with the Latin dances like the tango and samba.

As Cliff made it clear to me, all that would come if I worked hard enough, and work I did.

4

Future "Shuffle King"

I learned everything there was to learn about hard work from my dad—or so I thought. Looking back, I'd have to call Cliff Hurter a visionary. He was the coolest of the cool and the jazziest of the jazzers, but he wasn't much for rock and roll. At the same time, he saw that rock was exactly where popular music was heading in those early years of the 1960s, and he knew that I wanted to be there for the ride, so Cliff brought in the best man he knew to teach me.

Mabry Smith lived in Tuscaloosa and was well known in the surrounding states for pretty much one thing—his rock and roll drumming.

At the beginning of my first lesson with him, Mabry said, "Cliff tells me that you know how to play some dance music, some swing, jazz, and Dixieland, but do you know any rock and roll beats?"

This was the first time a drummer or any musician had ever asked me that. I answered, "Well, I've just tried to copy what I'm hearing on the radio, but I've never played a rock and roll song with a live band."

"All right," he said. "I'm gonna show you a couple of exercises to work on this week. With these two rhythms, you can play just about any rock and roll song that's out there."

Mabry sat down behind my drums in the little lesson room at Lively Music, and suddenly there was a confidence that came across his face as if he was a championship bull rider at a rodeo and had just mounted a bull before coming out of the chute. He placed just the top of his right foot on the bass drum pedal. Not the whole foot, as I had been doing, but just his toes. The way he placed his toes on the pedal looked like a ballet dancer before beginning a routine. He planted his left foot firmly on the hi-hat pedal, much like I did, but he adjusted the distance between the two hi-hat cymbals farther apart. "Why did he do that," I was wondering.

Mabry tested the bass drum with a double beat, using his toes. I saw then why he was placing his foot on the pedal like that. He could use the bounce back of the first beat quicker to execute the second beat with his toes, rather than using his whole foot. Then Mabry pushed down on the hi-hat a couple of times real hard. Now it was obvious why the cymbals were farther apart: they could be played with more force, rendering them louder. As he started this boom-chic, boom-chic rhythm with his feet, he began playing a straight beat on the bell of the ride cymbal (the top of the largest cymbal) with his right hand, with a hard and loud backbeat on the snare with his left hand. Once all his limbs were moving, the rhythm sounded like a train coming right at you, and there was no stopping that driving rhythm.

"Do you see what I'm doing?" asked Mabry. "This is the basic rock and roll beat that you need to get down, and then you can expand on it, like this."

He pulled his right hand from the cymbal beat and did this single-stroke roll on the snare drum, staying within the same rhythm that the beat was going, and then his right hand went back to the cymbal without losing a beat. He kept the beat going for a time, then he started on the snare with a single-stroke roll, but this time proceeded to do a roll around both the tom-toms and then back to the basic rhythm that he had set up again, and that driving train never stopped.

Then he started playing twice as many beats with his right hand on the ride cymbal bell. Kind of a ting-a-ling-lingy thing, and I could see that he was using his back two fingers to retrieve the bounce of the stick.

"Incredible," I thought. In just a couple of minutes Mabry had answered many of the questions I had about certain songs I'd been hearing on the radio.

"Now, you sit down, and we'll take it from the beginning. I'll show you how to start practicing this technique," instructed Mabry, "but don't worry about any double-bass-drum stuff or double-cymbal stuff right now. Let's just get the basics of this beat for you to practice at home. And, hey, man, I think another way to best understand how this works is to see it played live with some other cats. You busy Friday night? I'm playing at a fraternity party out at the university. You can come and sit near me. I know you're just twelve, and those frat guys can get pretty wild and obnoxious, but the band will watch out for you. That'll be a better lesson than I can give you here in this little studio room. It'll be a rock and roll drum lesson, and a lesson of what to expect when you play a fraternity party, because you'll probably play some one of these days."

"What's a fraternity?" I asked. Man, I was so naïve!

"Well," Mabry responded, "a fraternity is an organization of guys who live together in the same big house and go to the same school, such as the university. They sleep there, eat there, study there, and party there. If you're in a frat, you live the life of that frat. To each his own, and I know a lot of nice fraternity guys, but I've never wanted to be in one myself. Number one, I don't want to live with a hundred other guys, and number two, I want to live my own life, *and* number three, it costs quite a bit of money to be a member, and I don't have that kind of money. You need to be from a family with money in order to pay the dues. How do you think they're able to afford a live band tonight? I tell you how—with Daddy's money, and my dad has already passed away," snickered Mabry.

My folks knew Mabry's relatives, so I was fairly sure that if they had allowed me to play nightclubs with Cliff that they'd let me go to a University of Alabama student party with Mabry. Anyway, how much different could it be? These were college-age people attending the university for a higher education; they weren't hillbillies.

Then Mabry chimed in. "Bill, these fraternity parties are a lot different from the jobs that you've been playing. These kids get crazy. They haven't been drinking long, and most of them don't know how to handle the stuff." I was thinking that my father had attended the University of Alabama a couple of years before he went into the army, so he should know what went on at these parties.

Back home, my dad angrily raised his voice. "They can act like a bunch of heathens. They'll be throwing and breaking beer bottles up against the wall and picking fights."

But then my mother jumped in: "Oh, Al, they're just young people like we once were, out for a good time. Just don't you be drinking any of their beer, Bill, or smoking, or you won't be playing anywhere again until you're grown up and moved out. I know Mabry won't let you do any of those things and will keep you out of trouble. Let's let him go, Al. Mabry did say it was part of his lesson, and he sure wouldn't have asked Bill to come along if he didn't think that he would learn something."

Dad replied, "OK, Jeanne, but Bill, you stay close to the band, you hear?" My dad reiterated and continued, "I don't think this rock and roll music will last, anyway. So, go see what it's all about and get it out of your system. To me, it's just another passing fad. If you're going to do anything more in music, you're gonna have to go to school and learn how to read it, and even doing that, you're going have to study something else to fall back on."

I was glad they were letting me go, but I wondered if my dad was right. I had heard of a popular local swing band called the Alabama Cavaliers that musicians would kill to be part of. Many of the members were University of Alabama students, including the drummer, and even he read music. They were much better known around here than Elvis Presley or Little Richard, but all that was going through my head was the driving beat train that Mabry had taught me. What could be more fun than playing in a band with that rhythm going? I was extremely fortunate to have Mabry teaching me rock and roll drumming at such a young age. "Thanks, Dad. Thanks, Mom," I said.

That Friday afternoon, with his station wagon loaded with drums, Mabry picked me up, and we headed for the University of Alabama campus. On the way, Mabry told me that it was summer "Rush Week," the time when all the fraternities recruited new members. He explained that fraternity members knew that the best way to get someone to want to join their fraternity was to convince them that their fraternity had the best parties on campus.

We drove onto the campus, down an alley, and pulled into the back parking lot of this big house that was located in a row of other big houses. Each house was decorated with a theme, and the one that we pulled up to, Sigma Chi, was decorated like a jungle village. A stuffed gorilla figure stood at the entrance, and spears and shields hung from the bamboo wall that the guys had built toward the back of the fraternity. The hi-fi system was playing rock and roll with the volume turned up to "Good God Almighty" high.

The members and their dates were hanging around outside with their native costumes on, holding a beer or a drink in their hands. The house next door was having what Mabry called a "toga party." The fraternity brothers and their dates were all draped in sheets to look like they were from ancient Rome. This group looked to have been drinking all afternoon.

It appeared that the house next door was trying to play their rock music louder than the Sigma Chi house. The music of the two houses was running together, so it was hard to distinguish one song from the other, but neither houses' members—nor their dates— seemed to mind. I was glad that my Nanny Connell wasn't along; she would have said it was the devil's work! Mabry and my dad were right; it was *wild*, but in an interesting sort of way. It was more en- tertaining than any circus I had ever been to; this was an entirely new world compared to playing at the Elks Club or the Moose Lodge.

A fraternity member came up and asked Mabry if we were with the band. Mabry said, "Yeah, man," and the member said, "I'm the president. Glad you could make it. Are you ready for a crazy party?"

Mabry said, "Yeah, man, are you guys ready for a crazy band?"

"Sure are," the president responded, "I'll show you where to set up. Follow me."

We were directed into a large living room where the furniture had been cleared out. The president continued: "We thought that the band could set up over there in front of the fireplace. Won't need no fire tonight; it's hot as hell, isn't it?" he said chuckling.

Mabry shouted over the loud music that was playing, "Sure, man, that's fine as long as there are enough electrical sockets for our equipment."

"Let's see," said the president. "There are four double plugs along that wall. Is that enough?"

Mabry said, "Super! That's all we need, and the rest of the band will be here any time now. What time you want us to start?"

"We wanted you to start at 8:00. All the guys will start getting pissed off if there isn't any live music by then," the president smiled.

"You got it," Mabry shouted again.

Mabry and I continued to load his drums in as the other band members arrived. There were no electric instruments in the other groups that I had been playing with, but as these guys came in, so did the amplifier cabinets, with speakers in each. On the front of each cabinet was the name Fender. Mabry's band had a public-address, or PA, system and several vocal microphones. *Neat!* This band's setup was like nothing I had seen in my long musical career of one year!

One member opened his case, which held an electric guitar with the name Fender displayed near the tuning-key area. It also featured the name Telecaster. He took it out, plugged a cord into it, plugged the other end into the guitar amplifier, and then turned the cabinet on. He turned a knob and *wang*! He hit a chord that shook the glass in the windows. l didn't cuss much, but I instantly thought, "*Shit!*," as my mother would say. This was the loudest instrument that I'd ever heard—it sent a chill up my spine.

Then this other musician pulled out an even bigger electric guitar from his case, except this one only had four large strings. The guitar with the big strings also boasted the name Fender. I figured this must be an electric bass guitar, but it was nothing like the upright acoustic bass I was accustomed to. He plugged the cord into his cabinet, which was larger than the six-string-guitar's cabinet, turned it on, and out came these low notes that not only shook the glass in the windows, but caused Mabry's snare drum to start vibrating as if Mabry were playing a long stroke roll. I flashed back to Tut Yarborough's upright bass volume in the swing band—it didn't come anywhere close to this electric bass guitar's volume.

The guitar player and this other guy rolled in a piano that was in another room of the fraternity house. This new guy had to be the piano player. When they found a location for it, the piano player, who had been supplied with an amplifier, placed a microphone down into the piano and anchored it at a position that amplified the piano's keyboard perfectly. The piano was now at a volume level that could be heard and would blend in with the electric guitars at the same time.

The vocal microphones were plugged into another amplifier that was smaller than the guitar amplifiers, then the speakers for vocals were placed on each side of the band. The PA amplifier had the brand name Bogen on it. They turned the microphones on, and there was a squeal at first. The guitar player made an adjustment on the vocal amp, and the squeal went away, resulting in a clear vocal amplification. The guitar player spoke loudly into the microphone, "1, 2, 3 mic check, 1, 2, 3." He adjusted the sound system's volume until it was at a level that the vocals could mix well with the other instruments, but this would not always prove to be the case. During the microphone check, the microphones sounded as loud as the speakers used by the announcer over at Denny Stadium during a Crimson Tide football game, but when the band started up, the guitars drowned out the vocals.

The guitar player spoke to the other band members, saying, "Let's run through a few verses and see how the level is. How about 'What'd I Say?'"

Mabry seated himself behind his drums, taking the same position with his feet and hands as he had done in our small lesson room (the "riding a bull" position). The guitar player, who was also the lead vocalist, yelled, "1, 2—1, 2, 3, 4!" I had heard this song on the radio before, and even though Ray Charles was not present, it sounded so dynamic and exciting that I thought Ray himself would step out front any second. The excitement of Mabry's driving rhythm and the combination of the electric guitar, electric bass, and piano were so intense that the whole house started rocking.

The sound-level check began to bring the fraternity members and their dates into the large room, but when the real music began, they were shouting, singing along with the song, and dancing. There was no stopping this freight train now; the whole house was really rocking.

Next, the band started playing "Great Balls of Fire" by Jerry Lee Lewis, and again, it might as well have been Jerry Lee's band in the room. There was no air conditioning, and it was July. The sweat immediately started running down Mabry's face first, then down the faces of the rest of the band. By the third song, which everyone was dancing to, the whole crowd began to perspire.

No doubt, the huge amount of beer that they had consumed that afternoon was pouring out of their pores. Everyone's faces were wet, and then the guys' shirts and finally the girls' dresses were showing the darkness of sopping sweat.

After the first forty-five-minute set, the leader, who was also the guitar player and lead vocalist, asked the president if they had a couple of fans that could be aimed at the band.

The president reassured them, "Sure, we have some upstairs. I'll get a few members to bring down all that we have, and we'll aim a couple of them at the band and around the room." While wiping his brow, the band leader said, "Man, that would be a lifesaver. We're about to die up here, and I see the crowd isn't doing much better either since they're dancing to every song."

Mabry came right over to me when they took the break, and said, "As you can plainly see, rock and roll gigging, especially without air conditioning, takes a lot more stamina than playing ballads in the country clubs, huh? Bet I'm in better shape after a few of these summer fraternity gigs than most of the athletes at your school after spring training. One of the hardest parts about playing drums in a situation like this is having your hands sweating so much that you can hardly hold onto your sticks. I keep a towel on my knee and wipe my hands after every song. This is why I wanted you to come see what playing a fraternity was like."

Mabry continued, "There are a lot of little tricks to pick up on if you have your mind set on playing this kind of music. Keep a couple of sticks within easy reach in case one happens to slip out of your hand. This is also a good rule to follow when you break a stick while playing so hard, which all of us rock and roll drummers do. Knowing how to toss a broken stick and pick another one up without missing a beat and not confusing the band is an art form. You're going to learn a lot of tricks tonight, Billy. Just keep watching and learning. We'll talk on the way home and at the next lesson about what is going on here tonight. Sure glad you could make it; you won't regret coming over here tonight. It's a hundred lessons in one four-hour session. I'll keep giving you pointers as the night goes on," Mabry said with a big, proud smile.

The next set started with a song called "Snake Eyed Mama," which I had never heard. The crowd was very familiar with it, though, yelling, singing along, and encouraging the band on. Mabry had a unique but difficult part to play on this one.

The song began with Mabry doubling up playing sixteenth notes on his snare drum with his left hand along with playing sixteenth notes with his right hand on his floor tom-tom, which sat on his right side. On the chorus, he went into standard rock and roll beat on the bell of the ride cymbal accompanied by a hard backbeat on two and four on the snare drum. I know you nonmusicians are scratching your heads, but this was a physically demanding drum part to maintain.

Then, on the next verse, Mabry went back to the same pattern that he started on the first verse, with sixteenth notes on both the snare drum and floor tom-tom. He played these parts back and forth, back and forth. I couldn't see how his wrists and arms held up, but the crowd was going wild. If I had to play this song with a rock band in the future, it would take a great deal of practice and stamina to pull this off successfully.

None of the frat guys got out of hand. There were a lot of spilled drinks, sometimes on one another, and several students lost their footing and fell on the floor, which probably had at least an inch of spilled beer and liquor standing on it. A couple of guys and girls wanted to take over the microphone and sing, but the lead singer in the band, who was a tall, large fellow, discouraged it until one of the last songs of the night, and then he let a few come up and sing along in unison to a song entitled "Hot Nuts." The chorus was "Nuts, nuts, red hot nuts. Get 'em anyway you can."

This was obviously a fraternity anthem. All the drunken members and their drunken dates thought they were singing a very racy song about a male body part even though the song was actually about buying hot peanuts from a street vendor. This was a song that they knew that their parents wouldn't approve of—especially their interpretation of the lyrics. The rebellious tone of the song must have given them the feeling of breaking away from their parents' values. Being away from home and in a college-age environment allowed them an escape from their families' ways of doing things. If a rock and roll band played "Hot Nuts" at a frat party, they knew that they had a good chance of being booked there again. Hey, I was learning about how the biz worked along with learning drumming techniques.

What an evening! What a multitiered lesson! What a great band to introduce me to rock and roll, and I was convinced that there could be no better R & R drummer than Mabry Smith. If I couldn't learn the tricks of the trade from Mabry, they couldn't be learned. Besides, he was just a plain old nice guy; he didn't have a huge ego, he didn't brag, and he didn't cuss or drink. Mabry played with the utmost confidence, and, from what I noticed, never seemed to make a mistake, or if he did, he sure knew how to cover it up. Mabry was my mentor, and I was going to have to try with all my heart and soul to apply what I would be learning from Mabry over the next few weeks. If I could learn to play half as well as he did, I'd be able to play in a rock band someday. Playing for the older crowds at the nightclubs around town definitely provided me a way to improve my learned drumming techniques and fulfilled my obsession to play drums well. I made a lot of money for my age doing it, but that night, I discovered that the younger crowd loved rock music; they didn't give a dang about swing or Dixieland music. In a year or two, all of my friends would be absorbed in rock and roll as well. Wouldn't it be great if I could play the music that the kids around my age wanted to listen to? Was it possible for me to make the amount of money playing rock music that I had been making playing dance music for the older people? Could I someday make a living playing rock and roll?

The next Tuesday, Mabry came into the lesson room and said right off, "I know that at the fraternity house you were mystified with the sixteenth-note rock and roll thing that I was playing on 'Snake Eyed Mama.' You may remember we worked on sixteenth notes on just your cymbal last week, but I know it was a little over-whelming for you to see it in use with both hands...my left hand playing sixteenths on the snare drum while my right hand played sixteenths on the floor tom at the same time. Playing with both hands at the same time takes a lot of endurance."

Mabry continued, "I know you also got thrown off on that shuffle beat that my band was playing every now and then as well. That's the other beat that's a *must* to learn if you're going to play in a well-rounded rock band. I guess it's really more of an R & B beat, but all the rock bands play R & B songs, too. That's really a large part of where rock and roll originated. Have you ever heard of Jimmy Reed?"

I quickly replied, "Sure! I hear his stuff on the radio all the time, and it's great. A couple of my friends and I got together and tried to play a song of his called 'You Got Me Running,' but I just played the same old swing dance-band beat with it. It didn't really fit, but I couldn't remember what you had played on the same tune the other night."

I was familiar with a shuffle beat from listening to Mabry play, even though I hadn't attempted to play one. Mabry played a driving rhythm at the fraternity house, but I just couldn't figure out why my interpretation of that shuffle beat didn't have the same drive. Mabry, however, made it very clear.

"Here's the difference between a swing beat and a shuffle: a shuffle has one more lick than a swing beat. It's more of a continuous beat instead of having a break in it—that's what gives it that constant drive. A swing beat sounds like this on the ride cymbal: tee dota tee dota tee dota tee, while a shuffle goes tadot tadot tadot tadot without the single tap between the dotas or a space filled with a single tee. More can be said with a demonstration instead of my 'tee dota' talk. Here, let me show you. I'll only need to show you one time, and you'll have it. Just practice it this week a lot to get it even and in meter. Give that left hand a hard lick on 2 and 4, or what we all call the backbeat, which is what the audience hears and dances to."

Mabry sat down as if he were mounting that bull at the rodeo again. All of a sudden, the train that no one could stop started rolling down the track again. Mabry was the wizard of driving rock and roll percussion.

Damn. You either had it or you didn't—and Mabry had it in spades. Later, I heard a couple of local "so called" rock and roll drummers at my class dances, and none of them had the drive that Mabry had perfected. They were still playing that swing-band rhythm on rock songs, but their interpretations just didn't work. The drum part on the song "Snake Eyed Woman" would be way beyond their endurance. Playing drums in a rock band was completely draining; I never broke out in a sweat playing in a swing band. These new rock and roll beats and the physical energy required to play them made for an entirely different experience compared to playing the old music!

Mabry set me straight, however, on how much finesse was necessary. You don't really break into a sweat doing a shuffle, but I had to learn it anyway. He gave me a brief demonstration, and I picked up on the concept almost instantly. I took Mabry's place behind the drums. It was a little awkward at first, but as I continued to play, it became more fluid and consistent. Mabry soon exclaimed, "That's it! You got it man! Keep working on that at home. Now, let me hear the other sixteenth-note beat." Mabry had a kind yet demanding smile on his face as he spoke.

I then changed over to the other beat, which I had spent hours working on at home. Mabry told me, "Dang if you haven't mastered that, too. Give me a little roll and get back into it." I started the rhythm, broke it up with a roll between my snare drum and small tom-tom, and then went right back into the same rhythm.

"Double dang, you have that nailed too!" Mabry raised his voice with excitement but without cussing. I never heard Mabry cuss. He then told me, "And, as I said, with these two beats, you can now begin to expand by playing variations of fills like you just did with the roll between the snare and toms. Use taste and compliment what the other musicians are doing—don't ever take away from what they're doing. Listen to the vocalist or lead instrument being played, and don't get in their way. You'll acquire the technique of when and where to put in a lick to transition their changes and when to lay out. A good rule here is 'When in Doubt, Lay Out.' Understand?"

He taught me to play a shuffle using both hands. Before this lesson, I had been playing a shuffle on the ride cymbal with my right hand, and a single backbeat on the snare drum with my left hand, as most white drummers were doing. He also had me playing a shuffle on my bass drum on a couple of tunes. Man, that was really hard to do. It took strong right-leg muscles, which eventually I developed, making my right leg more muscular than my left. I still use that shuffle. Mark Jackson, a saxophonist I later played with for years in a band called Apollo and the Death Horns, still calls me "the shuffle king." That's one hell of a compliment.

5

Audition for a Rock and Roll Band

It was August and school was just around the corner. I couldn't wait to tell all my eighth-grade classmates that I'd been to a University of Alabama fraternity party—except most of them wouldn't know what a fraternity party was. In fact, most of my friends didn't know that I'd been playing in a dance band. Some found out when their parents told them that they'd seen me playing at one of the nightclubs or country clubs in town. I knew I'd have a lot of questions to answer once I was back in school.

A few weeks before school began, I was called to the phone by my mom. She said, "It's Mabry, and he's got a question to ask you."

I headed to the phone, wondering if Mabry was going to have to cancel next Tuesday's lesson. I took the phone from my mom. "Bill, Mabry Smith here. How's it going? Got that shuffle down pat?"

I responded, "I think so, but when playing a shuffle, the fills between my snare drum and tom-toms are coming a little slower than they did with the sixteenth-note stuff."

Mabry said, "That's OK, those fills will come after you've played for a while with a band that does some shuffles. Listen, a musician named Fred Styles who goes to the university called me. He and some other musicians I know are putting together a new rock and roll band called the Pacers. Fred wanted to know if I was available to play. As much as I'd like to, I already have more jobs than I can handle right now. I'm calling is to see if you might be interested in auditioning for the gig. I told them your age, but that didn't seem to matter to them since you've been taking lessons from me. I told Fred that you were as capable as anyone around, and he said, 'That's good enough for me.'

"I know the guys who are going to be in the band. They're all good, up-and-coming musicians, and I know they'll get even better.

If you want to switch from swing to rock and roll, this is your chance. They already have some jobs lined up and you might earn even more than you have at the nightclubs. Are you interested?"

There was a short silence on my end of the phone. A lump came in my throat and butterflies entered my stomach. "You really think I can do it, Mabry?" I asked.

"I wouldn't be calling if I didn't. You've already got more potential than some of the other local drummers that are trying to play rock and roll," Mabry replied. He continued: "I'll tell you what. I'll go with you to audition, and when you get to a part that you're not confident playing, I'll get you back on track right then and there. I think that if they see that I'm going to help you work into the band and learn the right parts to the songs, they'll be very receptive. Like I said, they're great guys. You know what? I think you're ready to play a fraternity now, and that's what they have booked. Since you've had the courage to step up and play in front of a crowd with a dance band, you can do this for sure."

I came back with, "What's an audition?"

Mabry explained, "An audition—sometimes called a 'try-out'—is where the band sees if you're capable of doing the job, and if you'll fit in. The try-out is tomorrow night in the Union Building on campus. They're using the ballroom, which is a good-sized room with a stage. I'll pick you up and carry you home. What about it? Are you ready to play some rock and roll for some good money?"

My twelve-year-old brain whirled as I was contemplated this decision. Mabry asked me as if he had all the confidence in the world in my drumming. How could I say no to "The King of Rock and Roll Drumming"? He was offering me a job that he had to turn down. Suddenly, my dream was happening fast...too fast. I was ecstatic and flattered by Mabry's gut feeling about my capability to get this job. He never made a mistake drumming, so I figured he must be right about my being able to play with this band.

"Yes, Mabry! If you think I'm ready, then yes, I'll audition," I answered in a somewhat quivering voice.

Mabry said, "Alright then, hoss. See you tomorrow."

I talked to my parents, and although they were a bit skeptical, they trusted Mabry and gave me their blessing.

Going to sleep that night would be near impossible. Before cutting off the lights, I'd practice those rock and roll beats until my folks screamed for me to stop and go to bed. Then I would lay there and, in my head, go over all those rock and roll exercises that Mabry had taught me.

Late the next afternoon, Mabry arrived and helped me load my drums into his station wagon. We drove onto the University of Alabama campus and pulled up at the back of the Union Building.

"The ballroom is on the third floor, and there's no elevator, so we'll have to take your drums up some stairs," Mabry pointed out. "No big deal—I've had to haul mine up many a flight of stairs over the years. If you stay in this business, you'll be doing the same thing many, many times. Unloading, setting up, taking down, and loading is the hardest part of gigging to me. Playing is the reward."

We got up to the third floor and opened the ballroom door. On the far side of the room, up on the stage, were two guys with guitars. One of guys was tall with an Elvis-style haircut. He was playing an acoustic guitar, not electric, and singing while the other guy played along on his electric guitar. When they heard the clunking of the drum cases coming into the room, they stopped playing and turned toward Mabry and me.

"Well, if it isn't ole Mabry Smith himself," the taller guy said, "and this must be Bill Connell. Glad you two could make it." He turned to me and extended his hand. "Hi, Bill, great to meet you. I'm Fred Styles and this is my roommate and the lead guitar player, Doug Hogue."

Doug stepped over and shook my hand, saying, "Mabry's told us a lot about you. I tell you what, Billy boy, you've got the best drummer in the South for a teacher. Wanna play a little tonight with us?"

I nodded and asked, "Sure, where do you want me to set up?"

"Right back there in the middle of the stage," Doug told me.

The first minute or so after meeting Fred and Doug, I instantly sensed their confidence. Fred appeared to be in charge. It was obvious early on that he was the driving force in the band. As it turned out, he was good at creating playlists for his audiences. Fred also had a high ideal to practice, practice, practice, even if it was just him and Doug at their apartment. Fred had booked a lot of jobs, but so had his roommate, Doug. They lived together in a garage apartment behind a fine old home close to campus.

Fred told me, "Our piano player and bass player should be here any minute, so go ahead and set up your drums." As I began to set up, in came a short guy with a short haircut similar to mine. Fred yelled, "Here's one of them now! Mr. Piano Man, Sam Hill himself." Sam stepped up on the stage with a smile on his face.

Fred said, "Sam, you know Mabry, and this is Bill Connell, whom Mabry has been teaching." Sam put out his hand, first to Mabry and then to me. Sam said with a smile, "Sorry I'm running late. I keep forgetting how long it takes to walk over here from the dorm." He sat down at the upright piano located on the left side of the stage.

Sam began to warm up by playing small bits of this and that. I soon found out that he was a music major who lived in a dorm on campus and didn't own a vehicle. He quickly earned my respect since he was the consummate "can play anything" piano player. Later, when the band began rehearsing at my family's house, my mom just fell in love with Sam. They spent many a night swapping licks and playing together.

"All we need now is Johnny," Fred said as he turned to me. "Our bass player has to drive from Gordo, which is Doug's hometown, too. He's one of the best harmony vocalists you'll ever hear. He also performs occasionally with another guy from Gordo named Jerry. Naturally, they call themselves Johnny and Jerry. Hope we can get Jerry to eventually come sing a few tunes with us. When they sing together, they sound better than the Everly Brothers."

Doug then interjected, "Hey, Bill, I know you've heard the song 'The Twist' by Chubby Checker. Want to give it a try with just the four of us until Johnny gets here?"

Fred asked, "Oh, man, Doug—do you really think we're gonna have to do that song?"

Doug replied with, "Sure! Everybody's requesting 'The Twist' at all the band jobs that I've been to lately. Anyway, it'll get Billy boy warmed up with something kinda easy."

Just then Johnny came in the door, and Fred said, "Oh, thank God. Let's give Johnny a second to get set up, and we'll do a song with some harmony. We can do 'The Twist' in our sleep. Is the PA hooked up, Doug? Doug built these speaker cabinets, and they look great. Now if they just work as good as they look," Fred said with a chuckle. "I'm kidding Doug! They sounded great at the apartment. I just hope they'll fill up the rooms that we'll be playing. Tonight should be a good test here in this big room."

Doug stepped over to the PA amplifier and said, "Check the mic, Fred."

Fred replied, in a steady cadence, "Mic check, 1, 2, 3." Then he sang a little of an Elvis tune: "Return to sender, address unknown, no such number, no such zone. How does it sound out there, Mabry?"

Mabry had strolled out to the middle of the ballroom and said, "Comin' through loud and clear out here."

Johnny put his amplifier onstage and looked toward me.

Fred stated, "Johnny, this is the drummer that Mabry was telling us about. Bill, this is Johnny Duran."

Johnny said, "Glad to meet you, Billy. Ready to try some songs with us?"

"Yeah, you all are gonna have to teach them to me," I said. "See, I've been mostly playing swing and Dixieland and really haven't played much rock and roll—except at Mabry's lessons and playing along with the radio."

Mabry stepped forward and stated, "I'm gonna help him tonight when he needs me, but I know he's not gonna have much of a problem with the different beats and rhythms. He just needs to learn the arrangements."

Fred said, "Alright then, why don't we start with 'Hit the Road Jack' by Ray Charles. It has a sort of swing beat like you're used to playing."

Doug added, "Yeah, that's a good one for him to start with. Ole Billy boy should be able to ace that the first time through." Doug turned toward me and gave a big "I know you can do it" grin.

Fred counted it off, and I began a swing beat as the other guys played the parts they already had down pat. I knew I was playing the right part because I looked over at Mabry, and he was smiling and nodding his head with a "Yes."

"This is great," I thought, "my part is working." I was playing my first song with a real rock band. The short introduction to the song was filled by Sam's piano part, and then Fred started singing. Johnny and Doug stepped up on either side of Fred when the chorus started, and all three sang into the same microphone. "Hit the road, Jack, and don't you come back no more, no more, no more, no more. Hit the road, Jack, and don't you come back no more."

Fred did a line by himself, "That's what I say," and then the others sang the chorus with him again, "Hit the road, Jack..." All three singers used just the one microphone because that was the only one the band owned at the time.

The only catchy part was the ending. We had to run over it a couple of times until I finished the song with everyone else. When it was over, Fred told me, "Great, Bill. Nice job," while Doug added, "Yeah, good job, Billy boy."

Sam turned from the piano, smiling, as was Johnny. "Oh, please God," I said to myself, "Please let all the songs go this well. I love playing with these guys already, and I really want this job."

Mabry gave me tips to help add a little spark to certain songs. He also had to show me a part on "What'd I Say" by Ray Charles that required a different beat from anything else that was rehearsed. I had to play one backbeat on the snare drum and the next backbeat with two licks on the tom-tom while doubling up my licks with my right hand on the cymbal bell, which sounds like mumbo jumbo to anyone but a drummer. It was a difficult part that I was going to have to really work on at home, but everyone in the band knew I understood the concept.

At the end of the audition, Fred came over and asked, "Would you like to play in the group?" The other members were all in agreement that I was able to play the type of tunes that they wanted to perform.

I answered with an affirmative, "Sure, I'd love to play with you all. I just need to work on 'What'd I Say' at home the next couple of days."

Fred simply said, "Then it's a done deal." And I was screaming in my head, "Rama Lama Ding Dong!"

Doug asked, "Can you practice day after tomorrow up here again?"

I could hardly form the words, but I managed to say, "Sure. Same time? I don't think Mabry can bring me again, but I'll get one of my parents to bring me over."

Fred snapped back, "No you won't. I'll come get you and take you back home—just give me directions."

Mabry and I loaded the drums and started back to my house, and he said, "I told you, man—you had nothing to worry about. You're gonna fit into this group real well. Heck, you already fit into this group. Fred took me aside and thanked me for introducing you to them. They're glad to finally have a drummer." Then he said, "I don't think you need any more formal lessons. But if you have any questions about anything in the future, you know that you can call me up and I'll help you, right?" Mabry looked over and waited for my response.

"OK, Mabry, and thanks so much for getting me this job," although I could hardly answer with such a big smile on my face. Mabry just laughed and said, "Hey man, you're doing me a favor. I can't hardly play two jobs at once!"

6

Right Corner, Right Time, Right Bus

Just like he said he would do, Fred picked me up at my house for our next band rehearsal. He was driving an early '50s white Chevrolet convertible, and he looked so cool driving it. I had never been in a convertible before, much less known someone who owned one. There we were, going through town with the top down, the drums in the back seat, and Fred and me up front. This was a real thrill. I felt like I had grown up a bit by accepting this new job. I was playing with older guys and now riding through Tuscaloosa with the leader of the band in his cool convertible.

For the next couple of weeks, the Pacers practiced several times until we were confident that we had enough material to make it through a gig. A seamstress made matching green jackets with "The Pacers" embroidered on the front for all of us, and Fred had the cool idea of applying Day-Glo paint on top of the band's name on each jacket and then hanging a black light up above us. The Pacers name glowed while we were playing. We thought this little gimmick would put us a step ahead of the other rock bands in the area.

The British Invasion was still further down the road at this time, so all our tunes were rock songs of the late 1950s and early 1960s. I could tell Fred really admired Elvis and his music, and who didn't?! He played an acoustic guitar while doing all the lead singing out in front of the others in the band; hence, I learned the phrase "front man."

Fred was the definitive leader of the band, on- and offstage. He sang all the songs, made all the microphone comments, kept up with the band's future bookings, and handled the money; he'd collect our pay from the various establishments and distribute our share to each of us. He also took the audience song requests, birthday announcements, anniversary announcements, etc.

Our song requests were for artists of the period and included Ray Charles, Little Richard, Jerry Lee Lewis, James Brown, the Four Seasons, Otis Redding, and Elvis Presley. Our most popular tune during the holidays was, of course, Elvis's "Blue Christmas."

As I prepared for my first time playing in public with the Pacers, I was stopped cold by Fred's and Doug's announcement about where our first gig would be played: we would be performing after the University of Alabama's Crimson Tide football team's first pep rally of the season in the huge Foster Auditorium. My first rock and roll gig was going to be in the largest hall in town with a huge crowd. This was where Alabama basketball games were played and where all the big concerts were held. This was the stage where I later saw powerful acts perform, such as Ray Charles, James Brown, Little Anthony and the Imperials, B. B. King, and many other huge acts. Our gig here was a giant step up from playing the small nightclubs in town, but I wasn't about to bother Fred and the other musicians with the fact that I was scared to death!

Not only would the auditorium be filled with excited University of Alabama students, it would also be teeming with numerous Crimson Tide fans from the community, including most of my friends and their parents. Crimson Tide pep rallies always drew a large crowd. I was twelve years old—a mere kid—performing in front of so many people. I thought, "I will want to just melt if I make a mistake!"

The big night finally came. We all arrived at the auditorium well before the pep rally began to meet with the coordinators of the event, and we were told where to set up after the pep rally was over. The only piece of professional equipment that I did not own was a legitimate drum stool. I was using the red wooden stool that sat in my family's kitchen while I was growing up. That was alright, though, because no drummer around Tuscaloosa at that time really knew what a professional drum stool was or looked like. I had noticed other drummers sitting on chairs, pieces of hard luggage, and even Coca-Cola crates turned up sideways. The stool was the least of my worries: the important thing was that I played the right parts without a mistake that night.

In 1961, being in a rock band was a *big* deal. None of the other members seemed intimidated by the large auditorium or considerable crowd that hung around for the "show and dance." Fred, Doug, Johnny, and Sam seemed to take the whole event with a grain of salt, but they were much older than I was. Somehow their confidence must have rubbed off on me, though, because after the first song was counted off, we performed just as we had rehearsed in the Union Building's ballroom. Our regular rehearsal space was a great place for a performing band to practice since it had a stage in front of a large ballroom, which meant I was accustomed to playing in a relatively large room. But the ballroom did very little to prepare me for playing in an exceptionally large arena—and this was my *first* rock and roll gig.

About one third of the crowd that attended the pep rally stayed and got right into our music. Was this great or what? I glanced out of the corner of my eye and saw several of my twelve-year-old friends sitting on the bleachers to the left of the stage. They were watching, smiling, and pointing at me. Somehow, in one year I had rapidly progressed from banging on that Sears and Roebuck red plastic snare drum to playing a large university auditorium with a full set of professional drums. I owed it all to my family's generosity and understanding and the musical guidance of Cliff Hurter, Eddie Welch, and Mabry Smith. University of Alabama pop culture professor Dr. Jim Salem told me years later that my good fortune and lucky breaks could be summed up like this: "It's having your bags packed and being on the right street corner at the right time when the right bus comes along."

All my music teachers made sure I was prepared. They had become my dear friends, and I loved them. They can take a big bow for instructing me in so many ways, from how to set up and tune my drums to teaching me how to play with other musicians in front of a crowd. When they heard that I was only twelve years old, they could have said, "No way! I'm not gonna babysit a kid who would rather be home watching cartoons or roller skating." I will never forget their never-ending patience and terrific confidence in me.

After that night, the gigs came flying in: fraternity and sorority gigs, civic club events, country club dances, high school proms, private parties, and a couple of unusual jobs. If the money was right and the venue safe, the Pacers would play it. Mabry had been correct; I was making a lot more money playing rock and roll than playing with a swing dance band.

Since we had a baby grand piano in my living room, the band began to rehearse there whenever we needed to work up some new songs. My parents didn't mind at all. As a matter fact, they reveled in the fact that the college guys were comfortable rehearsing in their home. Sometimes my mom would drop down on the piano bench with our piano man, Sam, and sit in on our rehearsals. We would all have *big* fun playing, singing, telling jokes, and snacking on the food she served us.

Every now and then, I went to Fred's and Doug's apartment to learn songs they wanted to bring to our next practice. They lived in a small, two-story apartment with a kitchen and dining area on the first floor and a small living room and two small bedrooms on the second floor. It was too small to set up my drums and even if there had been space, the next-door neighbors would surely have complained.

The first time I walked in their front door, a foul smell hit me. As I continued up the stairs to the living room, the odor went away. This was my first visit to a university student's apartment, so I was very curious. When we took a break, I went back downstairs to the kitchen and was hit again by the foul smell. I began to look around, and my nose finally led me to the kitchen sink. In the sink was a huge stack of dirty dishes that were caked with decaying food. This is where the smell was coming from. How long had they been there? Was this how university students lived? My mom would die if she walked in and smelled and then saw this. Well, if it didn't bother Fred and Doug, who had to live there, I figured I could tolerate being there for a few hours—if I just stayed away from the kitchen.

So, I headed back up to cleaner air and joined the band upstairs again.

That first holiday season, we landed a remarkably high-paying job on New Year's Eve in Montgomery. We were all elated about the idea of bringing home more money than we had ever played for before, but an unknown complication was headed our way.

Everybody in Alabama loved to see a few snowflakes in the wintertime because it rarely snowed there. A light dusting would send everybody crowding the grocery stores to load up on bread and milk because the streets would be shut down whenever we received only a half inch of snow. I could not understand the milk and bread thing—soft drinks and donuts seemed more important!

Well, the weather reports the day before New Year's Eve spoke of the possibility of some snow. Everyone in Tuscaloosa became excited, and it was all anyone could talk about. In the meantime, while I was loving the opportunity of making big money playing in Montgomery the next day, I was also a little disappointed that I wasn't going to be in town to see some snow. Montgomery is farther south than Tuscaloosa, so I knew that they weren't going to see even one snowflake.

The next day, the weather reports said that snow was beginning to fall just west of us in Mississippi. A little later, a few flakes began falling here. By afternoon, the snow was falling in large flakes and sticking to the ground. When the other band members arrived to pick me up, there were several inches of snow on the ground and streets, and it was still snowing extremely hard. The radio announced that if the snow persisted, all highways leading out of town could be closed—that is, if it persisted.

Fred and Doug were not going to miss out on this huge-money gig, so they were ready to hit the snow-covered roads leading out of town and head to Montgomery. To my surprise, we learned that it was snowing just as hard in Montgomery. My father said that it would be impossible to negotiate the small, snow-covered two-lane road to Montgomery and that we would find ourselves stranded with no water, food, or heat. Fred kept insisting that we could make it because he and Doug had dollar signs in their eyes. As the snow continued, my father kept laying out his dangerous scenario. It came down to a duel between my father's position and Fred's. As the debate reached a feverish pitch, an alert came over the radio. The announcer said, "All roads are closed."

The verbal bout was over, and Fred had lost. He had to call the venue and tell them that the snowstorm was too bad for travel. Fred went into the next room to make his call, and when he came back into the living room, he had an expression that I had never seen before. He paused and then said, "Our New Year's Eve gig was canceled several hours ago."

The high-stakes return was not meant to be. If there was a plus in our disappointment, we saw the most beautiful deep snow any of us had ever seen. As we all relaxed, Mama Connell whipped up a bunch of party treats, and we celebrated New Year's Eve in front of a fire while watching the snow that continued to fall.

7

Changing Players in the Pacers

The summer after the Pacers' first year of playing, one of the members decided to leave the group. Bass player Johnny Duran gave his notice. He had been driving fifty miles round trip from his home in Gordo, Alabama, to every practice in Tuscaloosa and to our gigs around the state. He had a wife and children, so playing in a band that rehearsed and played a good distance from his home just wasn't working out.

There was a "big decision" band meeting the night that Johnny left. We had let a saxophone player, Alvin Harbin, sit in at a couple of our gigs, and he really added a lot to the band. In the early 1960s, a sax solo was heard as often—or more often—as a guitar solo on the rock and roll songs being played on the radio, so someone in the band meeting asked, "Why don't we add Harbin on sax and forget about having a bass player? Having a sax would give our band an edge on getting more jobs."

Well, that question was not from me. I knew that a bass was a "must" instrument in any band because the bass and the drums laid down that solid beat needed in any rock band. As outlandish as it sounded to me, all the other members pondered the idea of adding a sax and not having a bass player. They debated and debated about the possibility of getting more gigs for more money, which seemed preposterous to me!

Our rock and roll band might appear a bit more "now" with a sax player, but we would lose that driving rhythm without a bass...duh! After using a great deal of time debating the sax option, the others finally came to the same conclusion. Now the band began thinking about how to find a bass player.

Suddenly, Doug had an epiphany. He had seen this new University of Alabama freshman from New Brockton, Alabama, who played electric guitar better than anyone he had heard in the area.

So, Doug said, "Why don't I switch to playing bass and we try out this Paul Hornsby guy on guitar?"

We all agreed that this was worth a try. Doug said he could adapt to playing bass easily and would improve with more experience. Trying out this hot guitar player sounded like a good strategy. If he was as good as Doug indicated, he might help us evolve into a more dynamic act.

After tracking him down, Fred and Doug asked Paul over to their apartment a couple of nights later. Paul played a few tunes with them, and the decision was immediate. This guy was incredible. If he didn't know a certain song, he could listen to it one time through and have it down. In addition, Paul knew a lot of songs that the band could add to our song list.

The Pacers began its second year as a new-and-improved dynamic rock and roll band. We began to get more out-of-town gigs and gained more confidence as we became tighter each week. When a band has an outstanding player in the group, each of the other players strives to play better, too, which is an incredibly good thing.

Paul was raised in a small farming town in southeast Alabama, close to Enterprise and Dothan. He grew up on a farm as a country boy, playing country music and bluegrass with his dad and neighbors, but his musical future would have no bounds.

In addition to being a superb guitar player, Paul supplied the band with a never-ending string of funny and amusing tales. He not only told funny stories, he sometimes *became* the funny story.

At the time, Paul drove a sharp, black two-door Pontiac. As we began to make more and more money, Paul treated himself to a gift and ordered fender skirts for the car. As luck would have it, when the shipment came in, only one fender skirt arrived.

We had seen a little of Paul's temper when things weren't going so well for him, but when he opened the package and found only one fender skirt, he went ballistic. How could he drive around town in a car with just one fender skirt?! That would be downright embarrassing! We tried to convince him that people could only see one side of the car at a time, so he should attach the one fender skirt until the second one came in. We all got a big chuckle out of the situation, but it wasn't funny to Paul. He wouldn't listen to our nonsense and insisted he had to have two fender skirts if he was going to proudly drive this sharp, black Pontiac around town.

After the other fender skirt finally arrived, Paul enjoyed his car more than ever, but this story lived on for quite a while for the band. Naturally, he didn't tolerate our continued ribbing about it very well, either.

In yet another example of Paul's amusing predicaments, the Pacers and several other bands—some we knew and some we didn't—ended up playing gigs on the same night at the university during a busy weekend. During one of our band breaks, we all went next door to catch what we had heard was an incredible band from Dothan called the James Gang. Paul was really impressed by the guitar player, John Rainey Atkins, and everything about his performance. So much so that during the Pacers' next job at a small coffee house, Paul tried to emulate one of John Rainey's showstoppers by putting his Fender Jaguar guitar behind his head while playing. (This was a trick later used by Jimi Hendrix and eventually the great Stevie Ray Vaughan and his brother Jimmie). Much to all our amazement, the fishing net that hung above the bandstand was lower than Paul anticipated. As he lifted the guitar over his head, the tuning keys got stuck in the net! It turned into a literal showstopper since we had to take a break while Paul untangled his guitar. Damn, playing with Paul was always entertaining in every way imaginable!

As 1962 rolled by, I was now fourteen years old, learning more and more, playing better and better, and growing more and more confident. By the next year, 1963, Sam Hill, our piano player, left the band to teach music. He was replaced by a keyboard player we knew named Paul Ballenger, who brought not only his fine piano-playing ability with him, but also a great voice: he was an excellent singer.

The Pacers began that year with Fred Styles remaining as the front man and singing most of the lead vocals with some help from

Paul, the new piano man. Paul Hornsby was still tearing up on guitar, Doug Hogue was improving on bass, and I wanted to think that I was making positive strides on drums.

We were playing a lot of jobs in and out of town, and the money continued to be good, but for this now-fifteen-year-old drummer, the money was better than good—it was extraordinary. I was rich!

It was also in 1963 that the Beatles released "I Want to Hold Your Hand," which became a huge hit in early 1964. The Beatles quickly began to launch a music, fashion, and lifestyle revolution for young people all over the world.

They emerged with quite a different hairstyle on men. It was long, cleanly washed, and combed toward the front and sides of their heads, unlike the previous pop stars of the late 1950s and early 1960s, who wore their hair combed back from the front and sides, sometimes in a ducktail, and held in place by greasy hair tonics. The Beatles had a completely different look. Their hair resembled a medieval bowl cut, whereby a bowl was turned upside down and put on one's head. The hair that stuck out from under the bowl was cut off. After being cut and the bowl taken off, the front had bangs and the sides covered the top half of ones ears...no white sidewalls here, where barbers shaved around the top of men's ears with a straight razor.

Worldwide, girls went wild over the Beatles' hair, and men began to let their hair grow out a little, keeping it clean and grease free. Musicians jumped on this longer, clean hair first. As the Beatles continued to have hit after hit, their hair grew longer and longer, as did that of other musicians and nonmusicians.

With all the changes that the Beatles' captivating music, long, clean hair, and Fab-Four fashions ushered in, a true cultural revolution and evolution boldly arrived onto the scene, unleashing sexual freedom, drug use, and the British Invasion. After the Beatles rose to fame, Great Britain experienced a surge in the production of hit records by a multitude of new bands, and all these new groups wanted to come to America and tour. When these new bands came across the pond, they quickly won popularity in the United States with their cool accents, unique hair, and new mod clothes.

No one in the Pacers had gotten up the nerve to grow their hair a little longer, styling it with bangs and wearing some of it over their ears. No one but me, that is, and that happened very quickly.

One weekend, as the Beatles were becoming a pop fixture, the Pacers were headed out of town to play a gig. We heard through the grapevine that a local five-and-dime store was selling Beatle wigs. Enough said: the band car and trailer made a beeline to the store. Paul Hornsby, Paul Ballenger, and I went in, and we each purchased one of the wigs. The Beatles' merchandising phenomena had begun.

Our wigs, if you could call them that, were basically skull caps with about two-inch-long, deep-black, cheap artificial hairpieces attached. We thought that from a distance the audience would think this was our real hair. We got back in the car and put them on. They looked ridiculous, but we were going to follow through wearing them that night. When the show and dance began, there we were, the three of us with the Beatle wigs on. Fred and Doug had refused to buy one...good idea. Not a single head was turned when we walked onstage to play. Our big Beatles hair debut was a complete failure. After having a few beers that he had been hiding behind his piano, Paul Ballenger grabbed his wig and threw it up in the air— our charade was officially over.

As Paul continued to put away beer and get a little more drunk, his bladder became painfully full. When our forty-five-minute set came to an end, Paul couldn't hold it any longer—not even long enough to make it to the bathroom. He casually walked over to the steam radiator beside the stage and began to pee right on it. The piss steamed up from the radiator, and it was a long piss, right there in front of everyone. Fred and Doug went berserk. We knew that we were fired without pay, right then and there. Luckily, no one in an official capacity saw him, but I thought Doug was going to kill Paul. Unlike the rest of the band, Paul Ballenger loved to drink on the job, and a six-pack a night was the norm for him. On any given evening, there was no predicting what Paul B. might say or do. If he hadn't been so damn good and entertaining onstage, Fred and Doug would have fired him several times!

In the spring of 1965, Fred Styles, Paul Hornsby, and Paul Ballenger began tossing around the idea of going down to the beach resorts on the Gulf Coast to play all summer. That sounded like a lot of fun; I'm sure it had nothing to do with all the girls who would be down there!

Of course, my parents wouldn't allow me to go down to the beach and live with college-age guys, and bassist Doug Hogue had a job with the Alabama Power Company that paid well, so the Pacers broke up. The new beach band that formed from what was left of the Pacers was going to need a drummer old enough to travel with them plus a bass player, so they began their search. I was heartbroken, to say the least, but, as they say, when one door closes, another one opens.

8

With the Nightcaps

In 1965, the formation of two new beach bands from Tuscaloosa marked a pivotal moment in Southern rock and blues history. It was the beginning of what eventually evolved into the large family of musicians who launched the Southern rock movement.

At this time, another band out of Tuscaloosa called the Spooks had a fine guitar player and singer named Eddie Hinton. I knew Eddie's name because he had played basketball for Tuscaloosa High School; I hadn't known that he was a singer and musician, too.

Having never heard the Spooks play before, one night I headed to a fraternity house on the University of Alabama campus to hear them. When I got there, I thought I must have been given the wrong address because I could hear a black man singing, and he was belting it out. Once I got inside, I couldn't see the band because they were not on a stage; they were set up on the floor. A huge crowd of students blocked my view, so I pushed and shoved my way up front, and there he was. I could see the singer now, but he was no black man. The man singing was Eddie Hinton, the white basketball player who had played for Tuscaloosa High School!

Any musician who heard Eddie Hinton was instantly impressed and fell in love with his voice and guitar playing. That's what happened when Fred Styles, Paul Hornsby, and Paul Ballenger heard him. They wanted him to join their new band, but there was a problem. If they added him, then they would have two out-front men and still no bass player. Then Fred had an epiphany similar to the one Doug had when Paul Hornsby was hired by the Pacers: he should switch from playing acoustic guitar and lead singer to playing bass. That would work, so they approached Eddie with the idea of heading to the coast for the summer to play, and he accepted the offer. Wow!

Now, what about a drummer? Between the four of them, they began coming up with names. One of the names was someone Fred and Paul Hornsby had never heard of, but Eddie and Paul Ballenger had. He was a drummer from Decatur, Alabama, who came highly recommended, and his name was Johnny Sandlin. They called Johnny, and he accepted. Now they were set to begin rehearsing. The new band would be made up of Eddie Hinton, singing and playing guitar; Fred Styles, singing and playing bass; Paul Hornsby, playing guitar and some keyboards; Paul Ballenger, playing keyboards and singing; and Johnny Sandlin on drums. They also added a saxophone player named Charlie Campbell, which made for an outstanding lineup. They named the new band the Five Men-its and quickly landed a job at Pensacola Beach.

Since Doug Hogue couldn't go to the coast with the rest of the guys, he decided to form a band with some younger musicians from Tuscaloosa, including singer Johnny Townsend (who would later head up the Sanford-Townsend Band, which had the smash hit "Smoke from a Distant Fire" in 1977); guitarist Tippy Armstrong, who would later become a major recording-session guitar player and writer in Muscle Shoals; keyboard player Danny Marchant; and a drummer named Poodgie Poole. Poodgie had been playing with another local group who called themselves the Playboys.

They named the new band the Nightcaps and began rehearsing in Poodgie's parents' basement. After the band had rehearsed for a few days, Poodgie decided he didn't want to play in a band after all because he was deeply dedicated to his studies at the University of Alabama.

Doug asked Poodgie if they could they still practice in the basement for a few days while they worked to get a new drummer worked in. He agreed, and Doug went right to the phone and called me. "Sure, I'll play," I answered. After all, I didn't have a drumming gig, and I had liked working with Doug in the Pacers, and he liked my drumming.

We rehearsed diligently, and when we were prepared, we began picking up some fraternity gigs that the Pacers had played in the past, but with the small summer-term student population, these gigs were few and far between.

Doug came up with an idea one afternoon in rehearsal, and said, "I can't take off and live on the coast, which is where the jobs are this time of year, but I can go down and try to book us some weekends. We can play down there on the weekend and come back to Tuscaloosa during the week. Playing just weekends, I can keep working at Alabama Power."

This sounded like a terrific plan to the rest of us, so Doug took off to the coast and came back with a couple of job prospects. The job that sounded the most desirable was playing weekends at the Dauphin Island Casino, which was located just south of Mobile.

My grandfather made an equipment trailer for us by shortening the tongue of an older boat trailer and mounting a four-by-six-foot, water-tight metal enclosure onto it. This was a great step up because we had been having to carry our equipment in several of our personal cars. Thanks to the trailer, we ended up only having to take two cars instead of four, which saved us a lot of gas.

Before leaving for the Dauphin Island job, the band had the trailer painted light blue with the name the Nightcaps in dark-blue letters on each side. In small letters on the bottom, we put "Music City." Why? I can't remember, but it's funny to think about now, and it was funny then, when Fred Styles and Eddie Hinton saw it down on the coast. They gave us hell for putting "Music City" below the name of our band. Eddie kept singing "Music City" over and over.

I pulled the trailer with my light-green 1957 Plymouth, which had huge fins on the back and a push-button automatic transmission. The bench seat on the driver's side had broken to where the back of the front seat would collapse all the way to the back seat. To remedy this, Tippy Armstrong and I jammed a two-by-four-foot piece of lumber between the bottom and the top of the front seat from the rear in order to hold it up. Now I could drive without falling backwards. I mean, we were looking at some kind of rig job for pulling the trailer and carrying our equipment, but hey, it worked.

The weekend of our first performances, the band left very early on Friday morning for the 250-plus-mile drive south from Tuscaloosa through Mobile and onto Dauphin Island. When Doug confirmed the gig with the management of the casino the week before, they told him about a house across the street from the casino where the band could stay in free. Wow! Free! That sure gave us a lot more profit.

Arriving a little after midday, we drove up to the casino, which was a large concrete building built right into the sand dunes that led to the beach. After Doug informed management that we had arrived, we began to set up for that night's performance.

The hall and stage where we were to play was upstairs, and as we walked in, our footsteps alone told us that there was going to be a terrible echo. We set up and ran through a few songs to balance the instruments to compensate for the horrific echo in this solid concrete room.

After doing this sound check, Johnny Townsend walked over to the far side of the room, where he found a hidden four-foot-high wall with an opening to the first floor. He got very excited, and started whispering loudly, "Come here, you're not going to believe this!"

The opening was directly over the girls' dressing room, and he was watching girls getting undressed and putting on swimsuits. Now, this was an added benefit of playing a beach gig! Johnny's discovery dubbed him with the name "Dirty John" from that day forward. We even began referring to the band as Dirty John and the Nightcaps. Of course, we actually should have named the band the Dirty Nightcaps or Dirty John and the Peeping Nightcaps!

Off and on that whole first weekend, all of us would go over to the club and peer through the opening to get a peep. That is, all of us but Doug. Doug was not that kind of guy. He was just so nice and squeaky clean. Peeping was indeed shameful, but we did have raging teenage hormones.

The band next drove over to the house where we would be staying. As soon as we exited the cars to enter the house, a cloud of mosquitoes attacked us. We ran for the front door, getting bitten all the way. Doug fumbled with the keys to the house as the rest of the band screamed for him to hurry up as we were slapping mosquitoes that were biting us right through our clothes. Finally, Doug got the door open and everyone rushed in, shutting the front door quickly. For a couple of minutes, all you could hear was the sound of hands slapping at the mosquitoes that were still perched on us. There was a lot of cussing going on!

We were not as anxious playing that first night as we were getting from the front door back to the car to return to the casino; those mosquitoes were relentless. We had to come up with a plan on how to survive this mosquito infestation that weekend, so a number of mosquito repellents and in-house mosquito killers in spray cans were purchased. We must have smelled like a walking poison factory over at the casino. Nevertheless, it was a free place to stay, so we were taking home more money.

The Friday-night performance wasn't too tough because there wasn't much of a crowd, but as word spread, the crowd picked up on Saturday night, and we had quite a large audience on Sunday afternoon for the matinee. Johnny and I spotted two attractive girls the first night, and it turned out that they were sisters. Johnny took up a conversation with the older sister, and I did the same with the younger. These two girls lived just right up the road on Wolf River, between Dauphin Island and Mobile, and they continued to come every weekend to see the band, and particularly Johnny and me; we just called them our dates each weekend.

Four of the members of the band traveled back and forth from Tuscaloosa to Dauphin Island every week, but Danny, our keyboard player, landed a job right there at the concession stand, where he worked all week during the day and then would play with the band on the weekends.

This was the period in the 1960s when the British Invasion had begun to spread. All these English bands had long hair, so all of the members of the Nightcaps, except for Doug, began growing our hair out. Danny became so obsessed with his hair that he would play his keyboard with one hand and continuously comb his hair with the other. This infuriated Doug as well as the rest of the band.

Even with the mosquitoes and that 500-mile round trip every week, we loved playing on the beach each weekend, and Danny had no complaints about making more money than the rest of us by working the concession stand.

We were always playing pranks on each other when we were on the road—maybe out of the boredom as we waited to play each day, or maybe just for the fun of having a little mischief. But the humor never let up on Dauphin Island that summer. Our guitar player, Tippy, always wore white, sleeveless undershirts that resembled the jerseys basketball players wore, but the rest of the band wore regular T-shirts with sleeves.

One morning before Tippy woke up, Johnny and I removed all of his white undershirts from his suitcase and hand-painted big numbers on each and every shirt, topped off with his name across the top of the backs. We then put them back into his suitcase. When Tippy woke up, took a shower, and went to get an undershirt from his suitcase, he went berserk. We had never seen him that mad! Johnny and I finally had to buy him new undershirts to keep him from leaving the band, but he would have his revenge.

Johnny had been studying art at the University of Alabama and decided one morning to paint this modern art piece on the back of our trailer. As soon as he finished his proud artwork, out of the front door ran Tippy with a large pot of hot grits which he threw—pot and all—over the painting. The paint was still wet, so the grits became embedded into it with no hope of repair. Johnny didn't get as mad as Tippy had when we ruined his undershirts—he just laughed uncontrollably. The grits-enhanced modern art stayed on the trailer for years and became a conversation piece and great reminder of the days we played Dauphin Island.

Dauphin Island had very few businesses besides the casino in 1965, just one convenience store. One afternoon, Tippy, Johnny, and I went down to get a few drinks and snacks. Johnny attempted a little humor by sticking a pair of kid's sunglasses in his pocket. The humor went beyond fun, unfortunately, when he went to the counter, paid for his other items, but not the sunglasses. Not half a minute after we walked out of the front door, two police cars pulled up with sirens blaring and lights flashing.

The storekeeper came out and pointed at Johnny. "He's the one."

The police put him up against the store wall and discovered the sunglasses in his pocket. "He was stealing those," the storekeeper yelled.

While all the questioning and handcuffing was going on, I called the casino, where I relayed a message to Doug. He was older and more mature than the rest of us, and he came right down to help Johnny. Doug talked diplomatically with the cops for a while, and they finally let Johnny go. Johnny later swore that he meant to pay for the sunglasses but forgot. Of course, no one believed him because while he had been putting them in his pocket, he had looked back and grinned at Tippy and me.

Playing Dauphin Island spawned some fun adventures for the band, but this wasn't one of them.

9

Joining the Men-its

After the Five Men-its concluded their summer gig on Pensacola Beach, drummer Johnny Sandlin decided to leave the group. His home was in Decatur, and it would be a six-hour round trip drive to play jobs in Tuscaloosa. Paul Ballenger, the Five Men-its' keyboard player and singer, also left the group to pursue an accounting career in his hometown of Birmingham. Charlie, the sax man, had taken the job just for the summer, so he wouldn't be staying with the group either. This left the Five Men-its with three musicians: bass player Fred Styles, guitarist Paul Hornsby, and Eddie Hinton on guitar and lead vocals. All three were making their home in Tuscaloosa again.

Number one, they needed a drummer, so they called me. I can't tell you how excited I was. Their group had a leg up on the Nightcaps because of their very tight arrangements and distinctive and accomplished musicians. I said, "Yes, of course I'd be flattered to play with you all."

Johnny Sandlin was a great drummer, so replacing him was an honor. Johnny and I would find ourselves exchanging drumming jobs several times during the 1960s.

Paul had been playing some keyboards while they were in Pensacola, so he decided that he would play both guitar and keyboards in the new lineup of the band. It turned out that the new Five Men-its didn't need a fifth member; the band sounded full enough with just four musicians. We kept the name the Five Men-its for a little while until we got tired of the questions about where the fifth member was, at which point we dropped the "Five" and called ourselves just the Men-its.

A little 1960s Tuscaloosa music history is in order here to give prologue to what was to come, which helps explain why Tippy would later call Tuscaloosa the "Mecca of Music."

When I left the Nightcaps for the Men-its, they were left without a drummer. Instead of replacing me, the Nightcaps broke up. A new band was forming in Tuscaloosa at this time that was led by another Decatur musician by the name of Johnny Wyker. Johnny, who also played trumpet, wanted a horn band located out of Tuscaloosa, so he asked two Tuscaloosa saxophone players, Tommy Stuart and Denny Green, to come on board with him. Tommy would later become a prolific songwriter whose compositions were eventually recorded by Roy Orbison and Glen Campbell. Tommy was a music major who could play everything from flute, sax, keyboards, guitar, and bass—and the man had a great singing voice as well. Little did I know then how our paths would cross many years later, but I learned, as many musicians will tell you, that life in the music business can be a small world indeed.

After hearing about the Nightcaps' breakup, Johnny Wyker immediately grabbed Johnny Townsend to sing lead and Tippy Armstrong to play guitar. He added a keyboard player from Decatur, and their lineup was complete when they added a Tuscaloosa native, Jackie Sims, on drums. The new band called themselves the Magnificent Seven.

The Magnificent Seven became one of the hottest and most popular bands around. Not many bands had a vocalist who could match Johnny Townsend's voice or a guitarist as excellent as Tippy Armstrong. Plus, they had a horn section.

After rehearsing and playing live for a short time, the Magnificent Seven went into to the studio and recorded a song written by Johnny Wyker called "Let Love Come Between Us." The record got some backing and was soon a Southeastern hit, which brought about a large number of gigs for the band.

An interesting side note is that the Hollywood studio that produced the movie *The Magnificent Seven* got wind of the band's name and demanded that they drop it or face a lawsuit. The band didn't contest it and changed their name to the Rubber Band.

So, back to the Men-its. Eddie had a blues-inspired vocal style that was almost scary coming from a white guy, while Paul was comfortable playing both keyboards and guitar by this point. The Men-its did songs by Otis Redding, James Brown, Sam Cooke, and many other rhythm and blues artists. We also did some pop tunes as well, including a twenty-six-song Beatles medley. That's right; twenty-six Beatles songs in a medley! It took us night after night of rehearsal to get those down, but what a showstopper!

Paul Hornsby married a great young woman from Sylacauga, Alabama, whom he met while attending the University of Alabama his freshman year. They got a house trailer, which they parked on the southside of Tuscaloosa. Paul had decided after his freshman year that college wasn't offering him what he wanted to pursue, so to supplement their income, he began teaching guitar lessons at the new Tuscaloosa Music Service. This allowed his wife, Jean, to continue attending the University of Alabama.

The man who gave me my first paying job playing drums with a band, Mr. Cool Daddy himself, Cliff Hurter, had recently bought his employer's music store, Lively Music. He moved the store to a larger building only a couple of blocks away and changed the name to Tuscaloosa Music Service, and this is where Paul was teaching. Cliff's store not only gave Paul a job, but he also let the Men-its rehearse there after the store closed in the evening. We spent many an hour rehearsing in that store, and Paul spent many an hour teaching aspiring young rock and rollers to become guitarists, some of whom became very good musicians.

It was also during this phase of the Men-its that Eddie and Paul began playing harmony guitar parts. The first song that they used harmony guitars on was a John Lee Hooker tune entitled "Dimples." This was pretty revolutionary, as rock and roll guitarists playing in harmony was almost unheard of at this time.

Fred and Eddie had rented a house together after they returned from Pensacola, so I would hang out there sometimes because they were always satirizing everything and everybody and just plain cutting up. They would keep me in stitches with their style of sarcasm, and I was usually their target when visiting. We rehearsed at their house frequently, too.

Besides being a great singer, Eddie was also a very good drummer. He would listen intently to the drum parts on R & B and blues
records and pull from them. Eddie often gave me drum-part lessons
on the tunes that the Men-its would be learning, and he owned a
new set of Ludwig drums that he special ordered, with an eighteen-
inch bass drum, two mounted tom-toms, and a floor tom. All the
drummers at that time were using twenty-two-inch to twenty-four-
inch bass drums, so his bass drum looked tiny in comparison, but he
got such a great sound out of it. I finally had to order a set just like
he had, and I could kick myself for later trading them in for another
set out in Hollywood. You don't know what you've got until you
lose it, right?

10

Reconnecting with Duane and Gregg

About six months later, on a typical low-key Tuscaloosa Saturday afternoon, Tippy called me, bursting at the seams. "Hey, man, you ain't gonna believe who I just ran into downtown—Duane Allman!"

Tippy and I weren't playing together anymore, but we continued hanging out all the time. "The Allman Joys are playing a fraternity party tonight on campus," he told me. "They want you to come over to their motel. They've been trying to find you but didn't have your number. They really want to see you. You're in demand, boy! They're just here for tonight and leaving right after the gig. Duane told me they've been playing up in New York City. New York City, man!" Tippy was all but shouting, "Man! Wait until you see Duane's hair and what he's wearing—you're gonna shit. Get your little ass on down to meet them."

I jumped in my '63 Ford Fairlane and headed to the Town House Motel, which provided the finest accommodations in town, so I knew from this alone that they must have been doing quite well. I had just traded in my old faded-out 1957 Plymouth Savoy (the one with the huge back fins and push-button drive). We had called it the Road Rocket, and that old car ferried the Nightcaps to a lot of gigs, including back and forth to Dauphin Island the summer before, which is when we met the Allman Joys. It completely died just after I drove it onto the used-car lot, but only after I had already reached a deal and completed the paperwork for the Ford Fairlane. I drove away from the lot a winner—and I'm usually never a winner when it comes to cars.

Finding their room number, I knocked on the door and Duane quickly opened it, greeting me with his big, happy smile—I suppose he knew it would be me. Damn! His hair had grown down to his shoulders like Tippy had said, and he certainly hadn't found the clothes that he was wearing anywhere around here! I had seen new top rock groups wearing similar threads on their album covers or on TV. He must have shopped at the same store where New York's Lovin' Spoonful bought their attire, including long-sleeved striped T-shirts. Duane's shirt had blue and brown horizontal stripes. He also had on these fine, tight black pants with huge bell-bottoms. Gregg was sitting on a bed with hair just as long and wearing similar pants, just a lighter color. His white button-down shirt had big blooming long sleeves. I had seen that distinctive new British singer Tom Jones wearing a shirt just like it. Man, New York City must be the new mod trendsetting fashion capital of the world.

"Well, look who's here," Duane said. "The old Nightcaps' drummer himself. What's up, Billy?"

Ever since our first meeting on the Gulf Coast, Duane and Gregg had called me Billy instead of Bill. I had always been called Bill by my family and friends (although my father had called me Monkey since I was born), but it was kind of neat being called something different by great musicians whom I really liked and respected—both for their music and friendship.

"Have we've got some things to show you and some stories to tell!" Duane said. "We've been playing up in New York City, and that's where it's all happening for sure! We've never heard so much great music in our lives. The whole city has so many fantastic musicians playing in clubs and music halls—it's unbelievable, man. So, how you been, Billy? Still got those great chops you had playing on Dauphin Island last summer?"

"I've learned a lot of R & B drum parts from Eddie Hinton, our lead singer and guitar player," I told him. "Eddie's a real good drummer, too, and he's become one of my greatest influences and inspirations. He has analyzed and applied the drum parts on a bunch of the best R & B records and taught me some great drumming techniques. I've been learning how drummers backing up R & B and blues singers are doing what they do. I think my chops are better now than when you last heard me."

Duane said, "Well, Billy, that's just what we wanted to hear. Matter of fact, I asked Tippy to call you to come down for two reasons. The first being that we really wanted to see you, just because it's been a while, and the other...well, let me tell you something while our drummer's out and about. Knowing him, he's probably trying to track down peach sodas and pralines. Really sweet treats are his weakness, and that's leading to his downfall with the band."

I kept listening.

"As you noticed when we last saw you, he didn't have good teeth and no front teeth. He still doesn't. We all chipped in money for him to fix them, but...well, he took all our cash and spent it on fucking sweets that continue to rot his choppers. He can't brush enough to get all that sugar off them. When he smiles, he looks like a damn hillbilly idiot, and that's not us. We're pissed...really ticked off. We've reached our limit with his disregard for the band's image, so this has gotta end. He plays good drums, but with the aspirations that we all have...well, a toothless drummer just ain't gonna make it. Tippy told us you were playing with some great musicians, so we wanted to ask—would you consider playing with us?"

I almost fell backwards.

"What?! Wait a minute... Man! Damn! You gotta be kidding?!"

"You'll have to leave home here in Tuscaloosa and live with us on the road full time," Duane said, "but believe me, we're gonna make it. You've got my and Gregg's word on that, Billy."

Then Gregg spoke up. "We liked the way you played the first time we heard you and have been thinking about you since. Don't you want to get out of this Podunk small town and play with us alongside some of the best musicians out there? You ain't gonna get extremely far in the music business staying here. We've been thinking for a while that a 'yes' answer from you would make our group finally come together like we've wanted it to for a while. Plus," Gregg laughed, "you got teeth. All the girls out there are gonna love you." It was like Gregg was laughing for me as he pondered the thrill and excitement of fighting off all those girls.

"We've been around some great musicians and bands," Duane said, "but we're convinced they've got nothing on us. We're just as good as any of them, and besides, we've got a standing invitation to play anytime we want in a shitload of top clubs and halls in the Big Apple and beyond. We've also got one of the most prolific hit song-writers in Nashville ready, willing, and able to take us in the studio. He's vowed to produce the band a hit record, and we believe in him. You may have heard his name, but if not, you've definitely heard his songs being sung by a ton of famous people. There's a tune he wrote that was released by the Nashville Teens called 'Tobacco Road.' You've heard that one, right, Billy? It's on our song list, but we do it with a little psychedelic touch."

Gregg chimed in, "Funny thing about the Nashville Teens—they're from England. Go figure."

Duane laughed along with Gregg. "The writer I'm talking about is John D. Loudermilk," he said, "but his friends all call him John D. He's one fine dude, man."

"Damn," I was thinking. "They've got it all going on." I was speechless.

"I know it's a lot to throw on you all of a sudden," Duane said, "but at the same time, it's a pretty fucking and exciting and reward-ing musician life we're offering. I bet when you woke up this morn-ing you didn't have a clue that we had a net out trying to run you down to see if you'd play with us, huh? Listen, Billy, we know you'll have to give this some serious thought. What we're simply asking is...would you—or could you—leave the band you're with and hit the road with us full time?"

Duane said he figured I might need a little time to think about it, but told me, "There's not a single drummer even in the running for this gig. You the man, Billy. I'll be calling in a couple of weeks to see what you've decided. We're dead serious about everything we're telling you. We're making good money, so you won't be bum-ming. The gigs and studio sessions are there—we just need you there. There's no turning us back, and we're headed to the top.

Maybe, I thought to myself, Gregg and Duane see me as John Lennon saw Ringo Starr. John once said, "Pete Best is a good drummer, but Ringo is a good Beatle." They knew Maynard was a good drummer, but I would be a good Allman Joy.

My musical destiny was hanging right there and then in this small motel room. I sat frozen in the chair, starring into the carpet with my brain just spinning. I was having an overwhelming yet sensational feeling contemplating this "out of nowhere" job offer and life change. It was truly remarkable that at seventeen I was being asked to join the best band that I'd ever heard.

"Damn, son, get a grip," I said to myself. "Duane and Gregg Allman have chosen you to play with them above all the great drummers they've seen from Miami to New York City. Stand up straight, hold your head high and shoulders back."

I couldn't turn this down, and I almost yelled out, "OK, oh yeah, I'd love to play with you all!"

We all began shaking hands, hugging, and laughing. Then suddenly I realized there was a huge dilemma. Slowly, in a depressing tone, I spit it out. "There's a snag. I'm only a couple of months away from graduating high school, and my parents might as well have their hearts ripped out if I don't suffer through the next several weeks and graduate."

"No problem," Duane said. "Last year we waited on Gregg to graduate until we hit the road full time. I understand, *but* the day after you graduate, a plane ticket will be waiting for you to come join us. As far as I'm concerned, you're already in the band."

I wanted to scream and yell. I had the best band job ever! Damn! I was one fortunate, grateful, and excited son of a bitch drummer! I was going to be hittin' the road with the best!

When I told my buddies in the Men-its, they were disappointed at first, but the guys knew it was a no-brainer for me. It turned out to be a smooth transition, as they called their original drummer, Johnny Sandlin, and he agreed to come back.

After playing the fraternity gig that night, the Allman Joys packed up and left town. A few weeks later Duane called.

"Hey, Billy. You haven't backed out on us, have you?"

"Naw, man," I said, "I wish I was playing with you right now."

"Good deal—we do, too. Listen here! We're up in New York playing a club in Greenwich Village called Trude Heller's and staying at a place called the Albert Hotel. It's just a few blocks away from the club. The Albert's rates are reasonable, and the accommodations are pretty nice, and they're clean. We're in a suite which is pretty roomy. Better than a motel room. You'll love this. We got wind of this hotel because it's renowned for being home to some really good musicians and bands. There are great musicians everywhere."

That's one thing Duane didn't need to tell me. I had visited New York City a few years earlier with my dad and my brother. It was a thirty-three-hour, one-way bus ride from Tuscaloosa. My dad was the Exalted Ruler of the Tuscaloosa Lodge of the Elks and had to attend a national convention in New York. He decided to take my brother and me with him since the World's Fair was also happening there. It was an eye-opener, to say the least. The city and the fair had a lasting effect on me.

The first thing I decided was that I never wanted to ride on a bus ever again. The next thing I decided was that I wanted to become a drummer like one of the incredible musicians I had seen performing and thriving there, far-fetched as that seemed at the time. We were on a shoestring budget for the trip. Shit, we were on a shoestring budget back home. Dad was extremely frugal, and while we were in New York, we had to eat at self-serve "Automats," where we ate standing up. Hot dog venders were numerous throughout the city, and we hit nearly every one of them. One day, we passed a Chinese restaurant while walking around, and, to my surprise, Dad said, "Let's go in and try this place out. It looks like it could be fairly reasonable and the food smells really good from out front here."

We had a terrific meal. I marveled at the fact that my father had suggested we get a meal at a place where we didn't have to stand upright to eat and whose food didn't require ketchup, mustard, or pickles. This was an eatery that had waiters who brought your food. Of course, we didn't order anything separately. Dad had them bring us one large dish that we all shared, but I do remember getting my own eggroll.

In addition to our walking tours to see the Statue of Liberty from across the water, the United Nations, and, amazingly, the top of the Empire State Building, the biggest thrill of all was my father taking us to the World's Fair. There were plenty of exhibits to see, but there were a multitude of live bands performing as well. One of these groups was the Young Rascals, and besides being really great, they had this drummer who not only played impressive drum parts that I had never heard executed before, but he could twirl his sticks, throw them up in the air, and catch them without missing a beat. What a showman!

When I got back home and behind my own set, I tried and tried to duplicate his stick twirling, throwing my sticks up in the air and retrieving them. There was no way. I dropped a million sticks, and the ones that I threw up in the air usually landed back on my head. Ouch.

Later, I heard records by the Young Rascals and saw them on *The Ed Sullivan Show*. They had made it, and the drummer still twirled his sticks, threw them up in the air, and retrieved them again without missing a beat. If I ever had the chance to be in the music business in New York City, I decided right then and there that I would not pass it up.

Duane called constantly, relaying songs that I needed to learn, so I would either pick up the 45-rpm records, buy the albums that had the tunes on them, or borrow records from friends as I continually worked on these drum parts.

So, the week before graduation day, I called the Southern Airways ticket counter at the Tuscaloosa airport, and what do you know? There it was, waiting for me: a plane ticket with my name on it. A few days later, Duane Allman and friends were greeting me at LaGuardia Airport. My road education was about to begin.

11

A Meeting with Some Yardbirds

One night after we had played one of our sets at Trude Heller's in Greenwich Village, Trude Heller came backstage and said that two English guys wanted to meet us. So Duane said, "Come on, Novice, let's see who these dudes are."

We approached their table and introduced ourselves, and one of the guys said, "Thanks for coming out. My name is Jeff and this is Jimmy."

Their long hair, English accents, and very cool clothes branded them as being in a popular British band—we just didn't know which band right off. By their first names, we couldn't place them, but then they said that they had a group called the Yardbirds and were in the States to play some shows. Which meant, of course, that I had just met Jeff Beck and Jimmy Page.

I can't remember which one of them asked, "Where did you learn what you're doing with the rhythm and blues?"

What a shock: they wanted to know how we had learned to play soul music so well. We always included some R & B and blues in each one of our sets, including tunes by B. B. King, Marvin Gaye, Little Anthony and the Imperials, the Four Tops, the Temptations and many other black artists. Duane handled their questions eloquently as they listened intently. In part, he told them that we had grown up in the South, so listening to and seeing R & B and blues acts was just a part of our musical experience and heritage. The conversation wasn't very long because we had to get back onstage to play another set. They listened to us, but there was not enough time for us to ask them anything.

Duane and I came back onstage very proud of being noticed by famous English musicians who were drawn to our ability to pull off performing black music. It made me think of how we all took for granted what a blessing it was to have grown up around soul music.

Gregg's vocals, even at his young age, had a real soulful flavor on all the traditionally black music that we were playing. We and all the Southern musicians we knew were immensely proud of our soul music roots.

Duane and I talked later and realized we had forgotten to tell Jeff and Jimmy that we were doing a couple of their tunes. It was a challenge because their songs were so different from any of the other English groups that we had heard so far. One of their guitars would sound like a violin and the notes sustained forever—that was Jeff Beck.

Duane had already been captivated by the guitar work on their records, and he wanted to learn how they were getting their guitar sounds and parts. It was a bummer since if Duane had had more time to talk with them, it would have opened a brand-new door for him. Even more depressing was that they left during our next set because Duane had just as many questions for them as they had for us. Now he had the task of figuring it out for himself, and this became his obsessive project.

Duane had learned about a device called a treble boost from a couple of guitarists in the Village band the Blues Magoos, so he bought one and began to experiment. Slowly, he came up with new guitar sounds that he began to work with, and these new sounds were like nothing any of us had ever heard. No doubt these sounds would be captivating to everyone in our future audiences—especially musicians and guitar players. This was when Duane's guitar playing evolved from good to "one of a kind." This was way before all the guitar pedals began to come out that gave guitarists different sounds. He began trying all sorts of devices to create more inventive, new sounds. Duane began to play the guitar parts necessary to cover the Yardbirds' songs exactly, and I never heard another band duplicate a Yardbirds song like we were able to do.

I never asked why, but soon after he began using the treble boost, he drew a picture of a hand giving the "bird" on the tape that was holding his treble boost on his guitar... Funny.

12

Village Adventures with the Blues Magoos

For Duane, next in importance to my needing new clothes to fit in with the band's onstage persona was the need for me to experience what they called their "most tasty Greenwich Village discovery."

One day, we were walking through the Village when Duane suddenly shouted, "There!" He pointed to an Orange Julius stand that wasn't as big as my family's kitchen. A couple of employees were busy making orange-colored drinks. My family hadn't bought a blender yet, so this drink that they were making, using these huge spinning machines, was all new to me.

The workers poured fresh-squeezed orange juice into one of these large blenders, added this powdery "secret" potion and some crushed ice, and then turned it up to a speed that I could only describe as "Good God Almighty" high. They then poured the drink into large cups, and voilà! It *was* the best-tasting drink I had ever put in my mouth.

After my introduction to the Orange Julius stand, I went there every day. I became an Orange Julius addict. This was the only Orange Julius stand in the world—well before the business was franchised, made it out of Greenwich Village, and, eventually, all across the globe. It was sad when, in a few years, I began seeing these stands popping up all over; I wanted it to stay a big secret that could only be found at that one spot in Greenwich Village, but the inevitability of a huge profit took over.

One day, while sitting by myself at the Orange Julius stand, I began thinking, "How the hell did I get to this point in the music business at the age of seventeen?" Here I was, in the middle of Greenwich Village, in New York City, with a gig that all the drummers back home were envying.

While playing at Trude Heller's, we had Sunday nights off. My first day-off adventure took place in our band's hotel suite, which was five stories up in the Albert Hotel. We were hanging with some members of the Blues Magoos. The Magoos were a talented, innovative group that was nevertheless struggling and obviously couldn't afford the nice Beatle Boots we were wearing, so they had to wear sandals, which they made out of old automobile tires that were cut up and lashed together with rope. Man, they would probably have been filthy rich if they had only patented their sandals before the later influx of Mexican imports of the same kind arrived.

The two bands spent this particular Sunday making smoke bombs from commercial fireworks with a cigarette fuse attached. The slow-burning fuse allowed the smoke bomb planter to get back upstairs to watch the show that would unfold below. The escapade went as follows: someone would place the smoke bomb in a phone booth down on the street, light the cigarette fuse, run back upstairs, and then we'd all watch while laying over the ledges of our hotel room windows as it went off. The smoke bombs didn't explode with a loud violent blast, but rather with an almost silent ignition as a huge smoke plume would rise from the phone booth. We would all cackle as pandemonium broke out down on the street as smoke poured from the phone booth. Can you even imagine pulling this kind of stunt today after 9/11?

The smoke bomb was made from an empty cardboard toilet paper roll which was packed with gunpowder from firecrackers and cherry bombs, then wrapped with various smoke-causing materials, and finally sealed with masking tape with the cigarette fuse sticking out.

Duane assured me that the cops couldn't find a lone bunch of smoke bombers in a four-block area of a zillion people. Being the Novice that I was, I believed him, and thankfully no one was ever caught, or even confronted by the hotel staff. Nevertheless, we were so stupid sometimes... Stupid, stupid, stupid!

One night at the club, it seemed like the gig just wouldn't end. It felt like we played a hundred sets. I was dog-tired walking offstage and quickly split outside to get out of the smoke. The "Novice" didn't smoke yet. There, leaning up against the stone wall of the club, was this very beautiful lady who was adorned in the finest fashion styles of the day. She looked a little older than me. She seemed to be alone, and it was about four in the morning.

I went over to her, and we began to chat and laugh, and it was obvious that we were going to get to know each other better that night. Right at the end of that thought, Duane came banging out the front door of the club. He made it down about ten steps in two bounds, grabbed me by the arm, and threw me into the back of a waiting cab. He got in and quickly and loudly gave the cabbie directions to our hotel.

I abruptly spoke up and demanded to know why he had messed up my action. I didn't know what his reason would be, but I certainly wasn't expecting his answer. I asked him, "Didn't you see how beautiful that lady was?" Duane said calmly, "Novice, that wasn't a she. You get it?" The Novice still had some growing up to do. This experience left me dumbfounded and embarrassed.

I was a member of the musicians' union, as were all the rest of the guys, but one night a gentleman came backstage and asked all of us to show him not only our musician union cards, but also our New York City cabaret license cards as well. I had been trying to sneak around not being of age because a musician had to be eighteen to play professionally in the city, and I was only seventeen, so I had no license.

So, this was the swan song for our playing in NYC at that time. I heard that the same thing had happened to George Harrison of the Beatles when they were playing in Germany. The Allman Joys could have hired another drummer who was of age, but instead they decided to keep me and go with another plan. Again, they must have liked my drumming a whole lot.

We hadn't told Trude Heller about my age and not having a cabaret license, so those Allman brothers came up with a plan. We went back to the club late that night. The custodian was still there, and he unlocked the club doors to let us in. We packed up all of our equipment, loaded the band trailer, and left town then and there, without giving any notice to the club or paying the hotel bill. The smoke bombs were bad enough, but now, at seventeen, I really felt like a New York City thug.

13

John D. Loudermilk and the Nashville Scene

Duane and Gregg had become acquainted with a notable songwriter in Nashville a while back. He was John D. Loudermilk, who was a legendary fixture in town, so the Chevy station wagon, the trailer, and the band began an adventurous journey directly to Nashville for the help that the Allmans knew he could give.

Earlier in 1966, before I joined the Allman Joys, John D. Loudermilk had walked into a small club in Nashville to have a drink. Up on the bandstand was what looked like just another of the thousands of teenage rock bands of the era. When they began to play, however, Loudermilk realized that they weren't so typical after all. The two front men were both light-haired and made quite an impression. One played a stinging guitar and the other sang in an anguished, world-weary voice. John D. wondered how these two young guys played like they had years of performing and road experience. That was the night he became interested in the Allman Joys. Loudermilk wanted to see if the boys were interested in going into the studio and cutting some tunes. Of course they were, but they had to keep working to support themselves, so they stayed on the road and ended up in NYC.

The night we left New York, Duane and Gregg indicated that they were relying on Loudermilk to help the band land a gig and the recording opportunity that he had promised.

None of the other members of the band seemed too bummed out about abandoning our gig at Trude Heller's, but I felt guilty for being the reason that we left.

The next morning, we found ourselves going through the Shenandoah National Forest. Mike Alexander had saved some cherry bombs that were left over from our smoke bomb escapade, so, being bored with the long drive, he decided to light a few and throw them out of the car windows. They started to go off on the highway behind us, but all of a sudden, we couldn't see where a couple of them had exploded. We were still young, reckless, and stupid, but we were concerned about where they may have landed, so we turned around and went back to where they had been thrown out.

We pulled over and quickly discovered that some of the cherry bombs had bounced off the road and rolled down the side of the mountain we were traveling down, starting two small fires. Duane said, "Grab the blankets and get down there fast. We got to try and beat the fires out."

Even though it was a short distance down to the fires, by the time we got there, the flames were spreading fast, and our frantic blanket beating showed no hope of putting the fires out. Although we were stupid, we were not heathens, so we ran back up the hill, piled into the wagon, found a phone booth, and called the Forest Service to report the fires. We were all overly concerned and felt really bad about being such gourd heads for throwing the cherry bombs. Starting fires in the beautiful Shenandoah National Forest filled all of us with terrible guilt.

Duane tried his best to calm us. He said that the Forest Service would have one of their tanker planes fly over and dump a fire-retardant solution that would extinguish the fires in one swipe. I still find myself wondering what happened with the fire and how much beauty had gone up in smoke. We were responsible for destroying that beauty. Stupid, stupid yet again! Oh, our guilt was really raging.

We traveled continuously day and night, with two of us up front and alternating drivers while the other two slept in the back seat until it was their time to drive, until we safely reached Nashville. Duane called John D. Loudermilk as soon as we arrived, and John was ecstatic to hear that Duane and Gregg and the group were in town. He gave us the name of a reasonable motel to check into.

The Anchor Motel would be home for us now and on many other visits to Nashville. It was an older motel, right in downtown. We found that it had a reputation for housing many of the top country artists that came to Nashville to record. In fact, it wasn't just all country artists who stayed at the Anchor because we heard that Elvis Presley stayed there when he was in town.

We checked into a single room with two double beds, which we would always do on the road. We would sleep two to each double bed and save money by not having to get two rooms. We went to bed early and got some much-needed sleep.

The motel had three wings that were situated in a horseshoe configuration. The office was located on the front of the right wing, the left wing had rooms around back as well, and the far wing had a swimming pool out front. The rooms that were on the back of the left wing faced a prominent Italian restaurant where we would see country music stars and local elected officials showing up to dine. We would always select a room on that back side because of the privacy.

After waking, Duane called John D. again, and he gave us the name of a booking agency in town for us to contact. John had already arranged for us to have a meeting with them. The organization was called One Nighters, Inc. We went to their office and met with the head of the agency, Billy Smith. Billy was a great guy, and for John, he wanted to do everything he could to help the group even before hearing us.

Billy immediately booked us a gig at a local club, the Briar Patch, and scheduled a photographer to take promo pictures of the band for distribution to other venues that might be appropriate for us to play.

Billy Smith had played with a group called the Casuals who had backed up Brenda Lee, so Billy knew the road. One Nighters, Inc., had another agent working for them named Bill Fennell who became a big fan of the Allman Joys and helped us a great deal while the agency was booking us.

14

Rock and Roll at the Briar Patch

On our first Monday night in town, we began playing at the Briar Patch, which was located just a short distance up a hill from downtown Nashville and not far from our motel. It was a club that catered to a crowd of all ages, but its clientele was basically made up of people in their early twenties to their mid-forties, with some illegal teenagers thrown in. The Briar Patch was nothing fancy. It had a single glass-door entrance, and, upon entering, the clientele would approach a counter where they paid the cover charge. The floor was not carpeted, and the tables and chairs looked a lot like what I'd seen in an Elks Club or Moose Lodge. A dance floor was located in front of the stage, and the bar was up against the far wall facing the stage.

Our contract with the club had us playing from 9 P.M. until 2 A.M., Monday through Saturday. The music that we had to play at the time to make a living was referred to as "cover music," songs that were popular on the radio or had become standard rock and roll, R & B, or blues tunes. We learned them using single 45-rpm records or 33 1/3-rpm albums that we would buy, so we always carried a portable record player with us for learning songs off the records that we bought.

Our repertoire had to be extensive because of the competition in the band-club business. If you could play a large variety of popular songs that your audience recognized, you had a better chance of being booked into the kinds of clubs that paid best. We were professional musicians, so our livelihood depended on staying on top of all the songs that were popular everywhere that we would be booked. We drew from the music of the British Invasion artists and American recording artists, especially those from Motown, the Philly Sound, Memphis, Muscle Shoals, and the new West Coast rock. Thinking back, the Briar Patch and the Allman Joys were probably instrumental in beginning to bring a different music to Nashville.

Our song list radically deviated from tunes that had that "Nashville sound." We were in the "Country Music Capital of the World" trying to get into the rock and roll music industry; now ain't that a trip?

Here's an example of some of the songs in our repertoire and the artists who introduced them:

The Beatles: "Paperback Writer," "A Hard Day's Night," "Baby You Can Drive My Car," "Money Can't Buy Me Love," "Tax Man."

The Yardbirds: "Shapes of Things," "For Your Love," "Over Under Sideways Down," "I Ain't Got You."

Little Anthony & The Imperials: "I Do Love You."

The Four Tops: "Reach Out and I'll Be There."

The Nashville Teens: "Tobacco Road."

The Blues Magoos: "(We Ain't Got) Nothin' Yet," "Gotta Get Away."

The Byrds: "Hey Mister Tambourine Man."

Ray Charles: "Georgia."

The Animals: "House of the Rising Sun," "Boom Boom," "Blue Feeling."

Paul Revere and the Raiders: "Kicks."

The Troggs: "Wild Thing."

Bobby Bland: "Turn on Your Love Light."

The Young Rascals: "Good Lovin'."

The Righteous Brothers: "Ol' Man River," "You're My Soul and Inspiration."

The Left Banke: "Walk Away Renee."

Wilson Pickett: "Land of a Thousand Dances."

The Outsiders: "Time Won't Let Me."

The Lovin' Spoonful: "Summer in the City."

The Shadows: "Gloria."

Bob Dylan: "Like a Rolling Stone."

Percy Sledge: "When a Man Loves a Woman."

Billy Smith, president of One Nighters, Inc., John D. Loudermilk, and the manager of the club were all there that first night to hear us play. Billy said that there would be no trouble keeping us working in various venues and in several states. The manager gave us a two-week stay, which relieved all of us because we were flat broke. The manager was also kind enough to front us some money, so now we could eat.

As word spread about the great new band playing at the Briar Patch, the club was filled with customers by the weekend. Every night the crowd grew larger until it was standing-room only with a line out the door. The manager was so happy with the turnout and the bar sales that he offered us an open invitation to come back and play anytime we wanted. The Briar Patch would become our security blanket when we had open weeks. We made many new friends while playing there, musicians and customers alike.

While in Nashville for a few days, we found a restaurant a few blocks over from the motel named Ireland's. This restaurant's specialty was steak and biscuits—we're talking a *huge* mound of steak and biscuits. The food must have been a foot high, and the price was almost rock bottom: $1.25 a plate.

When we finished the meal we also ordered their specialty dessert of hot fudge cake with ice cream, which was also huge. I don't know how we got up and walked out of the place. More than going to a restaurant, eating at Ireland's was like being at a party because it was such a fun place to go to. We always sat in the corner booth that was in a semi-circle, and Ireland's became our premier place to eat.

Another restaurant that we frequented to get our supply of vegetables was Morrison's Cafeteria. Morrison's was in the center of downtown Nashville, and it seemed that we were always seated at a table smack dab in the middle of the restaurant whenever we ate there. The restaurant was always full when we chose to eat there, and we became like the stage show. All the other patrons would stare at us and point and talk amongst themselves about our peculiarities in dress and our long hair. Duane nicknamed the restaurant "the Fishbowl" because we were like the goldfish that would be watched as they swam around in their bowl, but that didn't stop us from going there frequently.

Besides these two restaurants, after getting off at the Briar Patch late at night, we would sometimes go to a twenty-four-hour restaurant that was also located in downtown Nashville. After eating there one night, we stepped outside, and everyone except me started smoking. I asked why all three of them had lit up cigarettes when we walked out of the restaurant, and Duane said, "A cigarette really tops a meal off. It adds a little something after a meal and to the flavor of a cigarette."

So, for some reason, I became bold enough to ask Duane if I could try one of his cigarettes. This was the first cigarette I had ever smoked, and from that night on, I began smoking Salem menthol cigarettes.

Another first for me in Nashville was having an alcoholic drink. It came about one night at the Briar Patch after we played a set and took a break. One of the patrons came over to my table and said, "Damn, man, you play a hell of a set of drums. I bought you a drink; I figured you might like a whiskey sour."

The man sat down with me and began talking, so, not wanting to be impolite, I began sipping the drink. After about five or ten minutes, I noticed I began adding more to our conversation and laughing at the funny things he was saying. I have to admit that my whole body was feeling really "good." After just having that one drink, I got back onstage and playing seemed to be more fun too. On the next break, I went to the bar and ordered another whiskey sour. From that night on, I guess you could consider me a drinker.

After a few nights of playing at the Briar Patch, we noticed that the same three girls were coming every night. We struck up a conversation, and Gregg took an interest in one of them. The topic came up about where we were staying, and we said if they waited until we finished our last set, we would show them. So they stayed, and we all drove back to the Anchor Motel together.

The three girls and the band just shot the shit for a couple of hours, and then the girls left. The next day, they came by the motel in the late afternoon after they had gotten off work. They stayed until we had to head back to the Briar Patch, and they came along with us. This type of schedule repeated itself over the course of our first engagement at the club. After several days of seeing the girls, both in the afternoon and at night, it was obvious that Gregg and one of the girls were becoming very tight. They soon become an item.

In the mid-'60s, all the guys with long hair also had bangs. Each time that we were in town, these girls would be our barbers, cutting our bangs when they began to get in our eyes. The girls became our best friends, but Gregg's girlfriend became a little more than that.

Also, during our first week in Nashville, John D. and Billy Smith booked us a spot on a popular local early-morning TV show hosted by Ralph Emery. I have forgotten the songs that we played, but I am sure that we sounded awful. We really didn't want to do the show, but we owed John and Billy. Having to get up ultra-early to make it to the TV studio on time left us with about three hours of sleep.

During the second week at the Briar Patch, John D., as we called him, brought Chet Atkins down to hear us, and there could not have been a more prestigious guest. I think that it was on this night that Chet offered the RCA Studios to John for us to record in when we had enough original material together.

Neither Gregg, Duane, nor Mike had tried writing songs yet, so John D. invited us to come stay with him to get our original material together. The arrangement was that we would all get together and either approve songs by other writers that would fit our band or write some new songs with John D. so that we would have enough material to go into the studio.

John D.'s wife and children were going to visit their hometown, Chapel Hill, North Carolina, in a few weeks, so the timing worked out perfectly. Until then, Duane and Gregg suggested that after we finished the gig in Nashville, we should go to Daytona Beach to play a club called the Martinique, the most popular hangout in town. Now we had a plan.

15

Down to Daytona

During our first road trip together, traveling from New York to Nashville, I became well-versed in Duane's "Rules of the Road." First of all, there would be two of us in the front seat, with one person driving and the other one talking to him, changing the radio channels when a signal was lost, and suggesting we pull over to get some coffee or whatever it took to keep the driver awake and accident-free. After a couple of hours, the two would switch places. The passenger-side dude would drive while the new passenger would keep him awake, while the two on the back seat would be catching some shut-eye. After several hours, the two in the back would switch to the front, and vice versa, because we did not want to find ourselves in a ditch in the middle of nowhere. The interstate system was not fully in place in the mid-1960s, and most all of the highways to our destinations were two-lane roads. There was also nothing open past about 7 P.M., and that went for gas stations and garages, so when traveling at night, we had to make sure that we had a full tank of gas in the early evening.

To me, one of the hardest parts of trying to get some sleep in the back seat was battling for that perfect foot position with the other guy. From the very start, Duane and I partnered up. Duane frequently wanted to listen to classical music. Funny, huh?! I often wondered if he was listening to violins and string parts to get ideas for guitar parts, but feeling it was a private and maybe sensitive subject for him, I never asked. That aspect of Duane has always raised my curiosity.

Another hard-and-fast Duane rule: starch. We took our clothes to the nearest laundry weekly to have them dry-cleaned and then lightly starched. I can close my eyes and still hear Duane: "And remember—lightly starched!" He insisted that we look crisp and clean onstage, and in the heat and humidity of Florida and the South, that meant starch—but only light, since we couldn't play if our clothes were stiffly starched.

Some of Duane's rules were serious and some were hilarious. I was initiated into one of his musical rituals on my first trip to Florida with the guys. After we crossed into Florida and approached a bridge over the Suwanee River, Duane made us *all* sing, "Way down upon the Suwannee River," the famous lyrics from Stephen Foster's "Old Folks at Home," the official song of the state of Florida. Every time, whether we were going south or heading back up north. Tired? Too bad. Headache? Too bad. Brutal cheap-wine hangover? Too bad!

When light broke, we were driving into central Florida down US Highway 1, which runs parallel with the Atlantic coast for 2,369 miles from Key West to Fort Kent, Maine. While observing the terrain and foliage, I marveled at all the small roadside stands I saw along with the abundance of quaint accommodations available for tourists. This Florida portion of the trip was becoming a favorite of mine, running a close second to my adaptation to the bohemian life in Greenwich Village. Duane and Gregg were continually telling me about certain episodes that happened in their youth in the different areas that we passed through. One place was Tomoka State Park, which they called "To Smoka State Park." Get it?

We finally arrived in Daytona and drove into the driveway of their home, which was a three-bedroom house with a double garage in which their mother's automobile was already parked on one side. When Duane and Gregg entered the house, an exuberant mom shouted with joy at the sight of her boys. It felt like I was home, too, when she gave me a big motherly hug as well. Everyone was full of stories, so it was quite a while before we stretched out for some much-needed sleep after our grueling, straight-through drive from Nashville to Daytona Beach.

Geraldine Allman (often called "Jerry") instantly appeared to be another wonderful band mom. Her enthusiasm for the group's work reminded me so much of my mother. She managed a local prominent restaurant in Daytona called the Bali and brought home wonderful food for us every evening. My favorite was the chilled boiled shrimp because they went well with the Daytona Beach heat. Then again, there were plenty of mouthwatering homemade pies and desserts. Lovely girls with great personalities and senses of humor were also plentiful. That house was always jumping, day and night. It was really a big kick being in Daytona Beach with all the live bands at the numerous clubs and halls, and then there was the beach itself.

Ms. Allman had a 1965 Oldsmobile 98 Rocket Convertible, which she allowed me to drive occasionally. Daytona's beach was made up of the kind of sand that you could drive a family car on. I learned the beach was once used for stock car racing and helped launch NASCAR and the Daytona Speedway.

It was too much fun to take a lady for a drive on the beach with the top down, driving in this happenin' Olds, or "Short," as the Daytona Beach kids called a car. One of the first girls that I took a liking to happened to be the daughter of the race car driving guru Fireball Roberts. He was famous, but I never in my wildest dreams thought that one day I would be dating his daughter. It didn't take but one nighttime ride on the beach in the Oldsmobile Rocket to win her over. Gregg was seeing an attractive old girlfriend who looked like she could be Cher's stand-in, and Duane was also seeing his old girlfriend, Patti.

The Allman Joys were the most popular band in town when we were in Daytona. Our first gig on this trip was at a popular club and live music hall called the Martinique. Every night playing the Martinique was an adventure and a whole bunch of fun. The club was packed every night, and a good deal of the clientele were local musicians. It was a highly lucrative gig since we worked for a percentage of the cover charge at the door. Making a great deal of money while playing in a hip joint where everyone hung out only added to our excitement.

The stage was exceptionally high, making the previous club stages that we had played on seem tiny, maybe because it was really a music hall with a large bar. The stage rose about five feet off the floor, so the band could see the entire crowd, all the way to the back wall.

On one of our later visits playing the Martinique, we were asked to back up a visiting recording artist, B. J. Thomas, who had a hit record with a Hank Williams tune entitled "I'm So Lonesome I Could Cry." This was a first for me—backing up a star! We would play a set, then back up Thomas on a set. While backstage on one of our breaks, B. J. Thomas and the Allman Joys watched the Rolling Stones' first television appearance in the United States on *The Ed Sullivan Show.* This was where the Allman Joys had set our goal: to become a big enough act to make it on *The Ed Sullivan Show.*

The band visited and played Daytona Beach frequently when we had an open week. The Martinique was our club of choice, but when they were booked up with other bands, we would play at a club and music hall located on the long pier stretching out into the Atlantic Ocean called, fittingly, the Pier.

There were a number of good bands around Daytona Beach. On one of our first visits playing the Martinique, we played sets opposite one of those groups called the Night Crawlers. They were having a lot of success around Florida with their new 45, "Little Black Egg." The Allman Joys' previous bass player, Bob Keller, was playing with them. Bob had been playing with the Allman Joys in Mobile when I first met him. I had always thought that Bob Keller was the perfect bass player for the Allman Joys because of his showmanship and vocal harmonies. I was disappointed when I heard that he was no longer with the group and had been replaced by Mike Alexander. (Later on down the road, Duane and Gregg realized how valuable Bob had been, and he would once again join the Allman Joys.)

Playing alongside Bob in the Night Crawlers was a young guitar player named Pete Carr. Pete was only fifteen years old but very, very good. Pete and I became great friends, probably because of our close age. We didn't know it then, but we had a lot of music left to play together in the years ahead.

After the week at the Martinique, the Allman Joys had to get back to Nashville to begin recording. The rest of the band left ahead of me in the Chevy wagon pulling the trailer, as I had decided to ride up with a new friend from Daytona named Don, who wanted to leave town for a bit and see Nashville. Don had just acquired a sporty new Chevrolet, which I thought would be nice and comfortable on the long ride back to Nashville.

Pete Carr of the Night Crawlers also wanted to leave Daytona and to come with us heading north. Pete had never been out of Florida before, so once we got a little inland, Pete began noticing these small hills, which seemed to make a big impression on him since all he had ever seen all his life was flat land.

Suddenly, Pete screamed, "Stop the car! I've got to climb up that mountain!" He was in such awe seeing these small hills that he actually thought they were mountains! We humored him and let him get out and climb up a hill. At the top, he looked down at us with this big smile, waving his arms. Little did he know then, but leaving Daytona Beach was going to change his life forever because Pete Carr was destined to become one of the most sought-after recording-session guitarists in the business.

16

Working with John D. and Chet Atkins

After arriving back in Nashville, I called the Loudermilk home to get directions. John D.'s home was in Brentwood, Tennessee, and at that time, Brentwood was outside of town and really considered to be in the country. (Today, Brentwood is part of the vast area of metropolitan Nashville.)

In the 1960s, Brentwood was dominated by beautiful, undisturbed rocky hills with an abundance of stately trees and thick foliage. John lived on top of one of these large rocky hills overlooking the scenic valley below. His driveway was very narrow, and you had to negotiate carefully when driving up to his home. He had horses stabled in a large flat area of his acreage, halfway down to the valley.

John's home featured a scenic view of the valley below and the tall hills beyond. His place wasn't a country music-star mansion, it was simply a very nice two-story house with a songwriting studio upstairs. The band felt right at home, and the house was an extremely comfortable place for us to work while we put together our recording song list.

The first gold 45-rpm record I ever saw was hanging on John D.'s wall. It was the record awarded to him for writing the song "Tobacco Road," which was a bigger-than-huge rock hit. Funny thing, though: it had been recorded by an English group who called themselves the Nashville Teens. John D. had a terrific reputation in the country music business, but "Tobacco Road" opened his eyes to a whole new outlet and industry for his songs. That hit inspired him to try his hand at producing a rock band, and who did he pick? The Allman Joys.

John was a gracious host and incredibly fun to be around. The first night there, we had a blowout party. But the next morning, it was down to business. Remember, his reason for having us stay with him was not to have parties, but to get us ready to go into the studio to record. He not only had the resources to produce us, he also had an abundance of original songs for us to pull from. As stated earlier, we didn't have even a smidgen of our own original material. So first, the obvious thing to do was listen to some of John's songs and pick and choose those that could fit our band.

In addition to picking tunes, John spent a great deal of time giving Gregg songwriting lessons. Gregg later told me that he recognized John D. Loudermilk as a mentor for helping him learn how to write songs and for giving him tips that he put to good use in the years to come.

There was one song that we had played around with while rehearsing at the Briar Patch that we were convinced we could turn into something powerful if given the chance in the studio. The song was an old Willie Dixon blues tune called "Spoonful." We rearranged it from a laid-back blues tune into a fast, powerful, and upbeat tune with a psychedelic arrangement. This was the only song we had to offer John as being somewhat original. John D. allowed it to be added to our list, and it was later picked to be our first 45-rpm single and distributed to radio stations.

Later, we all felt bad about drastically changing the arrangement of this wonderful blues tune into an unrecognizable lemon. We took this song in the wrong direction, trying to make it a hip new-day popular hit. This was the first record release for all of us, and we were young, doing what we thought it took to have a hit.

One evening, John revealed that he was a member of Duke University's staff of psychic research. He told us story after story about ghosts, bizarre events, and his investigations of the weird with the staff. Some stories were unbelievable, and others were downright terrifying. He would just laugh and laugh each time he got our gander up. John D. was some kind of funny and very interesting, too.

Contrary to what I was told when we first arrived to stay with John D., it was *not* going to be all business. It turns out that there was never a dull moment while staying up on that high hill at the Loudermilk Tennessee ranch. On one such occasion, while upstairs in John's small studio, our bass player, Mike, announced that he could fart songs.

Everyone said, "Sure you can—that's a bunch of bullshit." He got down on his knees and elbows and actually began farting tunes that we recognized. Our stomachs cramped from laughing, and our eyes began pouring with tears. As entertaining as his performance was, these were not tunes that could be considered for our album. We forwarded them on to recording artists who were looking for unique songs of this nature. Naw! Just kidding!

Early one morning, John D. invited us to have breakfast at a real down-home restaurant in the little town of Brentwood. As we were driving down, he said, "By the way, Chet Atkins will be joining us." We were all stunned. Each of us well remembered how he had been in the audience one time when we played at the Briar Patch, which was when John introduced him to us between sets. We were trying to be on top of our act that night after hearing that the great Chet Atkins had come to hear us. This was Mr. Nashville in the flesh. Chet Atkins had played on so many records, and he was un-doubtedly one of the most well-known musicians not only in the United States, but worldwide. Now we were going to have breakfast with him. Unbelievable, just unbelievable...sitting at the breakfast table with Chet Atkins.

Conversations with Chet were a lot like having breakfast with our own families or friends. He was a kind, down-to-earth person who had not let fame go to his head or change him into an egotis-tical snob. He came across as a good old guy who wanted to be our friend. Chet had the ability to make everyone around him feel right at home. You would never guess that he held the recording business of Nashville in his hands. When I reflect on our talking, laughing, and getting to know each other better that day, I hope he came away knowing that we were a dedicated band of young musicians who had a vision of where we wanted to go in the music business. I'm sure he knew how overwhelmed we were when we first sat down with him. I guess Chet had overwhelmed many other musicians before, but he was so humble that it did not take long for anyone to become comfortable around him, and that's exactly what happened to us. The ice really broke when we began to notice how attentive he was when we spoke. Of course, we hung on to every word he said.

Chet Atkins and his musical partners Floyd Cramer and Boots Randolph were legends in the business and had always been bigger than life in my parents' home. My mother had bought all their records and played them over and over on the record player and on her piano. Now Mr. Atkins, or Chet, had become a friend of mine and all the guys in the band.

Shortly after having breakfast with Chet, his daughter came over to John D.'s to meet us, too. She immediately got a little sweet on Gregg, who had no interest in taking their friendship to another level, but she would still hang out with us whenever we were in Nashville. Surprisingly, we now had both Chet and his daughter as our new prominent Nashville friends. She would often call my mother, and they would have long conversations. My mom was knocked out that she became friends with Chet Atkins's daughter. She loved talking to her and couldn't understand why I didn't develop a more-than-friendly relationship with her. Hmmm? Chet Atkins was the president of RCA at that time, so if I did, I might have become active in the RCA administration and its two studios... Hmmm.

One day, while I was staying at John D.'s, a friend from the Briar Patch called and said he had a good friend that he me to meet. He told me she was a girl that didn't live far from John Loudermilk's place, and that he was going to bring her over if it was OK. I said, "Sure, bring her over."

I waited out front for them to arrive, and when they pulled up, the most beautiful girl I'd seen since arriving in Nashville stepped out of the car. Wow! Her name was Julie, and she would come over any time, night or day! A courtship had begun...

I would take the band's Chevy wagon to pick Julie up, or occasionally she would drive over in her family's 1955 Ford. I don't know how her very strict father would let her have the car because she was only fifteen. In fact, he was so strict that she could never be seen with me. She would have to sneak out of the house when I came to get her; it was obviously because of my long hair and mod clothes.

Later on in our relationship, when the band was staying back at the Anchor Motel, Julie and I found ourselves alone one day. Before long we were under the sheets and we began to make love. This was my very first time, but I didn't ask about her sexual history. I was very awkward, but it was unbelievable. I had never imagined it being this good!

Suddenly, I heard my mother say, "A few minutes of pleasure can give you a lifetime of pain." That did it: Julie and I were not using any protection, so I immediately stopped. I hated to do it, but we had to talk about it. We both agreed that we certainly didn't need a baby when were this young. She was only fifteen, and I was seventeen. I was just out of high school, and she was still in high school. I told her that I would get some prophylactics before we got together again.

Well, I bought them, and the next time Julie and I were together, I tried putting one on. It was a real chore and just didn't feel the same, so I told a friend about our experience and problem. He told me about a foam solution that the woman could use that would prevent her from getting pregnant. This sounded like the solution to our problem, so I gave him some money and he picked up the birth control foam for us. This became the solution to our problem, and from then on, we were in the sack anytime we were alone. I had wonderful feelings for her, but we were way too young to even consider marriage.

After discovering the joys of sex with Julie, my hormones kicked into overdrive. I didn't hesitate to sleep with other women I found attractive, and vice versa. I went to bed with a famous country star's daughter in Nashville, a go-go girl in St. Louis, a nurse in Tuscaloosa, and on and on. Free love in the '60s was alive and kicking ass. As a rock musician on the road, well, all the cliches are true.

After spending several days up in John's studio, we finally picked the songs for our first recording session. John hadn't picked a recording date yet, so we went back to playing at the Briar Patch and staying at the Anchor Motel. Every afternoon we went to the club and practiced the songs that we planned on recording.

It was during this stay at the Anchor Motel that Duane and Gregg acquired motorcycles with John D.'s help. We must have scared the city of Nashville to death riding those bikes around town with our long hair blowing in the wind. There wasn't a helmet law, so our heads were fully exposed to the public. I'm sure the name "Hells Angels" was tossed around, but we were just young, lovable musicians who had a hankering for bikes.

After rehearsing for a couple of weeks, John D. announced that it was time to go into the studio. He hadn't selected Chet Atkins's RCA Studios for these first recordings, but a studio on the outside of town that sat in the middle of a large pasture. The studio was called Bradley's Barn.

17

Recording at Bradley's Barn

From the exterior, the building just looked like a big red barn, but once inside, it became a state-of-the-art recording studio. On the walls were pictures of all the country stars who had recorded there. Even though I had never been in a studio or recorded before, I still knew that this was going to be quite a different animal from putting a song across to a live audience. There was no crowd, no public address system, no stage, and, as I quickly learned, there was no covering up a mistake.

We glanced through the glass of the control room, and inside was a man talking with John D. He must be our recording engineer, who would be running the whole recording process. John had arrived before us, but somehow we had managed to get to the studio on time, which was extremely early for us, as we usually didn't do anything before the crack of noon! All of us were accustomed to playing until 2, 3, maybe 4 in the morning and then sleeping in. Getting up at 7 A.M. and being at the studio by 9 A.M. should have been a horrible jolt, but it wasn't.

Our adrenaline was in overdrive because we had the incredible opportunity to record and ultimately have some songs released, so getting to the studio on time and being ready to get to work wasn't a problem at all. Besides, we were young. How many other struggling bands would be given this break in the music business? Not many, and here we were.

As we entered the control room, our eyes must have been bugging out as we took in the state-of-the-art recording equipment in front of us. The engineer began explaining all the equipment to us, but most of it went over our heads. We were thinking about playing and getting our songs right, not about all the technical stuff.

Then we were escorted into the studio and shown our assigned positions. I used the drums that were already there because the engineer told me that they had been tuned for the studio and that the microphones were already in the correct positions for attaining the best drum sounds for recording. Bringing my drums in, setting them up, tuning them for this studio, and meticulously placing all the microphones in the best place on each drum and cymbal to obtain the best sound would have taken up half the day or more. Later, when I recorded at various studios with different producers, I would find myself spending hours to obtain an acceptable drum sound from my own drums; starting from scratch is utter torture. Tap, tap, tap, tune, tune, change microphone positions, change again...for hours and hours.

The drums were on a small riser about a foot and a half above the studio floor. With the riser, it was easy to see Duane, Gregg, and Mike in their positions on the floor. All the engineers and producers I've worked with over the years always started the recording session by getting a "drum sound." That was also true here, but these drums were ready, so this drill would be easy. I put on the headphones that had been rigged up for me, and the engineer gave me commands to hit each drum and cymbal individually and repeatedly. He then told me to play all the drums as if I were playing a song. Hearing my drums through headphones was something that took a little getting used to. Several years later, my guitarist friend Tippy Armstrong told me to cover one ear with the headphone and to keep the other free to hear the natural room sounds of the other instruments. I wish that he had been here with that information on this recording session to tell me that. Recording was much easier after he clued me in on his studio trick.

Once we had the drum sound that pleased John and the engineer, the process of getting the other instruments sounding their best began. Duane's, Gregg's, and Mike's instruments were put through their paces for getting the tones and volumes that pleased our control room patriarchs. Now, all was set both out in the studio and in the control room. It was time to run down the first tune.

The engineer asked if we could hear him through over headphones as he spoke through his microphone in the control room.

We all gave a nod and thumbs up. He then told us, "We're rolling," and that was the signal for me to count the song off. "1, 2,...1, 2, 3, 4," and we kicked it in—only to have to stop instantly because one of us had made a mistake on the very first note. We would find ourselves starting and stopping quite a bit that first day. My main mistakes were either counting the song off too slow or too fast. There were faux pas aplenty, like hearing that an instrument had become out of tune, hitting a bad note, playing where there should have been an empty space, breaking a string or a stick, forgetting where you were supposed to be playing a different part, and so on, and so on. I kept hearing it in my sleep that night: "We're Rolling; Count It Off, Bill."

Playing with headphones on in the studio *was not* like playing live. I could see right away that I had to make some adjustments. Where was that tip from Tippy? Ever so slowly, we ran through take after take, trying to get one song, then the next, down as best as we could. When we had a good take, John would call us into the control room to review it. If we thought that we could do it better, we went back into the studio until we all agreed that this was the best one.

I guess we handled our first recording session fairly well, given it was our first time in a recording studio. We had several days lined up to record at Bradley's Barn, as we could only complete just two or three songs in the course of a day. After getting the four instruments recorded without any mistakes on a tune, and all agreeing it was a keeper, then we had to do overdubs. When recording, the basic music track of our four instruments was completed first while the vocalist sang a rough vocal, which helped the band follow the arrangement. Once we had a good recording of the instruments without mistakes, the vocalists went into the studio and sang the song until there was a good recording on the vocals, and that take was the vocal that would be used on the final mix of the song.

One song required a gunshot sound effect. John D. had a pistol in his car, so Duane went out and got it. He shot it at the ceiling of the studio at the appropriate time in the song. John D. had been reluctant to use a real pistol, but he approved it. Several days later,

John got a call from Bradley, owner of Bradley's Barn. He said there was water coming from the ceiling. John D. had to pay to get it repaired and was probably thinking, "Damn those Allman boys."

Since I didn't sing, I would sit in the control room and listen to the final vocals as they were recorded. While I was listening, I would catch drum parts that should not have been played and think of other places where this and that should have played. I would also listen to the tempos and wonder why I sped up in some places and slowed down in others. Later, a prominent record producer told me that he didn't have a problem with it as long as it felt natural and worked with all the other musicians' parts.

In the studio, time is money, and it was a factor at Bradley's Barn, so John D. could only book us a week this first time. Our next recording sessions were in the RCA studios, where Loudermilk probably got a break on our studio time from his close friend Chet Atkins. We recorded in both of RCA's studios, Studio A and B.

Before we recorded at RCA, Duane dismissed Mike Alexander and brought back Bob Keller as our bass player. While we were at RCA, it was clear that Bob was in his ultimate psychedelic period. Psychedelic music was a new rock and roll genre that several groups were experimenting with. At first, it was mostly coming out of New York City and the West Coast, but soon it spread across America and Europe. Psychedelic music is just what the name implies: you played music in such a way that it would enhance your listeners' "trip" while taking LSD, mescaline, psychedelic mushrooms, or any other mind-altering drug. We began dabbling in these arrangements after being exposed to psychedelic music in Greenwich Village. Coming south, we startled Southern bands who were completely alien to it. They had not become "Experienced," as Jimi Hendrix put it.

As with Southern musicians, our Southern audiences had never heard this new psychedelic music, and we began to "lay it on" them. Duane and Bob especially loved to "blow their minds." Some folks in our audiences were receptive, some were in awe, and others were totally scared to death.

I was thinking that John D. wouldn't be receptive to our doing any of his compositions with a psychedelic touch, but I was wrong. When we recorded at RCA Studio A, he didn't oppose our recording his song "Tobacco Road" with psychedelic parts, and we took it way on out there.

RCA was located on Music Row in downtown Nashville. This was where all the record company offices and studios were located, and it was here in 1966 and 1967 that the Allman Joys jolted the Nashville music scene when we recorded some of our psychedelic arrangements. While recording in Studio A, we attracted country artists Porter Wagoner and Skeeter Davis to the control room. They went nuts as they watched Bob play his psychedelic parts—especially when he began to run the strings of his bass down all sorts of things out in the studio.

This psychedelic music fad bloomed in London and in California for the next few years, but it didn't last long down South, and we were glad about that. We no longer let the Village musicians influence our roots of R & B and blues; we were charting our own course now.

After the RCA sessions, John D. Loudermilk bowed out of producing the Allman Joys. He and the band were not making any progress toward recording a hit. He passed us onto one of his friends, Buddy Killen, who was president of Dial Records. Sadly, John D. Loudermilk passed away September 21, 2016, at the age of eighty-two. His influence will never be forgotten.

18

Sessions with Buddy Killen,
A Return to Tuscaloosa

In the summer of 1966, Buddy Killen decided that we would begin recording in earnest in his small studio, which was attached to the Tree Publishing and Dial Records building on Music Row. We would be working with their in-house producer, John Hurley. There would be no charge out front for the studio time used, but the bill would be paid out of our record's royalties later. John Hurley would take on the challenge of landing the Allman Joys a hit record. We recorded several songs in the Tree's studio, but none of these were considered worthy of a 45-rpm release or inclusion on an album.

Ironically, after the Allman Brothers Band became popular a few years later, an album of the songs we recorded in Nashville was released. In addition, a multidisc collection of the most notable songs by the many top artists that Duane had recorded with during his much-too-short life was also released, entitled *Skydog: The Duane Allman Retrospective*. This collection contains six of the Allman Joys' Nashville recordings from 1966 and 1967. I am honored and proud that six tunes I played on are part of this remarkable collection of Duane Allman's immortal recordings.

Although the songs we recorded in Nashville were not released as an album until the 1970s, one of those tunes—"Spoonful"—was released as a 45-rpm record in the summer of 1966. WTBC radio station in Tuscaloosa began playing the record immediately, and it started climbing the local charts. Fred Styles, the bass player with my former bands the Pacers and the Men-its, had gone into promoting local concerts with prominent bands from around the Southeast. His partner was Jack Garrett, a WTBC disc jockey.

Their turnouts performed well, so they asked if we'd come down and perform. My mom had given Fred the telephone number of the Anchor Motel, and all four of us were in the motel room when he called. After hearing about the large turnouts Fred was seeing, we agreed to work for a large percentage of all the door receipts. We didn't have a gig that particular night, so everyone said, "What the hell, let's go play it." In addition, we could all stay at my parents' home, just as we had stayed with Duane's and Gregg's mother's place in Daytona Beach.

So, one Saturday night after playing the Briar Patch in Nashville, we headed down to Tuscaloosa. For my parents and me, it seemed like years since I had been home, so we couldn't wait to see each other. Bringing down my bandmates—Duane, Gregg, and Bob Keller—to meet my Tuscaloosa musician friends screamed excitement. I knew they would love the Allman Joys and our musicianship. Could being seventeen years old get any better?! My homecoming...and our record was climbing towards number one on the regional charts. We were stars in my hometown!

Always being on the road, we ate wherever and whenever we got hungry. We would grab honeybuns from a gas station and burgers from roadside diners while traveling, and eat at local restaurants in towns and cities where we were playing. After seeing a restaurant in Paducah, Kentucky, advertising "Good Eats," Duane would always ask, when we spotted a restaurant anywhere, "Do they have Good Eats?" After coming across a diner with a Flamingo logo, he then changed his question to, "Do they have Flamingos and Good Eats?" Every time he asked that, we would howl with laughter.

My parents' house became a hangout for everyone who knew me. My mom couldn't have been more pleased to have us there and cook for us. At the time, I also had two grandmothers in town who could cook old-time Southern food that was just out-of-sight delicious, and they would not hear of us not coming over to their houses to eat also. Duane's and Gregg's favorite dish at my father's mother's house, Big Nanny, was fresh cut-up beans cooked with potatoes; they just couldn't get enough of them. Wonderful homemade desserts at both grandmothers' just properly came after the meal. By the time we got through with the meals, it was a task to get up from the table. Both my grandmothers, of course, were at our concerts, and I'm certain the volume of our music wrecked their ears!

We arrived on a Sunday, and the interstate from Birmingham to Tuscaloosa had been completed, so it felt as if I had been gone for a long time. We had all week to horse around with some of the musicians Duane and Gregg had already met when I was with the Nightcaps at the casino on Dauphin Island. Every day, Tippy Armstrong and Johnny Townsend were at the front door, and it was great catching up, no doubt.

One afternoon, while Duane was reading *The Tuscaloosa News* in my folks' living room, he looked up at me and caught me off guard by saying, "Hey, Novice, let's go downtown to the Bama Theatre and see Cecil B. DeMille's *The Ten Commandments*." So off we went. We ate popcorn and drank Cokes as Duane became totally absorbed in the movie. This was the first time I saw this side of him, although he and Gregg were not shy to tell you they were Christians.

Terry, my ten-year-old younger brother, had a large collection of comic books. Since our gig in Tuscaloosa was on the weekend, there was spare time aplenty. Early in the week, Duane and Gregg discovered all these comic books that my brother had stashed, so Terry decided to make some extra money himself. Instead of just letting everyone read his comic books, he would rent them, and the band did not mind paying.

Besides making some change from his comic book rentals, Terry recently told me that while we were all asleep, he would go through our pants pockets and take our coin change. He did not take a single bill, and we never missed our coin change. Now he doesn't remember how much money he lifted from all of us, but he said, "For a ten-year-old, I did quite well!" Was "quite well" five dollars or twenty-five dollars? Doesn't matter now, but it is actually quite hysterical today. I'd never known Terry to be dishonest his whole life until I heard about this small-time caper! He's been totally clean since, and Terry was laughing as he relived the adventure.

Comic Book Terry is now Dr. Terry Connell. His titles include professor of Microbiology and Immunology, director of admissions and recruiting in the PhD Program in Biomedical Sciences, director of the Summer Undergraduate Research Experience, at the Jacobs School of Medicine and Biomedical Research at the University at Buffalo, in upstate New York. He now resides in Buffalo, and I think he turned out OK!

Back to the music. In Tuscaloosa, some of the local musicians were beginning to let their hair grow out a little over their ears and wearing Beatles-style suits or dressing alike with matching bell-bottom pants and mod shirts. We arrived with shoulder-length hair, so we got a lot of stares but not as much harassment as we had received in Nashville. Most of the comments here were along the lines of, "Are you a boy or are you a girl?"

(Addendum: most all the bands in Nashville were country bands, and they still favored that slicked-back, greasy look. The country band image came complete with cowboy hats and rhinestone suits.)

As our Saturday-night concert got underway, the promoters, Fred and Jack, could not have been more shocked, because the venue, the Fort Brandon Armory, was packed. We were going to make a lot of money and play to a full house! What could be better?

My mom and Fred Styles had become very tight friends over the years since I began playing with Fred in 1961, so she helped rake in the money at the front door for him. She was all grins taking in all that cash for us.

Since Jack Garrett was a WTBC disc jockey, he had the band appear on his popular rock and roll radio show the week before the Saturday-night show. Jack had us do on-the-air interviews and phone interviews while playing our record, which helped tremendously to bring in the large turnout at our concert. Being live on the radio pumped us up and made us feel much bigger than we actually were. Hell, this was only one little local radio station in a small Southern town, but we loved it. My uncle Joe, who had not agreed with my parents' allowing me to go work in New York City, was also at the concert. Man, was his face red when he saw the huge turnout!

This was one of several shows that the Allman Joys played at the Armory in Tuscaloosa, and every show was a sellout. The large turnout was helped by there being no age limit to get in. The audience was made up of young teenagers, with some in their late twenties. Unlike our previous club crowds, there were no people in their forties to sixties, sitting at tables talking to one another while waitresses kept the drinks coming. This was a show, not a club gig. Groups began dancing together, and everyone was swaying to the music as they listened.

Unbeknownst to me at the time, one of the "regulars" who attended these Fort Brandon gigs was a young Chuck Leavell, who had a band in town called the Misfitz. Chuck primarily played keyboards, but he also played some guitar. The lead guitar player in the Misfitz was a fellow named Ronnie Brown, a very talented musician whom I would later play with in a future band called Sailcat. None of us met Chuck back then, as he was a quite a bit younger than we were, about thirteen at that time. I did get to know him some years later, and he went on to work on Gregg Allman's first solo album, *Laid Back*, in 1972. Shortly afterwards, he joined the Allman Brothers Band and played with them on their biggest album, *Brothers and Sisters*. Chuck stayed with the Brothers until 1976, and in 1982, he started working with the Rolling Stones. Today he is still with the Stones as their primary keyboard player and musical director. Chuck also had tenures with Eric Clapton, George Harrison, David Gilmour, John Mayer, and a host of others. Chuck and I are good friends today, and he has been instrumental in helping me make this book a reality.

At the end of the night, we received encores, and the whole band was drenched in sweat because we had played with a great deal of intensity. I can remember changing shirts a couple of times to try to stay dry and placing a towel across my lap to keep the sweat off my hands and sticks, just as Mabry, my rock drum teacher, had taught me. I played so hard that I bet I went through a half dozen sticks that broke from the force that I was exerting on every lick. We never had microphones on the drums, so I had to play that hard to be heard over the electric instruments. As usual, there were no monitor speakers onstage for the vocalists to hear themselves or each other. They had only the two small PA speakers that were pointed away from them toward the audience.

Everyone—including the band, the audience, and the promoters—had a wonderful night. Our pockets were full when the proceeds were distributed, and we began to see larger turnouts at our shows around the South, which was really a thrill for us and all the bands that were playing these types of gigs all over the US.

One night, some local musicians told us about a new store downtown called Varlow's, which they said carried clothes that were a little hipper than what could be found at a typical department store in the South.

So, the Monday morning after a gig at the armory, early-riser Duane shook me awake and said, "Novice, get up. We're going down to check out this store that those dudes were talking about."

He rushed me so quickly that all I had time to put on my feet was a pair of house shoes that my mom had bought me years earlier. We got down to Varlow's and started looking around. It turned out that the store did not have any clothes that came near the variety or quality of threads we had bought up in Greenwich Village.

One of the owner's daughters was working there and recognized us from our recent concert. She alerted her dad, Stan Weller, who was the owner of the shop. After his daughter filled him in about us, Stan came over and enthusiastically introduced himself. He looked down at my shoes and asked about them. I said, "Man, these are the latest craze in New York City."

On our next visit to play a show in Tuscaloosa, we went back down to Varlow's to see if Stan was selling any of the high-quality, hip threads that we were accustomed to purchasing in New York. I walked in, and there they were: Stan had racks of the same house shoes that I had been wearing when we first visited his store—but Stan was selling them as street shoes! Seeing the multitude of house shoes that were on the racks, we made a couple of complimentary comments and let it go. Duane and I nonchalantly cruised the store and held our laughter as Gregg and Bob were window-shopping. After leaving the store and getting well away, Duane and I began to howl and howl all the way back to my parent's home about all the house shoes Stan had on display!

Each time we came to town, a visit to Stan's store was always on our agenda. It wasn't really to buy some of his inventory, which we did out of friendship, but more because the band and Stan had become good friends. He was a good-natured and kind man, and I guess we all sort of loved each other, so we never told him about the house-shoes joke. He was always wanting to know about the band's travels and adventures, especially any funny stories about being on the road, or I should say, about being on the "chitterling circuit," as Duane called it.

19

Sessions in Birmingham

While on one of the Allman Joys' shows and stays in Tuscaloosa, we heard of a new recording studio in Birmingham. The owner, Ed Boutwell, had converted an old, deserted church into a recording studio. Even though the church floor was slanted from top to bottom, as they had been designed in an earlier time, recording there sounded challenging and interesting, so we decided to try our hand at producing ourselves. Off we went to Birmingham.

Over the past year, we had recorded in three different studios in Nashville, and I am nowhere close to being a technical person. I was a seventeen-year-old drummer—period—but here's how I found the finer studios were set up in Nashville in 1966.

Of course, they all had ultra-soundproof studios, equipped with the most modern and up-to-date recording equipment. Their tape machines and audio-mixing consoles could accommodate several instruments and vocals, each being recorded separately on different audiotape tracks, which allowed for repairing a single instrument or vocal until it sounded its best.

At Boutwell Studio, there was no repairing anything, except perhaps a vocal, which was on a separate track. If the vocal bled over on the instruments track, then you had to keep it. The studio only had a three-track recorder, but that day our recordings were right on the note, as Duane would say. We couldn't repair anything, but, hell, we didn't need to. The music was flawless and powerful—each one of us was on fire. I guess this happened because we were so relaxed and not nervous, like we had been in Nashville. The novelty of being the first rock band to record in Nashville brought a tremendous amount of anxiety for us. We felt we had to record everything perfectly, right out of the chute.

In addition, in Nashville, the ticking of time while recording equated to *big* \$\$, so recording was nerve-wracking as we were trying to beat the clock...rush, rush, rush and cha ching, cha ching, cha ching. Record-company bigwigs and Nashville hit-song celebrities were always in the control room while we recorded, and, man, that brought on a great deal of stress. These were the hit makers, so the atmosphere was anything but relaxed. Another crucial factor was that John D.'s songs had not been written for the Allman Joys. None of his tunes felt comfortable for the band to play and record, which just led to More Stress!

A few months after we recorded at Boutwell's, no one in the band could locate the copy of our recording session. I went back to the studio at some point and asked Ed Boutwell if he could make me a copy of the songs we had recorded there, but he couldn't find them either, which is still a great bummer.

More than sixty years after it began, Boutwell Recording Studios is still in business today but under new ownership. Ed Boutwell sold his studios to go into another business. Mark Harrelson, one of my best friends from the 1970s, is one of the owners. He is still active as an outstanding recording engineer there. In the 1970s, Mark was a superior audio engineer for several bands, including the group that he and I would later join, the Bobby Whitlock Band. Bobby, of course, was the keyboardist and co-songwriter on Eric Clapton's *Layla and Other Assorted Love Songs*.

20

Down by the River

On another one of our trips to Tuscaloosa, we decided we needed a break from all the people who were coming over to my parents' house, where we always stayed. My idea was to go down to my family's very secluded river house on the Black Warrior River. It was located about twenty-five miles south of Tuscaloosa, below Moundville and several miles southwest of Akron. It had no telephone, no address, and no directions! To get there, we had to go down a long and winding one-lane dirt road that had no landmark for an entrance. No one would ever be able to find us there...no one.

Finding the river house was impossible without detailed directions. My step-grandfather, Nelson Baud, whom everyone called Baud, had located this lot when I was quite young. He first put a small, old two-room house trailer on the lot, and we often stayed at the river on the weekends or for entire weeks during the summer. We would sleep overnight in the trailer, and my grandmother, who loved to cook those real Southern meals, stayed busy preparing breakfast, lunch, and dinner for us in the small kitchen.

After a catastrophic flood in the early 1960s, Baud, my father, and I launched a small johnboat at the start of the floodwaters and followed fence lines together with known landmarks until we reached our place, which we recognized by the trailer's stovepipe sticking out of the water. After the floodwaters subsided, we saw that the trailer was a total loss. Dark river mud coated the entire interior and its collapsing sides.

After losing the trailer in the flood, Baud would not be caught off guard by surging water again. He and my father built a two-story concrete blockhouse on the lot. The bottom story was built so that the metal windows and doors could be opened for the flood waters to run through if necessary. Later, when the floodwaters receded, the walls and floor could be washed clean with a hose leading from the deep water several feet below the property.

No furniture was kept downstairs. That was where we kept our outboard motors, fishing gear, and any other equipment that we could easily carry upstairs in case of a flood. We did have a shower and a toilet downstairs.

Thankfully, the river never flooded that high again. The upstairs featured a living quarters that could sleep up to ten people. It had a large kitchen, a large living room, bedrooms, and a half bath. Once my grandmother couldn't walk up the stairs to the living area, Baud had a small elevator built for her. That elevator was also useful in getting large loads of groceries, clothes, and living supplies upstairs without any effort.

The band set up our equipment for rehearsing downstairs, and we lived upstairs, where we could sleep, eat, and watch TV. We might receive a couple of channels on a good day, and maybe one more at night. There was no cable, just an antenna on the roof.

We would practice several hours during the day and evening, only breaking to eat periodically. When we did take a long break from rehearsing during the day, we watched TV, ate snacks, drank iced tea, shot the shit, or hit the river in one of our boats. We would rehearse at night until we all got sleepy, and then we would turn in, only to wake up the next day and begin practicing again.

My family had several boats. One was a typical johnboat that was outfitted with a twelve-horsepower outboard motor, one was a larger flat-bottom boat that had a steering wheel and fifty-horsepower motor, and the third was what we referred to as a "float boat." Fifty-gallon drums provided floatation for the deck that was attached to the frame. My father and Baud also built a small cabin on the top of the deck that was enclosed with screen wire to provide cover from rain or protection from mosquitoes. This boat, which had a forty-horsepower motor, was large enough to carry several people, and we would fish from the deck all around the cabin.

Sometimes when the band took breaks from rehearsing, we would get in the fast boat and go up and down the river and swim from the sandbars. Rehearsing in this remote location, we couldn't be disturbed by people dropping by, which gave us a lot of time to concentrate on our music while also having a lot of fun adventures on the Black Warrior River.

I had spent years with my family on the river. We took long cruises and fished all day on our "homemade pontoon boat." We would occasionally stay overnight on the boat and sleep in the screened-in cabin so the mosquitoes couldn't get to us. We used folding cots to sleep on and a Coleman stove to cook on. Most of the time, however, we found it easier to eat sandwiches, Vienna sausages, and left-over fried chicken.

We used the flat-bottom boat with the forty-horsepower motor to get around the river quickly and go to our favorite fishing holes. This boat was also outfitted for water skiing. I was allowed to take this boat on the river alone, and I would often swim off the sandbar across the way. Sometimes I brought my friends to the river house, and we would take that boat out and have a fun day of swimming and skiing.

A couple of families who had places in the area included some girls that I knew from high school. One girl's family had a large trailer on the river about a mile down from our place, and another girl's family had a cabin just across the little dirt road from us. My friends and I would often visit them and take them swimming. My high school girlfriend would also come down to our place and enjoy us taking the faster boat out and engaging in water sports while making the sandbar our launching and swimming place.

One day, while taking a break from rehearsing, Duane, Gregg, Bob, and I decided to take a ride down the small dirt road which led to the little town of Akron. There was only one little country store operating in Akron, which was almost a ghost town, with a lot of old buildings that were falling into disrepair from being deserted for years. The storekeeper must have thought that we had just landed from Mars because of the way we dressed and wore our hair, althhough we weren't hassled at all. I guess Duane's saying of "safety in numbers" held true.

I vividly remember one item that we bought and took back to the river house. It was a six-pack of glass-bottled soft drinks called Buffalo Rock Ginger Ale. Buffalo Rock is a locally produced ginger ale that's bottled in Birmingham. To this day, I don't think it's distributed very far out of Alabama. We chilled the six-pack down and later opened a couple. The other guys in the band had never tasted Buffalo Rock before, and they loved it. Buffalo Rock has somewhat of a hot bite to it, although it's not as intense as the Caribbean ginger ales that I have sampled since, which have a spicy ginger bite.

The guys were hooked! Some years later, Gregg had a backstage pass for me to visit him when the Allman Brothers Band was playing a concert in Atlanta. I brought a bottle of Buffalo Rock for Gregg, who had reserved me a room in the same motel that he was staying in. I didn't pull the drink out the night of the concert, but I had it chilled and brought it out while we were at the motel pool the next day. Mrs. Allman had come up from Daytona for the show and was sitting by the pool with us. Gregg placed a bottle opener over the bottle cap, but when he pulled to open it, the top of the bottle broke and came off with the cap. Gregg let out a few choice cuss words, and was so motivated to taste a Buffalo Rock again that he came up with the idea of straining the contents through a piece of cloth to catch any glass splinters that might have descended back into the bottle. Mrs. Allman went ballistic. She said that this idea was insane! She was so worried that Gregg was going to get glass in his throat and stomach, but her pleading didn't stop him from straining the drink and enjoying a Buffalo Rock Ginger Ale one more time.

A very young Bill Connell with Fred Styles
and the Pacers in Tuscaloosa, Alabama, 1961.
Courtesy Fred Styles

The Allman Joys: Bill Connell, Bob Keller,
Duane Allman, and Gregg Allman, 1966.
Courtesy Bill Connell

Duane Allman seated at the Connell family piano
in Tuscaloosa, Alabama, 1966.
Courtesy Bill Connell

Gregg Allman seated at the Connell family piano
in Tuscaloosa, Alabama, 1966.
Courtesy Bill Connell

Duane Allman at the mic, with Bill Connell in the background.
Courtesy Bill Connell; photo by Billy Howard

GIGANTIC
SHOW and DANCE
The Allman Joys

ATLANTIC RECORDING ARTISTS

Fort Brandon Armory
TUSCALOOSA
FRIDAY, AUGUST 19
Admission $1.50   8:00 — 12:00 —
Direct from Smash Shows with the Animals,
The Beach Boys, Sam the Sham and Others

Show poster for The Allman Joys at the Fort Brandon Armory
in Tuscaloosa, Alabama, August 1966.
Courtesy Bill Connell

Bill Connell keeping the beat in Nashville, Tennessee, 1966.
Courtesy Bill Connell

The Allman Joys. A promotional photo from Dial Records, 1966.
Courtesy Bill Connell

The Allman Joys on stage, 1966.
Courtesy Bill Connell

Bill Connell behind his kit, with Duane Allman's
12-string electric in the foreground.
Courtesy Bill Connell

Bill Connell at the Fort Brandon Armory, Tuscaloosa, Alabama, 1966.

Courtesy Bill Connell; photo by Billy Howard

The Allman Joys. A rare, autographed promo photo inscribed by
Duane Allman to famed Tuscaloosa DJ "Tiger Jack" Garretson.

Courtesy Tiger Jack Garretson

Duane Allman and bassist Bob Keller, 1966.
Courtesy Bill Connell; photo by Billy Howard

Gregg and Duane at Fort Brandon, Tuscaloosa, Alabama, 1966.
Courtesy Bill Connell; photo by Billy Howard

The Allman Joys. Bill Connell, front and center
in a promo shot from Nashville, Tennessee, 1966.
Courtesy Bill Connell

SHOW & DANCE

GIGANIC

RCA VICTOR
RECORDING ARTISTS

the ALL-MAN JOYS

ALSO

the 5 MEN-ITS

FRIDAY, JULY 22, 1966
8:00 — 12:00

Only $1.50

SPANISH VILLAGE PATIO
PENSACOLA BEACH

A great double bill featuring The Allman Joys
and The 5 Men-Its, July 1966.
Courtesy Fred Styles

Tippy Armstrong. Bill Connell's close friend and renowned Muscle
Shoals session player.

Courtesy Bill Connell; photo by Marshal Hagler

The late, great Eddie Hinton, Bill Connell's musical mentor.
Courtesy Fred Styles

Batter up! Paul Hornsby, Eddie Hinton,
Johnny Sandlin, and Fred Styles at the plate.
The 5 Men-Its in Pensacola, Florida, 1964.

Courtesy Fred Styles

Paul Hornsby and Chuck Leavell jamming at the
University of Alabama, May 1969.

Courtesy Bill Connell; photo by Marshal Hagler

Bill Connell and Mark Harrelson share a laugh after a rehearsal in
Tuscaloosa, Alabama, 1976.

Courtesy Mark Harrelson

Circled up with Sailcat. New York City, 1972.
Courtesy Fred Styles

A smoking gig with the Bobby Whitlock Band
at the University of Alabama, 1977.
Courtesy Mark Harrelson

Mark Harrelson and Bobby Whitlock
after the University of Alabama concert, 1977.
Courtesy Mark Harrelson

Bill Connell promo shot, 1984.
Courtesy Bill Connell

Gregg Allman and Bill Connell reunited
in Savannah, Georgia, June 2015.
Courtesy Nathan Connell

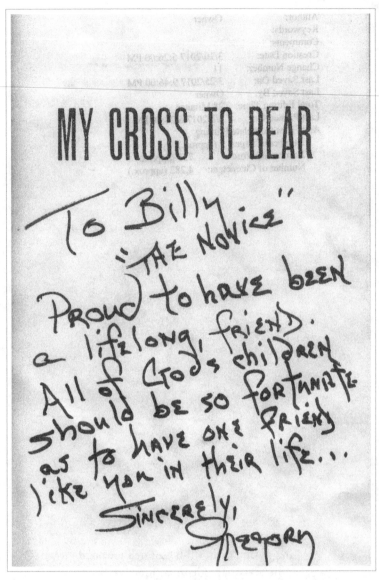

A copy of Gregg Allman's autobiography *My Cross to Bear*,
personalized to Bill Connell.

Courtesy Bill Connell

Bill Connell in front of The Allman Brothers Band Museum
at the Big House. Macon, Georgia, April 2021.

Courtesy Kris Hughes-Craig

Bill Connell visiting the graves of his musical brothers
in Rose Hill Cemetery. Macon, Georgia, April 2021.

Courtesy Kris Hughes-Craig

Bill Connell reflecting back on a life well lived, 2021.
Courtesy Kris Hughes-Craig

21

Duane's Big Surprise

One day, while we were playing shows at night in Tuscaloosa, Gregg and Duane thought that we needed to visit some of the music stores in Birmingham, which was a much larger city than Tuscaloosa. One of the stores that we walked into had a large display of English-made Vox Amplifiers. Guitar players in the United States had historically been playing through US-made amplifiers such as Fender and Gibson. Vox Amps were gaining attention lately in the US due to TV shows and newsreels showing the Beatles using them. This was the first time that we had seen them displayed for sale anywhere.

Duane and Gregg decided to trade in their Fender amplifiers and buy Vox rigs for the band's electric instruments: there would be one for Duane's guitar, one for Gregg's organ and guitar, and one for Bob's bass. Duane did all the haggling and negotiating. I don't know what he said, but we walked out of the store that day with all-new Vox equipment.

After playing Tuscaloosa, we didn't have a gig the following week, so we decided to head back to Nashville, where we knew that we could play at the Briar Patch. When we arrived and called the club, though, it turned out that they had already booked a band for the week, so we had a week off in Nashville before we could start playing again. The Anchor Motel became our vacation resort for that week.

One January morning, Gregg and I woke up and decided we would go get some breakfast. Duane was not in the room, so we thought he got up early and was in the motel office reading the newspaper. When we walked out of the room to go get him, we noticed that the Chevy wagon was gone. Figuring Duane had gone ahead of us to eat, we waited for him to get back with the car. An hour went by, then several hours went by, and we began to worry. It was a good thing we weren't playing that week because night came and still there was no Chevy wagon and no Duane.

We were walking the floor now, and we talked ourselves into thinking Duane had run off with a girl for the night. We were really pissed that he hadn't said anything to us about being away for this long with our only vehicle. Leaving the rest of us without a car just wasn't like Duane, but he did have his shortcomings, like we all do.

A day went by, then two days went by, but then, suddenly, on the third day, Duane busted into the motel room with a big smile on his face. Gregg yelled, "Where the hell have you been?!"

Duane responded, "I got married!"

There was utter astonishment on all of our faces. In disbelief, Gregg screamed, "You what?!"

Duane then began to tell the story. In a fit of missing her, three days prior, Duane had taken the car and driven all the way down to Daytona Beach to pick up his girlfriend, Patti Chandlee. They then drove a good distance up to South Carolina and got married before driving back to Nashville together. His trip over those three days covered a lot of miles. Duane had checked Patti and himself into another room at the Anchor before coming to the band's room with his big announcement. Gregg was flaming mad, as were Bob and I. This was over the line. Gregg let his big brother really have it, which I had never seen.

"Man, you know this won't work! We can't have her on the road with us. We can't afford it, it's too complicated, and it'll lead to bad feelings in the band."

Duane didn't say anything, but a few days later, he bought Patti a bus ticket back to Daytona. He didn't discuss it with us, and I never saw Patti again. As outgoing as he was, Duane kept his personal life away from us.

The next week, we were back playing at the Briar Patch, but we had added a fifth member who played guitar and sang very well. Duane thought extra vocal parts and an additional guitar would really fill up our already-tight unit with even more musical power. The new member, Tommy Tucker, was also from Daytona Beach.

After some rehearsals, the Allman Joys' harmonies were outstanding, rivaling all the four-part vocal groups that were monopolizing rock radio playlists at that time, and having Tommy on guitar gave the band even more punch.

During the beginning of this engagement at the Briar Patch, Nashville began filling up with Shriners and their wives. All the men were wearing their Shriner headwear fezzes day and night, and some were riding big Harley motorcycles. Over the next few days, every motel and hotel in town filled up with Shriners, and, man, there were fezzes everywhere. We soon found out that the Shriners had picked Nashville as the location to hold their national convention.

It was utter pandemonium because the Shriner bikers were behaving as if they were now the police force in town. These guys and their better halves drank all day, every day; it was a twenty-four-hour party. When we would try to drive into the motel parking lot every night after we got off, it was a challenge to negotiate our car through the mob to find a parking space. We ducked down in our seats so they wouldn't see our long hair.

One night, Duane and Bob decided to stay at the club after hours to have a beer without having to get back up onstage afterwards. They said that getting a ride back to the motel wouldn't be a problem. That night, the club was filled with all these mountain men who had come down to the big city to have some fun. These were some very tough guys, but they really liked our music and stayed there all night laughing, singing and dancing after they had made friends with us. They were still there drinking along with Duane and Bob when the rest of us left them.

Gregg, Tommy, and I headed back to the motel, doing our best to avoid drunken Shriners as we drove. When we reached the motel parking lot, once again it looked like there would be some difficult negotiating for us to get in. The Shriners were out there partying yet again.

Most people in the South—or nationwide, for that matter—had only seen men with long hair on TV or in magazines. Long hair was something happening far, far away, but I happened to be part of one of the few "long-haired bands" in Nashville. Some of our popularity with young people was partially due to our having the guts to wear our hair long like the British groups, and the Baby Boomers were becoming attracted to American bands that wore their hair like that. The older generation, however—some of whom, especially in the South, were beginning to be labeled "rednecks"— had no love lost for this new fashion revolution. Guys in Nashville either had crew cuts, flattops, or greased-back hair with the "white sidewall" around their ears. Most men wouldn't think of having hair touching their ears or shirt collar. As far as the locals were concerned, we were a dark sideshow. They blew their car and truck horns at us or laughed at us. Some even pulled our hair to see if it was real.

So, while the Shriners were there, we would drive into the motel parking lot ducked down in our seats, go to our room, and stay there all night and day, ordering room service from across the street and remaining out of sight.

This particular night, the crowd in the parking lot noticed us as we drove in and started heckling us about our hair and making it almost impossible for us to navigate. The car doors were locked, and we tried not to give attention to their drunken comments.

The motel's design had two stories of rooms in a half rectangle or semicircle, with parking spaces laid out in front of the rooms, and it was in this open semicircle parking area that the Shriners would party constantly. There were also rooms with more privacy around back, which was where our room was.

We finally made it to the room, but Gregg was furious. We still had a few cherry bombs in the car that we would set off for fun sometimes, so Gregg brought them in, lit a couple, and threw them over the motel roof, where they landed right in the middle of the crowd of drunken Shriners! After he chunked them, we all three ran into the room, cut off the lights, and got in bed.

Ten or fifteen minutes later, there was a deafening knock on our door. We tried to ignore it, hoping it was a one-time knock to scare us, but the pounding persisted until we heard a voice say, "This is the Nashville police, so open up this door before we have to kick it in."

The three of us got up and turned on the lights, and Gregg asked through the door what this was all about. The policeman said, "Just open this door *now!*" Gregg opened the door, and he was pushed violently against the wall as the room filled up with several very large and drunken Shriners. A couple of them took Gregg down and started beating him and pulling out his hair. I saw one throw Tommy across the room, where he landed on the sharp edging of the bathroom door and fell to the floor. I was at the back bed, and a couple more grabbed me and started hitting me, and I lost my breath. As this was going on, the two Nashville policemen stood at the door, just watching with a look of pleasure on their faces. After the police finally thought the episode had gone far enough, they stopped the violence, and one of the officers said, "Get into your car, *right now!* Forget your clothes and get out of town, or you're gonna get really hurt bad by these guys."

We jumped into the car and sped away as fast as that Chevy wagon would go; speeding wasn't even a consideration! All three of us were in shock and hurting from the beating that we had just gotten. Our only sanctuary was the Briar Patch. As we came in the front door, Duane was leaning against the bar facing the door, and a look came over his face like he had just seen a ghost.

"What the hell happened to you all?" Duane yelled. All the mountain men were still in the club, and when they heard Duane's loud and shaken question, they turned their attention toward us. We told them what had happened, and their faces quickly morphed to angry scowls.

One of them said, "Let's go get those guys."

They had us get back into our car, and we led these pissed-off mountain men back to the motel. The Nashville police had already left, so the mountain men got out of their trucks, grabbing clubs, tire irons, and anything else that they could find, and waded into the Shriners who were still gathered close to our room.

They tore into those Shriners so furiously that I thought they were actually going to kill them all. We stayed in our station wagon a short distance away from our room and watched, just riveted. I thought that I might still be in shock from the beating and seeing things, but not so. I could swear that I saw one of these mountain men bite down hard on a Shriner's ears and spit a piece of flesh onto the pavement. They just literally beat the living shit out of those guys.

The fight finally stopped when the mountain men were convinced that they had taught the Shriners a lesson. Words were exchanged and promises made, and the Shriners limped away with their tails between their legs. The mountain men came over to us while we were still a safe distance away from the altercation and told us that it was safe now to go back into our room and that the Shriners were not going to bother us again.

Both the Shriners and the mountain men had wounds that needed attention, so we weren't surprised to hear later that the two groups had gotten at it again in the emergency room! I wasn't about to stay at the motel that night, so I called a friend and asked him to come pick me up and let me stay at his place. I only went back to the Anchor Motel to get my things the next day. The other guys stayed there and thankfully didn't have any more trouble. For the next few days, the band picked me up at my friend's place to transport me to the gig every night. Gregg later claimed that a spot of hair on his scalp never grew back!

The Shriners are known for their charity work and contributing to many needy institutions. I would like to think that the faction of the organization that became violent at the Anchor Motel that night represented only a small group who drank too much, to the point of forgetting what they really stood for. My constitution tells me to forgive them and not to let this event forever have me holding ill will toward the Shriners as a whole.

I finally returned to the Anchor Motel to stay only after the Shriners were long gone from Nashville. After all this chaos, we were ready to get out of town for a while. The One Nighters agency booked us to play at a place called "The Bunny Club" in Paducah, Kentucky, after which we were scheduled to play at a club in St. Louis's Gaslight Square called Pepe's a Go Go.

22

Bunny Clubs and Abandoned Buses

The band was very excited about getting out of Nashville, not only because of the Shriners episode, but also because we were booked to play the Bunny Club in Paducah. We could just imagine all the female employees wearing those skimpy bunny suits, which would show almost everything except for those body parts that were outlawed for exposure in the 1960s. We pictured the club as being very classy with beautiful furniture, elaborate bars and restrooms, and possibly valet parking at the red-carpeted and canopied front door. We envisioned a plush dressing room and a really fine stage with its own state-of-the-art PA system. We had been told by our booking agency that an apartment was being provided for us, and we had already imagined that it was located in a high-end part of town with all the modern amenities.

Duane insisted on riding his bike all the way from Nashville to Paducah. We were traveling at night, and it was winter and very cold, but Duane made it there without turning into an icicle.

As we arrived in Paducah, we could hardly wait to see this incredible club, but somehow, as we drove closer to the address that we were looking for, the neighborhoods began looking more and more run down. There were cars on blocks in front yards, washing machines on front porches, and vacant houses with broken-out windows.

We finally pulled up to the club's address, and our big dreams of an exquisite club were promptly shattered. Outside, the club looked like the worst nightmare of a place to patronize; we were speechless. Walking in, our hopes of seeing a magnificent club went out the window. It was an ugly, dark room with non-matching tables and chairs and a biker-club type of bar, complete with pickled pig's feet and red plastic-upholstered stools. The stage was only about two inches above the dance floor, and the only waitress working that afternoon looked like she might have once been in a traveling carnival.

Duane looked at me with disappointment at first, but then he smiled, shook his head, and just kept smiling. He was indicating that we would play the job the best we could, pick up our pay, and continue on to St. Louis, where we were assured that Pepe's a Go Go was in the classiest club district in town.

After we set up, the manager gave us the address to the band apartment. As we made our way through the neighborhoods leading to our home for our stay in Paducah, the housing along the way didn't improve. The address that had been given to us led into the parking lot of a Chinese restaurant, and the apartment number was posted in black letters on the restaurant's door.

"What is this?" Gregg raised his voice in question.

Duane entered the restaurant, and we watched as he and a Chinese man talked. The man pointed to his right, and Duane came out of the door, walked to the corner of the building, and looked down what appeared to be an alley. He motioned for us to get out of the car and follow him.

Around the back of the Chinese restaurant was a door, and our key fit, so we walked in. It was quite the opposite of a high-end modern apartment. Like the club, all the furniture looked like it came for a variety of yard sales. We each picked out a bed in the four-room apartment, and then we heard Bob yell, "Get in here and check it out!" The window in Bob's room didn't look out into the backyard, but rather it looked right into the Chinese restaurant's kitchen. In addition, the main counter used for food preparation was located right under the window. Bob found himself face-to-face with one of the Chinese cooks; the two of them were within a hand's reach of each other. Instead of our apartment smelling of scented candles and incense, it smelled like Moo Goo Gai Pan and rice for the duration of our stay.

The first night that we played at "Hugh Hefner's worst nightmare," there may have been an audience of four people, and all of the weekday nights were like this. The band was also back to a four-piece, as Tommy Tucker had decided the road was not for him and went home to Daytona. The only redeeming quality of the week was that my girlfriend and Gregg's girlfriend were coming up for the weekend. The weekend audience was a bit larger, but still not a packed house, like we were used to at the Briar Patch in Nashville. We wondered how the hell the club stayed open. Maybe it was a front for something much bigger. Who could know?

Our engagement was contracted for two weeks, so the second week we came up with the educational and entertaining idea of leaving the cramped apartment to take in the wonders of Paducah. After being out and about town for a bit, we spotted an older Blue Bird bus for sale. Duane pulled our Chevy wagon over to take a look, and as we circled it, Duane said, "If this thing has a good engine and transmission, we could have it converted into a bus that we could travel in comfortably." We began to discuss how the interior could be remodeled with a travel-trailer-type of plumbing system installed and with beds and a kitchen built in. We could carry all of our equipment and luggage in it and get rid of our trailer. Living in the bus would also save us a ton of money on hotel expenses.

The exterior of the blue-and-white bus wasn't flawed, beyond a few scratches here and there. We couldn't get a good look at the interior because we had no way of reaching the height up to its windows. Duane took down the phone number that was on the For Sale sign, and we went to a nearby pay phone to make the inquiring call. After Duane's conversation with the owner, he said that the man on the phone who was selling the bus sounded of good character and not like an uneducated redneck. A meeting was set up for the next day, when he would go over the history and mechanical status of the bus and take us out on the road to see how well it drove and rode.

The next day, the gentlemen showed up on time and began giving us a rundown on the history of the bus. His information on the engine, transmission, and overall mechanical status sounded very encouraging, but it was just talk so far. After his informative oratory, we all walked through the bus as he pointed out different features. Next was the test drive, which revealed that the bus ran smoothly on the streets in town, and it rode very comfortably on the open highway as well.

We all began to smile at each other, and when Duane asked the about the price, much to our surprise, it wasn't so out of sight that we would have to walk away. The sale price was quoted at only $2,500, which was about the sticker price of a new automobile in 1966. We told him that were heading to St. Louis in a couple of days but that we would be back in touch with him very soon and asked him not to sell the bus until he heard back from us. We had first dibs.

We suffered through the next few evenings at the Bunny Club and then packed up and left for Gaslight Square in St. Louis. We were so, so happy to be leaving this awful engagement and terrible living quarters.

23

Playing at Pepe's a Go Go

The Allman Joys discussed buying the bus and its potential while back at the apartment in Paducah and when we were on the road to St. Louis. After driving for a while, we knew we were getting close when we could see the new arch off in the distance. After arriving in the downtown area, we followed the numbered streets until it was obvious that we were entering the club district, known as Gaslight Square. Gaslight Square appeared to be a huge step above Paducah since there were countless clubs, bars, and restaurants to choose from. The streets were manicured immaculately, with gaslight lanterns burning every few feet down the walkways throughout the entire district.

Pepe's a Go Go was the first club we saw when entering Gaslight Square. The side door employee's entrance was open, so we went right in. The stage was on a raised platform well above the dance floor, which meant everyone in the club could easily see the band.

I had only seen go-go cages with girls dancing in them on TV, but here they were, dotted around the club and suspended well above the crowd. It looked like this place was going to be a blast to play, and that proved to be true.

A man came from the back of the club and introduced himself as the manager. He was smiling and seemed glad to see us, another far cry from the Bunny Club. He went through the hours that we were to play and some of the basics of how the club operated. He told us that the crowd turned over quickly because most of the clientele in Gaslight Square did a lot of barhopping. We would play four or five musician-union sets of forty-five minutes during the week and a couple of extra sets on the weekend, and we would have Sundays off. He said he would call the man who owned the building because he wanted us to meet him.

We began bringing our equipment in to set up, and it was quite a chore climbing up the ladder-type stairs to the raised stage. A short time later, the building's owner, an exquisitely dressed black man, showed up. I suspected at the time that he was gay, and truth be told, I didn't know any openly gay men at that time, so he seemed different to me. Nevertheless, he was very friendly, and we soon accepted him as a new friend of the band. His name was Tyrone De'Lamone, and he shot the shit with us for a little while, telling funny stories about Gaslight Square and the club. He said he would show us the apartment upstairs when we were done setting up. Although the club was very nice, he let us know that the apartment was not a luxury suite.

The entrance to the apartment faced the main street, and a set of steps led up to the apartment. Tyrone gave us a tour, and I could tell by the looks on Duane's and Gregg's faces that they weren't pleased, but they didn't say anything in Tyrone's presence. After the tour, we went back downstairs. Tyrone gave us the key and left, at which point the band began talking about our accommodations. Duane, Gregg, and Bob talked about staying somewhere nicer, but I told them that since it was free, I planned to stay. So, the three of them got rooms at a nearby hotel, and I had the run of the apartment to myself.

That first Monday night wasn't slow like the Bunny Club in Paducah. There was a pretty good-sized crowd there all night, and I found it really interesting watching the go-go girls and seeing how the crowd seemed to enjoy them too. As the week went by, the crowd picked up and turned over several times each night. By the weekend, there was a line waiting to get in.

One day, Tyrone knocked and walked in with his arms full of groceries. He said, "I'm gonna make you my specialty today, chicken cacciatore." It had occurred to me that Tyrone might be gay, but he had never come on to me, and, of course, we didn't't' talk about it, so I wasn't sure. He was a great cook, though, and very generous with his time. He spent several hours in the apartment kitchen chopping, rattling pans, and talking to himself. Finally, he announced that he had finished and for me to come to the kitchen, sit down, and enjoy his famous chicken cacciatore. It was really great, and Tyrone was extremely proud. I ate leftovers for days because he cooked so much!

Throughout the next week at our gig in Gaslight Square, the band continued discussing the bus deal. We told Tyrone about it, including how it would need to be converted inside in order for us to be able to live in it. Surprisingly, it was then that we discovered Tyrone's chosen profession, aside from being a real estate mogul: he was an interior decorator, too! He said, "If you buy the bus, I can remodel it just the way that you want it." This made getting the bus even more exciting. So now the question was, how were we going to pay for it?

Duane and Gregg had been discussing the purchase amongst themselves. Their idea was that they could sell their motorcycles and the band trailer, which would result in enough money to buy the bus, and that's exactly what was done.

Duane called the owner as soon as he had the money in hand and told him we would take the bus and that we would be back in Paducah on Sunday to make the purchase. We headed back to Paducah early on Sunday, the gentlemen met us at the bus again, and then he asked who was going to drive the bus to St. Louis. To my complete surprise, Duane and Gregg pointed at me. Hell, I'd never even driven a truck—much less a bus—but the two of them would not hear otherwise.

We loaded onto the bus and the former owner got into the driver's seat and instructed me to stand next to him as we drove around Paducah and out on the highway. He showed me how to change the gears, and my head was swirling during the whole demonstration, but I made sure to pay strict attention. Luckily, all the cars that I had ever driven up to now had a straight shift, so operating a clutch wasn't new to me. The challenge was just being aware of the correct gear to be in at any given time, and when and how to gear up and down. Of course, I had to remember that this wasn't a car, so I needed to pay close attention to negotiating all the turns.

I figured at that point that since Duane and Gregg had come up with the money to buy the bus, made the deal for its purchase, and followed through on all the assigned title paperwork, driving it to St. Louis was the least that I could do.

We pulled over, and now it was my time to drive. My driving instructor stood beside me where I had been standing while he was driving. Patience. I ground the first gear a little bit, but after a couple of shifts, I began to get a feel for the clutch. As the gear-changing became more fluid, I suddenly had to divert my attention to turning a corner while driving this tyrannosaurus rex. The first obvious difference from driving a car was that the front wheels that turned the bus were located *behind* where the driver sat, instead of in front, and there was a lot of this dinosaur still behind the front wheels. Around and around Paducah we went, going down small streets and making turns, then onto larger streets with wider turns, and finally out on the highway. The bottom line is that I passed the bus-driving audition.

Driving the bus out of Paducah was nerve-wracking, but I made it without having an accident. Once on the highway, and having gone through the all the gears to get up to the speed limit, controlling the bus was a whole lot easier than making all the sharp turns and gear changes associated with driving in town. The trip went well all the way back until we entered the metropolitan area of St. Louis. The guys would jump out of the Chevy wagon and stop traffic to help me negotiate the small and sharp city turns.

Damn you, Duane and Gregg! Hey! I'm "the Novice"! What kind of bus boot camp did you think I could master? I'd only had an automobile driver's license for and year and a half at that point. Once in Pepe's parking lot, I felt like Lindbergh must have felt after crossing the Atlantic solo!

There was plenty of room in the parking lot for the bus. Tyrone came over Monday morning to give it a look. After his inspection, he told us that converting the bus wasn't going to be a problem. The agreement that we reached with Tyrone was that we would leave the bus with him after we completed our St. Louis gig, and when he completed the conversion, we would make arrangements to pick it up again.

During a performance one night at Pepe's, the cute, young actress Angela Cartwright, from the TV series *Lost in Space*, was escorted by some older people into the club. *Lost in Space* ran from 1965 to 1967, and it was about a space-colony family struggling to survive after a spy throws their ship hopelessly off course. Although Angela had been born in England, her accent was purely American, and Duane and Gregg would encounter her again one day, out in Los Angeles.

After our engagement at Pepe's a Go Go, we continued back on the road, playing one-night stands wherever our booking contact people could find us jobs in Tennessee, Alabama, and Mississippi.

As we continued to play on the road, Tyrone worked on our bus. During one job, the band got a message from One Nighters in Nashville that we had been booked back at Pepe's a Go Go. When we arrived, we got in touch with Tyrone, and he said that the bus conversion should be complete by the end of our engagement in St. Louis.

On the first Saturday afternoon in my St. Louis apartment, I was able to pick up the University of Alabama football game on the small TV set that was in the living room. The television wasn't hooked up to cable because cable wasn't even an option back then. Most houses or apartments buildings only had antennas on the roof, or individual TVs were equipped with rabbit ears. A better picture sometimes could be received by wrapping aluminum foil around one or both of the small rabbit-ear antennas. Watching the Alabama game gave me a little feeling of being back home in Tuscaloosa.

I had been eyeing this blond go-go dancer while we were playing at Pepe's. It got to where we would get together and talk whenever we both were on break. One night, we were hanging around the club after it had closed, and I asked her if she would like to come up to the apartment for a beer. She said, "Sure, let's go on up." Well, we drank, talked, and laughed, and eventually I got bold enough to kiss her, and then one thing led to another and we ended up in bed together. The engagement at Pepe's a Go Go had reached its zenith.

The end of our stay in town came, but Tyrone wasn't quite finished with the bus. We needed to return to Nashville for some business matters, so Tyrone proposed that I give him a bus-driving lesson so he could bring the bus to us. At the time, this sounded like a workable plan. So, I taught Tyrone how to drive the bus, and it looked like we would be traveling by bus beginning the next week. We left St. Louis and Pepe's a Go Go and were tending to our business in Nashville while Tyrone continued to work on the bus.

We stowed all of our equipment on the bus along with some personal effects, and then we headed to Nashville in the Chevy wagon. We had a decent amount of money in our pockets, so this time we checked into a much nicer motel than the Anchor. Once checked in, I called my girlfriend and invited her to come over to stay with me. She was excited that I was back in town and said she would pack a few things and come on over. We really enjoyed staying together the next few days in these nicer accommodations.

One night, while my girlfriend and I were sleeping, there was suddenly a loud banging on the door. I stumbled out of bed and opened it. It was Duane, and he was outraged. Tyrone had started driving down from St. Louis that day, but the bus had broken down out in the middle of nowhere on the back roads of Illinois. Tyrone wasn't able to locate anyone who could work on the bus, and I don't know if anyone in the sticks was going to help a feminine-sounding, black, "big city" man with a huge ego anyway. The big disappointment and shock was that Tyrone had deserted the bus and headed back to St. Louis. He had notified the Illinois Highway Patrol that all of our equipment and personal possessions were sitting in our bus, but with no one watching it.

Duane said, "Get up, Novice, put your clothes on, and pack your bags. The bus has broken down, and Tyrone has left it on the side of the road."

Duane had his drill sergeant face on, so even though I was bummed out about having to leave my girlfriend, there was no choice but for the band to hit the road in the middle of the night to save our equipment and personal effects.

I left my girl in the room and climbed in the car with the rest of the guys. It was a several-hour drive from Nashville to reach the bus in Illinois, and then it took us a while to find it. We didn't have a trailer anymore, so after we located the bus, we studied a map to try to identify a nearby town that would be large enough to have U-Haul trailers.

We drove into a fairly large town and looked around until we found a stash of U-Haul trailers. The only problem was that it was still dark and the business hadn't opened yet. The trailer that we needed wasn't chained and locked down, as they usually were, so we hooked it up to the car and drove away. Duane said, "We're just borrowing it. We'll take it back to a U-Haul lot and pay for the rental when we're finished with it."

The Chevy wagon and "borrowed" trailer headed back to the bus. We loaded all of the equipment and personal effects into the trailer and headed south to Tuscaloosa to figure out our next move. Thinking back, I don't know why we didn't stay with the bus and search for someone to repair it the next morning. All that I can conclude is that we were still young, impulsive, and very stupid.

The band had only one alternative now: return to my parents' home in Tuscaloosa and come up with a plan. When we arrived in Tuscaloosa, we unloaded the U-Haul trailer and later that night dropped it off at a closed U-Haul facility without paying. The Allman Joys were New York City thugs again.

During our stay in Tuscaloosa, we made some calls to not only One Nighters, Inc., but also to Fred Styles and any other people we thought could be helpful in getting us some work. Within days, we began getting one-night job offers from all over, and each was farther away from our bus.

Before we had to be back on the road to begin our one-night gigs, we went to a U-Haul dealership and legally rented a trailer to haul our equipment. A couple of weeks went by, as we were playing so many gigs. Duane and Gregg called their mom one day, and she

152

told them that a letter had arrived for them from the Illinois Highway Patrol. After the run was finished, we ended up back in Daytona. Duane opened the letter, which stated that if we didn't claim our bus by a certain date, it would be auctioned off. Since we had been on the road for so long, both the cutoff date for us to claim the bus and the auction date had passed, so we lost the bus.

On the previous engagement at Pepe's a Go Go, Bob had invited his wife in Daytona to come up and stay with him, but he hadn't discussed bringing her on the road with us. After she arrived, they began fighting, and the fighting somehow led to knives being pulled, although no one was cut. When the rest of the band heard about the incident, it didn't sit well with us, so Bob sent his wife back to Daytona after the gig. Even though his wife was back home, Bob was given his walking papers after our next show in Tuscaloosa. He didn't ask to be taken to the bus station, which we would have done for him, but instead set off on foot while we weren't paying attention.

When it came to replacing Bob, Duane and I thought of Ralph Bollinger, who was the bassist in a horn band that was playing in a club down the street from Pepe's a Go Go. Duane, sensing that Bob's days were numbered, had gotten Ralph's phone number when we went to see his group one night. We all liked how Ralph held that big band together with his solid bass lines. After Bob left, Duane called Ralph, offered him the job, and Ralph accepted. He hopped on a bus and arrived in Tuscaloosa the next morning.

24

Showstopper

In the late spring of 1967, we took a week off in Tuscaloosa to break in Ralph, our new bass player, and made good use of our time by rehearsing in my parents' garage. (And eating my mom's fabulous food, of course. Duane always helped Mom with the dishes.)

During a brief break one day, I wandered out to the mailbox and, in an instant, my whole world crashed in: there was a letter addressed to me from the federal government. It was my draft notice. I hadn't lived at home since I was seventeen, and since I'd turned eighteen, I really hadn't given it a whole lot of thought since we were constantly on the move between various cities and states.

But somehow I happened to be right there, at home, the day the Feds caught up with me. At this time in 1967, there was no draft lottery. When they said report, you had to report—or move to Canada.

With my father being US Army Major Albert Braxton Connell, who landed at Normandy, no less, I had absolutely no options. I walked back up the drive to the garage and into the house a different person.

Gregg immediately advised I drink as much iced tea as possible so that I'd fail the physical with signs of bladder problems, and Duane said, "Don't worry, Novice, we're gonna find a way for you to beat this," but I knew there was no way.

I called my father at his office, and he wasn't surprised. He'd been warning me that being out on the road with a rock band was not the same as being in college, and that I was going to be drafted eventually. The only consolation was that he said he'd try to keep me from being on the ground over there. Dad called our neighbor, Commander Whittle, who lived across the street. He was the commanding officer of the Naval Reserve in Tuscaloosa. About an hour later, Dad called me and said that Whittle had promised to pull some strings.

It was later that afternoon that I got the word: Whittle had found a billet for me, but I had to be sworn in immediately, which put a lump in the throat. Dad instructed me to meet him at Commander Whittle's office—as soon as I'd had my head shaved.

Commander Whittle met us with the same warm smile that I'd known all my years growing up. He told us that since my father was still active in the Army Reserve, he was eligible to do the swearing-in.

Dad was relieved and honored. I wouldn't be going to fight in the jungle, and he had the privilege of swearing me into the services, which I know was really important for him. I raised my hand, took the oath, and all the papers were signed before my father and I headed back home, where we found Duane and Gregg still rehearsing in the garage with Ralph.

In the time it took for them to practice a few songs, I'd gone from being the long-haired drummer of one of the best rock bands in the South to being a buzz-cut United States Navy recruit.

My government took away my hair and was going to take away my drumsticks, so the lump in my throat got bigger. That evening, we all talked about how my life as a professional musician was only temporarily on hold; I'd be back playing in a couple of years, and with the greatest musicians, in extraordinary venues and the most renowned recording studios around.

Down—not out. One door closes, another always opens...all the sayings meant to take the sting out of having your heart crushed and your dreams extinguished.

There was one reprieve: I was given a three-month deferment from active duty.

Several musician friends of mine had enrolled in a small college to avoid the draft. Livingston State College, now called the University of West Alabama, is about seventy miles west of Tuscaloosa. The college was on the quarter system, with each quarter lasting three months. One of my best friends there was Tippy Armstrong, previously of the Nightcaps, the Magnificent Seven, and the Rubber Band, and who in the future would become an incredible Muscle Shoals recording-session guitar player. Another friend attending Livingston was Tommy Stuart, who'd also been in the Rubber Band and would later continue to play live and record under the same name. He would write a multitude of songs, record them, and put them out on several albums, several of which Tippy and I appeared on.

Other fellow musicians from Tuscaloosa attending Livingston State College also encouraged me to enroll during my first three-month deferment. I could earn a quarter's worth of college credits before leaving for active duty, and we could all play music together in our spare time.

Bill Stewart, a musician who wasn't from Tuscaloosa but was an aspiring drummer, wanted to know everything that I knew about rock drumming, so it was both humbling and a lot of fun to go over to his apartment, where we would go over different beats and licks. While I was off on active duty in the service, he became a prolific drummer who would go on to play and record with many Capricorn Record artists. It turned out that I would be deferred three times, for three months each time, and during each deferment, I got another quarter of college on the books.

My grandmother had given me a 1950 Studebaker Champion, which was the model that had the nose cone on the front and the rounded back windows. People would say Studebaker had put the front on the back. It looked like a rocket ship, and it was a beauty! I drove it back and forth on Thursday nights to the Naval Reserve Drills and home on the weekends. I had it painted 1966 Corvette yellow with an upholstered black interior. I loved that car; it got me lots of stares and a few dates.

In the shock of me having to enlist, Duane and Gregg decided that there were no more Allman Joys, so Ralph Bollinger hopped on the next bus back to his hometown in Illinois. In the incredible, tight circle of musical talent in Tuscaloosa, the brothers Allman easily found their next step to stardom, however. They formed a new band with members of my old Tuscaloosa group the Men-its, including Paul Hornsby on keyboards and guitar, Mabron "Wolfman" McKinney on bass, and Johnny Sandlin on drums.

Men-its guitarist and singer Eddie Hinton decided to get off the road and go to the Muscle Shoals' studios and try his luck at becoming a recording-session guitar player and songwriter. Shortly after he arrived, he began playing on numerous recording sessions with many big-name and spectacular artists, including Wilson Pickett, Aretha Franklin, Otis Redding, and Boz Scaggs.

The new group rehearsed and hit the road immediately afterwards. They sometimes called themselves the Allman Joys at clubs where they had previously played or had a following, and they sometimes used the name of the Men-its at other shows where that band was better known.

One of their gigs was back at Pepe's a Go Go in St. Louis. It was there that Bill McEuen, the manager of the Nitty Gritty Dirt Band, who was in town, came into Pepe's. After listening to the show, he approached the band and introduced himself. McEuen saw so much potential in them that he made a business proposal on the spot. He told the guys that he would like to manage them—if they would relocate to Los Angeles. There he could obtain them a recording contract and have the band booked on well-paying jobs and in more prestigious venues.

It didn't take the band very long to make up their minds because they were tired of playing the low-paying bars and clubs east of the Mississippi River. They didn't have anyone interested in recording them, so they decided to head off to Los Angeles because they knew that some great acts had been turning out great records in California.

Since a couple of the old Men-its band members were married, they found separate apartments for Duane, Gregg, and Mabron, but all three apartments were in the same complex. Also, the apartments were located close to where all the music action was happening.

The promise of better gigs and a recording contract came true. The new band changed their name one more time; from now on they would be known as Hour Glass.

After recording their first album, Hour Glass hit the road to do a promotional tour, and one of their dates had them coming to Tuscaloosa. Tippy and I met up with Duane and Gregg and the other members of Hour Glass when they arrived to do the show. Duane had just had a falling out with their road crew and fired them all, so he asked if Tippy and I would drive their equipment truck back to Los Angeles, with a one-night stop in Las Vegas, where they would be performing one of their promotional tour shows.

After completing three quarters at Livingston, I was finally given my active-duty report date. It was a few weeks off, and those weeks happened to fall exactly when Hour Glass wanted Tippy and me to drive their equipment truck to the West Coast. There was also enough time left over for me to stay a couple of additional weeks in LA.

Tippy and I were very excited since neither one of us had been to California before, and we were aware of the incredible amount of phenomenal music coming out of there in 1968. To take this trip, I made a deal with the Naval Reserve Center to let me come in and work for several days so I could miss those Thursday-night drills for the next few weeks. This was one of what would become several of the navy's acts of kindness on my behalf.

25

Going to California

So, Tippy and I set off from Alabama to drive straight through to Las Vegas, and after the show in Vegas, we then drove to Los Angeles. That was one long trip. Nevertheless, the journey was well worth it once we arrived in California. Of course, we had to sleep for a whole day to get over the exhausting drive.

Once there, we attended numerous shows by top-performing West Coast musicians, and at every gig there were scores of rock and roll stars with hit records strolling around the various venues. We rubbed elbows with Stephen Stills, Neil Young, and David Crosby, soon to become Crosby, Stills, Nash, and Young; a couple of the Monkeys; Moby Grape; Mama Cass of the Mamas and the Papas; plus many others. We also attended a concert featuring Mike Bloomfield and the Electric Flag. Bloomfield was a renowned guitarist and leader of the group, which played fusion rock, jazz, and R & B. The Electric Flag also featured renowned keyboardist Barry Goldberg and the fantastic drummer Buddy Miles.

The California hippie scene was even more exciting than we had heard about. For one of Hour Glass's shows, we traveled up to Bill Graham's Fillmore West in San Francisco. We also visited the Haight-Ashbury district in San Francisco, which was the capital for the hippie movement in the United States. The recently released Scott McKenzie song that had these lyrics was so true: "If you're going to San Francisco, be sure to wear some flowers in your hair."

This was 1968, and the Bay Area was leading the way for a new cultural revolution. There were so many long-haired guys wandering around, and all the girls wore more creative clothes than what I saw the average girl wearing elsewhere, except for a few places like Greenwich Village and, eventually, Atlanta. Atlanta was quickly becoming the central location for the cultural revolution in the South.

The hippie-girl fashion was different from the miniskirt rage that emerged in the South the 1970s. In California, it was not unusual to see girls wearing skirts that went almost to the ground, with hippie-fashion tops, no bras, and lots of costume and turquoise jewelry. Turquoise jewelry was expensive for the average hippie, so only the elite hippies owned these necklaces and bracelets. "Peace" was advertised on bodies, walls, and Volkswagen vans, which every hippie desired to drive. The Volkswagen van was the ultimate hippie vehicle, mainly because several hippies could live in it.

One morning, after we had been awake for a while, Duane said, "Hey, Novice, get yourself ready. We're going over the Golden Gate Bridge to Sausalito to eat at a place famous for their fish and chips."

As we drove over the bridge, a couple of dudes in a van pulled up next to us and an arm was waving for us to take a huge joint from them. I took the joint, and we smoked it going over the bridge. It was the strongest weed that I had ever smoked, and the extreme high made the magnificent beauty of Sausalito incredibly intense.

Duane's promise of the best lunch on the West Coast was correct. The accepted way of serving fish and chips at this diner was to wrap the food in newspaper instead of in a cardboard or Styrofoam box. Actually, it was the best meal I had eaten in California since I had arrived, even though the band did take me to this incredible Mexican restaurant which was located in a shady part of LA. We ate those fish and chips as if it was the first bite we'd had in days.

The Fillmore West performance by Hour Glass was beyond superb, and the audience gave them ovation after ovation. This was when I ran into the members of Moby Grape in the dressing rooms. Moby Grape was a San Francisco group that was popular for their acid rock and psychedelic music.

When we got back from San Francisco, Gregg decided that he, Tippy, and I should go horseback riding out in the countryside where many of Hollywood's Westerns were filmed. Now, to use a few 1960s phrases, that horseback ride was hip, groovy, and out of sight! It was my first time on a horse, so it took a few miles before I got the hang of it. Man, my ass hurt for days.

In Tuscaloosa in the '60s, buying wine in grocery stores was unlawful; wine could only be purchased in an Alabama Beverage Control Store, which was operated by the state. One of the surprises that first blew Tippy and me away was that you could buy a gallon of wine for pennies at Ralphs, a famous grocery store in Hollywood. We found out that liquor, wine, and beer could be purchased in most California grocery stores. Ouch! Cheap wine hangovers are next to death!

While in LA, I bought some fine, mod hippie threads unlike anything sold back home in the clothing stores. Why I bought them, I don't know; I guess because they looked great on the rack. I was going on active duty within weeks, and these clothes weren't exactly navy issue! They went into storage until I was back stateside. By then, the clothes that I had bought in LA two years previously were just coming into style in the South, so maybe that was a good investment.

As I made arrangements to fly back home, Tippy decided to stay in California. I had to be back in Alabama to begin my two years of active duty in the navy. The trip back was much faster and more comfortable since I was flying in a big jetliner instead of driving all the way across the country. I was now preparing for my new navy life. Up until now, I had lived a wonderful musical career at a young age playing with the likes of Duane and Gregg Allman, Paul Hornsby, Eddie Hinton, and Fred Styles. A change was going to come, no doubt.

26

Active Duty

I arrived back in Tuscaloosa a few days before my deployment was to begin, which allowed plenty of time for packing my seabag. I packed one set of civilian clothes in case I could get leave in a foreign port. The civilian clothes I packed didn't include any of the mod clothes that I had bought over the past couple of years on the road; I knew that look wasn't going to cut it with my navy colleagues.

My entire family was at the terminal to say goodbye before my early-morning flight to Charleston, and yes, there were tears. The flights went smoothly to Atlanta and then to Charleston, where I was to get my final duty-station orders.

I had two weeks to cool my heels before receiving my orders, but there was a lot to see, and I got to play some drums at the base club. A navy cruiser had just arrived back from Vietnam, and most of the crew stayed in my barracks. Talk about an eye-opener about what was really going on "under the table" over in Southeast Asia.

That first early evening, the men from the cruiser in my compartment asked if I'd like to smoke some of the best reefer in the world. I asked, "Man, how are you able to have this weed in your possession?" They all openly laughed. This one guy said that I wouldn't believe how much they had brought back. They said that even the officers had big stashes of a little of everything. They opened a bag, and it was the strongest pot that I had ever smelled.

They assured me nothing was going to happen to me because all the SPs and MPs looked the other way, so what the hell. They said we had to take a ride on one of the military "jitneys" to get to their preferred smoking place, so into the vehicle I went. Their favorite party palace was on the base hospital grounds. I took one hit, and I have never been so blown away in my life. This reefer was stronger than anything that I had smoked in California, including the joint Duane and I were passed on the Golden Gate Bridge.

There was one downer: a groan or moan could be heard every now and then from a hospital ward. We continued for a bit then caught the jitney back to the barracks. We were howling all the way back! We did this for several nights until I got transferred out.

"So, this is the real navy," I said to myself. "It's not *that* bad."

When I received my orders, the guys in my barracks went insane. "That is the very best duty you could get," they hooted. I had been assigned to Naval Fighter Squadron 14, which, I was told, was the oldest naval air fighter squadron in the navy, stationed stateside in Virginia Beach, Virginia.

After arriving at the squadron's hanger, I was told that we would make a deployment on board the brand-new carrier, the USS *John F. Kennedy*, in a month. This would be the *Kennedy's* first time at sea. I became a plank owner, which is what you are called when you make your first voyage on a navy ship. All my crew was very excited because the ship was air-conditioned and would have the best food of any other ship in the US Navy.

Since I had already reached the rank of petty officer back at the Naval Reserve Station during my deferments, I could live off base when we were stateside in Virginia Beach. Two guys in my squadron asked me to share an apartment with them that was right on the Virginia Beach strip, where many clubs, pubs, and restaurants lined the street.

My first at-sea duty was a training cruise in the Caribbean for three months for air-combat training—bombing, missiles, etc. Our F-4B Phantom jet fighters flew down to Roosevelt Rhodes, Puerto Rico, to begin the training operation while the rest of the crew flew down in C-130 transport planes. We would be here for two weeks before meeting the *John F. Kennedy*. After the two weeks, the crew was again airlifted by a C-130 and taken from Puerto Rico to Guantanamo Bay, Cuba, to meet the *Kennedy*.

Our C-130s were outfitted with these sort of hammock seats that were made for transporting military personnel. They weren't very comfortable during the several-hour flight from Naval Air Station Oceana in Virginia to Puerto Rico and then to Guantanamo

Bay. When we deplaned the C-130 in Cuba, we were taken over to the aircraft carrier by small boats called "liberty launches," which were designed for ferrying sailors or materials from one location to another. I later understood why these small boats were called liberty launches: once we were given a day off to go ashore in a port, the liberty launches carried us on liberty, the navy's term for an off day.

When deploying anywhere in the world, all the departments in the squadron had to load every bit of our gear into cruise boxes for transporting. Moving all the gear needed to keep our F-4B Phantoms flying and the squadron operating was a tremendous task. These metal cruise boxes were large and heavy as hell when fully loaded with gear, and they only had one handle on each end, so that's just two men carrying each of these heavy metal boxes. Transporting scores upon scores of our squadron's cruise boxes from the Naval Air Station to the aircraft carrier was a real chore, especially when we were getting on board the ship. I thought moving all of a band's equipment from a trailer or truck to the stage was work, but this was way beyond that! We were endlessly going up and down steep ship ladders. Never having been inside an aircraft carrier before, I was amazed and somewhat bewildered by how large it was once inside, and what it took to keep these operations running smoothly. The topside, which was used to launch and retrieve planes, covered four acres, so multiply that by deck upon deck upon deck below. Our ship was home to 5,200 men. It was a small city. I lived on the carrier for more than a year and never saw the entire ship.

All our aircraft flew from Oceana, Virginia, to Puerto Rico and then from there to the carrier. The planes were recovered on the carrier once we were at sea. Pilots had to make sure that the tailhooks underneath the planes grabbed one of the cables that pulled them to a stop. I saw many planes miss all four hooks, at which point the pilot would have to put the pedal to the metal and come back around for another try—or go into the sea. My worst experience while watching a landing was when a small personnel transport plane missed all the cables and ended up in the ocean, drowning all twelve men aboard before any of the helicopters and rescue divers could get to them. While I served aboard the *Kennedy*, the ship suffered sixteen fatalities.

We did get a couple of days of liberty in Montego Bay, Jamaica, before sailing back to Norfolk, Virginia. Jamaica introduced me to reggae music, and I fell in love with it.

My second deployment was to the Mediterranean for nine months with 24/7 air operations. While in the Mediterranean for extended operations, I was ordered to the flight deck during flight operations with the ordinance guys for a while, lifting and mounting missiles and bombs. The squadron was then assigned to Vietnam just four days before my discharge, so they left me behind.

I really hated it when I had to leave playing with Duane and Gregg Allman to enlist in the service, but today, as I reflect back with honor on my tour of duty in Fighter Squadron 14 on board the *John F. Kennedy*, I am proud of my service to my country. I was shore-based for several months in the fantastic town of Virginia Beach. Then I got to travel the Caribbean for three months and the Mediterranean for nine months.

I missed playing with the best of the best, but I got both pleasure and an education by visiting Jamaica, Cuba, Puerto Rica, Spain, France, Italy, Greece, Corfu, Malta, Austria, Germany, and Rome, where I stayed for five days and traveled to the summer home of Pope John Paul II for Mass and his blessing. My leave to Germany was highlighted by traveling by train through the Alps and the Black Forest and a five-day stay in Munich. Of course, I met boo-cuddles of European ladies—I do love a European accent.

27

Stateside Again

The ship arrived back stateside just before Christmas 1969, and the squadron was given leave to go visit our families. The only means of transportation that would get me close to home was to hop a C-130 again that was going from Virginia Beach to a Naval Air Station in Georgia.

I called my parents and told them that the only chance of getting near home was to catch this plane and get a bus home. My mother said, "You will not take a bus. Your dad and I will meet you in Georgia."

As when traveling to Guantanamo Bay from Virginia Beach a year a half earlier in a C-130, this one was also outfitted with those uncomfortable, hammock-like seats. Flying in a C-130 is a far cry from a commercial airliner, but I was so excited about getting back home that I didn't care.

To my amazement, when the plane doors opened, not only were my parents there to greet me, but my girlfriend, Susan, was there, too. She had stuck by me during the two years that I had been away from home. While on active duty, she was constantly writing me letters, and I was ecstatic and overjoyed to see them all.

It was funny that my father, a stickler for detail, discovered, when showing his identification at the base guard gate, that his driver's license had expired. He joked about it, but I could tell he was a little embarrassed. I thought it was kind of fortunate because now I was going to get to drive for the first time in ages. Even though I hadn't driven in a year, it was just like riding a bicycle. I only had to stay extra alert and make sure that I obeyed all the signals, speed limits, and road signs because I knew my father would be back-seat driving. Besides the fun of being back in the driver's seat, the big thrill was having my girlfriend right next to me.

It was a terrific Christmas. Being with everyone that I loved, along with having all that homemade Southern Christmas food, was a real delight and a huge change. I had been eating with a bunch of sailors off of a chow-hall metal tray for a long time, and even though the carrier food was actually very good, Christmas dinner with my family brought tears to my eyes—tears of joy.

In a couple of days, after all the celebrating had settled down, I said to my father, "It's time for me to buy a car so I can drive back to the Naval Air Station at Virginia Beach." He knew how much money I had saved because I sent him a money order each month on payday for him to deposit in a savings account for me.

Dad asked what kind of car I was interested in, and without hesitation, I said, "That brand new Dodge Challenger, and I want to look at one today."

He said, "OK, then, let's go take a look."

I almost stumbled running to the door and out to his car. I had never been so excited about getting something new in my life—except for the Christmas I got my first new drum set.

We entered the dealership, and there on the floor it was: a 1970 copper-colored, straight-shift-on-the-floor, V-8 Challenger. I didn't take a look at another car; this was it. The sticker price seemed a little high at the time. It was listed at $2,750. After some haggling by my father, the price came down a couple of hundred dollars, and I put a thousand dollars down and financed the rest. My payments came to a whopping $97 a month. Who would have guessed that more than forty-five years later, a new Challenger would hit the market with exactly the same body style, starting at $27,000? The most economical Challenger is ten times the cost of what I paid in 1970.

As my military leave came to a close, I packed up my new Challenger with civilian clothes, a small record player, *and* my drums. I had to be ready to play in a band again once I was discharged later that year. The car rode like a dream all the way back to Virginia Beach.

As I noted earlier, because of my rank of petty officer, the navy paid for me to live off the Naval Air Station. A couple of my squadron mates and I found a fabulous two-story house right on the beach that was rented to us by a retired navy captain. Wouldn't you know it? Next door was a house occupied by four lovely ladies who were teachers in the area.

I set my drums up on the second story facing a big picture window that looked out over the beach and ocean, and I practiced every chance I got when I wasn't on duty at the base or sleeping or eating. Bringing my drums to Virginia was the best accessory I had packed after coming off leave. I was determined to be back in shape by the time I was discharged.

Astonishingly, soon after we moved in, a total eclipse of the sun was to take place right over Virginia Beach. Some scientists from around the country came to our house and asked if they could set up their equipment on our part of the beach to record the event. The eclipse was pretty spooky. My buddies and I had never seen one before. The day of complete sunlight turned into total darkness as the moon passed over the sun. All the birds even roosted.

Living on the beach in Virginia Beach in the winter was much different from living on the beach on the Gulf Coast. It would snow, and the sand on the beach would disappear under the snow. One of my roommates was from Maine, and he would get out his hockey stick and puck and practice on the ice on the driveway.

My girlfriend Susan, who was attending college in Columbia, Missouri, at the time, came to visit me. She flew to Norfolk, and a close navy buddy of mine from the squadron, Lieutenant "T" Green, a pilot and owner of a Cessna aircraft, flew me from Virginia Beach to Norfolk to pick her up. My spirits were lifted during her visit to the beach house. We were even talking of marriage after I was discharged. Life was good, even if I was still living the navy life.

Lt. Green was discharged that spring and began flying advertising banners up and down the beach. I would joke with him and say, "Your business has really taken off." His clients steadily increased, and he stayed on in Virginia Beach flying those banners and enjoying the beach life and all the girls well after I was discharged. "T" Green had flown many sorties, or aircraft attack missions, over Vietnam during his active duty in our naval squadron, Fighter Squadron 14. He knew he was fortunate to have made it safely back.

I had the opportunity to advance from petty officer III to a much better-paying position as petty officer II after passing a difficult written test and accomplishing several duties that the advanced position would require. I took the test just to see if I could pass it, but in order to accept the promotion, I would have had to reenlist in the navy for two more years. The extra benefits and higher pay didn't tempt me at all because eventually playing drums again would give me the extra benefits and pay I was looking for.

My squadron was ordered to deploy for Vietnam just four days before my discharge date, so the navy didn't extend my service time. Instead, they left me behind to be discharged. It seems I had fallen between the cracks, thank God.

28

Visiting Duane and Gregg in Macon

Ironically, I was discharged on the 4th of July, 1970. Independence Day took on a whole new and incredible meaning for me. I didn't think twice about what I was going to do or where I was going to go. I aimed my Dodge Challenger straight towards Macon, Georgia, where Duane and Gregg Allman were now living since signing a contract with Phil Walden and his Capricorn Records. Phil had managed Otis Redding and was building a nice stable of artists at Capricorn. Many of my musician friends from Tuscaloosa had moved there as well in order to take gigs around the area or do session work at Capricorn Studios.

As soon as I got into town, I headed to Capricorn and called Duane. He raced down to meet me and said, "Welcome to Macon, Novice." He was excited that I had been discharged, and he immediately took me over to the Big House, the ramshackle, 1904 Tudor mansion where the band, their ladies, and the roadies lived. It was the greatest homecoming ever, and I was so happy to be around all the guys.

Then, right up front, Duane told me, "Novice, I'm sorry that Gregg and I can't offer you a job because we've already got two drummers. But I will keep my eyes and ears open for a gig for you."

I wasn't surprised. I knew their hunger to reach the top in the music business would have them finding the best musicians available, which they did. After all, I had been away for two years, and there was no way they could keep a spot open for me that long.

I spent a few days in Macon with the guys and saw them perform at the Byron Pop Festival, which was about twenty minutes from the Big House. It was crazy hot, but so was the music. Aside from the Allman Brothers—who opened and closed the festival—I saw Jimi Hendrix, Spirit, Procol Harum, Mountain, Poco, Johnny Winter, Mott the Hoople, B. B. King, and so many more artists.

About 300,000 hippies descended upon Middle Georgia, and the locals didn't what to think, but to us, it was heaven. You had to be there, you know?

My sons have asked me what the '60s were like—and to me, the '60s were from about 1963 to about 1974—and I have always told them that they were magical. Like Byron Pop; things like that just seemed to happen all the time. Now-legendary events and moments were just another Saturday night for us at the time. But we had our troubles then, too. Georgia's governor at the time, Lester Maddox, had vehemently opposed the festival in general, and as a staunch segregationist, the presence of Hendrix atop the concert bill provoked another layer of outrage. I mean, you had Richard Nixon as president, Lester Maddox as governor, and a black headliner. Maddox did everything he could to keep that festival from happening. He even sent the State Highway Patrol down there, but they just stood around all day, not bothering anyone, because no one was doing anything wrong.

Still, despite the 1970 event solidifying the Southeast as fertile concert ground, and hundreds of thousands of people commingling peacefully for more than three days, the State of Georgia enacted stringent restrictions that made it nearly impossible for future music festivals to be granted a permit. No matter: Hendrix's Byron Pop Festival performance achieved legendary status over the years, and in 2015 became the subject of the Showtime documentary *Jimi Hendrix: Electric Church.*

After a few days in Macon and attending the Byron Pop Festival, I made my way back to Tuscaloosa. Almost immediately I was offered jobs playing in several local groups around the area, and my first gig was backing up blues legend Johnny Shines. Funny thing: he never counted a song off like "1, 2... 1, 2, 3, 4" to set the tempo and start the song. He just started a song, and you had to jump in!

I stayed in touch with Duane and Gregg, and the next time I saw them was in March of 1971. Duane had reached out to let me know that the Allman Brothers were going to play the auditorium in Tuscaloosa on March 24, so they would see me there.

Unfortunately, a few days before the concert date, the band was driving up from the Gulf Coast when they got busted in Jackson, Alabama. They all were thrown in jail, which is where those famous mug shots were taken. Eventually, they were released and made it to the gig in Tuscaloosa. I was at the venue when they arrived, and the first thing they asked me was, "Hey, Novice! Do you know where we can get some blow?" Apparently, all their coke had been confiscated in the bust.

I said, "What?," and they said, "C'mon, Novice—blow! You know, cocaine?"

I told them that I hadn't been home all that long, but we could try. So, they jumped in the car with me and we drove around looking to score some cocaine. There we were, in my new Dodge Charger, driving all over the place, but we didn't find any place to score. It didn't seem to matter, though. It was just good to be together again.

That night, right at the start of the show, Duane stepped up to the mic and said, "I sure am fucking glad to be here tonight!"

Everyone in the damned auditorium went crazy because they had all heard about the bust in Jackson, and then the band put on an extraordinary performance. I was blown away because I'd never heard music like that before in my life.

Later that summer, the phone rang, and it was Duane calling from Airport Motel in Birmingham. He and Berry Oakley, the bass player with the Allman Brothers, were on a long layover, so I headed right over there, and we had a great time. It was like hanging with my big brother. Duane made us all feel that way. He had so much charisma, and he could handle any situation. You always felt like Duane had everything under control.

Less than a year earlier, Duane had played with Eric Clapton on the classic album *Layla and Other Assorted Love Songs* by Derek and the Dominos, and he was very proud of that. So, while we were sitting there, Duane said, "Novice, I'm gonna get my guitar out and play you a lick that I came up with. I played it on the new Eric Clapton album. Tell me if you think it's any good and if you like it." He got out his Les Paul out and played his opening lick from

"Layla." I'll never forget that moment, and I'm still thrilled that he asked me if I thought those famous two bars were any good. He also told me that he played all the really high parts at the end of the song. Not long afterwards, "Layla" came on my car radio, and I knew instantly it was going to be a hit; I just didn't realize what a huge part of rock history his lick and that song would be. We didn't know it, of course, but that brief but memorable moment together in Birmingham was the last time I would see my friend Duane.

On October 30, 1971, I got a call from an old friend telling me that Duane had been killed in a motorcycle accident in Macon. I didn't waste any time. I packed a bag and headed to Macon. I had to be there because I loved him so much.

The service was held in a small chapel in downtown Macon, and the band was set up beside Duane's casket. As people were walking in, the guys started playing this real slow, bluesy music, and it gave you a lump in your throat. I saw Mama Allman come into the chapel, but I didn't want to bother her right then. After the service was over, the first thing I did was approach her. She had been like a second mother to me when I was in the Allman Joys, so I went up and wrapped my arms around her, and just squeezed her and squeezed her. Unfortunately, and to my horror, if there was any humor in this terribly sad situation, it came when my watchband got caught in her hair! It took the help of a couple of other folks to disentangle my watch from her hair, and it was so embarrassing, but it also seemed somewhat funny at the same time! Mrs. Allman just smiled and took it in stride, and eventually we got the watch band unhooked, but I'll never forget that.

I stayed in Macon for a few days to celebrate my friend Duane's life, but it was mostly a blur; everyone was lost. Duane Allman was an extraordinary man, and he touched my life forever in the brief time he was on this earth.

Also in 1971, a drummer in one of the local Tuscaloosa bands passed away from a drug overdose. The band was called Buttermilk, and the lead singer in the group was Johnny Townsend's brother Billy. The other members of Buttermilk were Ronnie Brown on guitar, Rodney Davis on guitar, Randy Reed on bass, and now me on drums. We were booked by an agency in Birmingham named Southeastern Attractions. They kept us fairly busy, and we made decent money. The band would play one-night stands as well as bars and clubs for a full week or maybe just on weekends all over the states of Alabama, Georgia, Florida, Kentucky, and Mississippi.

My old friend, guitarist Pete Carr, had climbed the ladder in the music business while I was in the service, and he had been getting a lot of work playing on major recording sessions in Muscle Shoals. Buttermilk had worked up an album's worth of original material before I joined the group, so after I was worked into the band and could play all their original material, I called Pete to see how we could get some free studio time to lay down some songs. It turned out that Pete had a recording arrangement with a new studio in Muscle Shoals called Widget that was owned by a gentleman named Ron Ballew. Pete told me to bring the band on up and he would record and produce us at Widget Studio.

Immediately, Buttermilk traveled up the road to Muscle Shoals to begin working with Pete. We recorded all of our original songs, hoping that Pete would be able to land us a record deal. Unfortunately, he never managed to find anyone that was interested in the band, but it did lead to the next story coming out of Widget Studio.

29

A Band Called Sailcat

In the 1960s, a guitarist/vocalist named Johnny Wyker led the group first called the Magnificent Seven, and later called the Rubber Band. In 1972, Johnny worked out an arrangement with Widget Studio-owner Ron Ballew and producer Pete Carr to record some of the original songs that he had been writing over the past several years.

So, now here's the story that reads like a movie script.

John "Johnny" Wyker III grew up in Decatur and attended the University of Alabama before striking out to build a career singing and playing guitar. He took up songwriting and cowrote the single "Let Love Come Between Us," which James and Bobby Purify took to number 23 on the Hot 100 charts in 1967. Johnny later moved to Muscle Shoals to write and play on recording sessions.

In 1971, Johnny Wyker met Court Pickett, a singer and bass player from the Decatur area. Court had just come back from Macon, where he had recorded an album with a band called Sundown. The keyboard player in Sundown was that young Alabama kid named Chuck Leavell who, years prior, had come to see the Allman Joys every time we played at the Fort Brandon Armory. As previously noted, Chuck would later join the Allman Brothers Band and, eventually, the Rolling Stones. Anyway, Court and Johnny began recording some demo songs that turned into an entire album that was themed around a biker named Red Rider, with Pete Carr working alongside them as producer. Pete had played in Hour Glass with Duane and Gregg but returned to Alabama to do studio work when Hour Glass split up. Pete met Johnny when he moved to Muscle Shoals, and Pete became the lead guitarist for the Muscle Shoals Rhythm Section. As the recordings progressed, Johnny brought in a number of musicians from Alabama to be involved, including Chuck Leavell and me.

While the sessions were going on, Russ Miller, a representative from Elektra Records in LA, was in Muscle Shoals on business. He dropped by Widget Studio and took a real interest in Johnny's project. A quick deal was written up in case these recordings were ever turned into an actual album. No one thought much of the idea at first, but we decided to keep recording. We even joked about the idea of these songs ever seeing the light of day. The project was titled "Motorcycle Mama" after a song Johnny had written, and Johnny came up with Sailcat for the name of the band.

After the recordings were completed, Johnny thought he needed a vacation on the Gulf Coast. He took his tent and camping gear down to a campground in Gulf Shores, about 400 miles away from Muscle Shoals. He called me to bring down my camping gear and join him. So, I loaded my 8- by 10-foot tent, a sleeping bag, and some cooking utensils, and drove down to join Johnny at the KOA Campgrounds.

It was a poor man's way of life; we were literally beach bums. The campsite was seven dollars a night, which included water on the site and the use of the communal showers and bathrooms. There was also a small store at the campground. We were at campsite number 1, right next to where the deep-sea fishermen cleaned each day's catch.

There was this one fish that all of the pro fishermen thought was poisonous and which they referred to as a "trash" fish: triggerfish. Johnny learned the local secret, though, that revealed that they weren't poisonous at all, but a wonderful fish to eat. Triggerfish are today a delicacy and very expensive in the restaurants all along the Gulf Coast.

Since we didn't even have enough money to eat at a burger joint twice a day, we would go up to every boat that pulled into the fish-cleaning station and ask for their "undesirable" or "trash" fish. They would look at us like we were crazy, but at sunset we would have a cooler full of triggerfish, which we would clean and cook on an open fire; they were delicious. Johnny and I had a budget each day that allowed us to buy two potatoes and a bottle of cheap wine to go with our fish, which we ate for breakfast, lunch, and dinner. We lived like kings every day: we had the beach, the ocean, a swimming pool at the campgrounds, great fresh seafood, new friendships with the other campers, and very few worries. We very well may have been the happiest and most blessed poor folks in the world.

Johnny and I would sit around the fire every night after dinner and listen to a New Orleans radio station on our transistor radio, and then one night came *the kicker*! We had been camping happily on the coast for a few weeks on our limited budget, but our money was going to run out soon. We would either have to find local jobs or go back home and find them. One night, after enjoying our trigerfish dinner, we were making small talk around the fire with the radio on.

The reception was not great, but then we heard it plain as day...the station was playing our "Motorcycle Mama" recording! We couldn't believe it! Unbeknownst to us, Elektra had taken a chance on the song and released it, and "Motorcycle Mama" just took off, steadily climbing the charts.

There was one pay phone at the campground, so we raced to it and called Widget Studio in Muscle Shoals. Ron Ballew, the owner, answered the phone. When Johnny said, "Hey, Ron," Ballew went crazy.

"We've been looking for you guys everywhere," he yelled. "You've got a big hit record! Elektra Records and Russ Miller want you in Hollywood immediately to form a band, have pictures made, do tours, appear on television shows, and make personal appearances. You don't know what a hot potato you guys have!"

If ever there was a rags-to-riches, real-life story, this was it!

Ron told us that a limo would be waiting to pick us up at the Los Angeles airport to take us to a fine hotel in Hollywood, and that some LA music stores were ready to outfit the band with all the new equipment that we would need to tour.

Ron barked, "You guys need to put a band together—*now!*"

30

Sailcat Meets Ziggy Stardust

Johnny headed north to Decatur, and I headed back to Tuscaloosa, both of us still in disbelief. It seemed like overnight we had gone from obscurity to being the guys with a Top-12 hit.

Of course, Court Pickett would have a place in the group as a singer and bass player, since he sang on "Motorcycle Mama." My first inclination was to commandeer Buttermilk's two smoking guitar players, Ronnie Brown and Rodney Davis. It hurt to break up our group, but Sailcat had a hit record, an album release, and touring dates.

Ronnie and Rodney both anxiously accepted the offer to go to California and play for much more money than we had ever made in the small-time, local scene. The huge challenge was that we had to work up an outstanding repertoire to go on tour, but we had absolute confidence that we had the right players who could perform all the songs on our album magnificently.

As promised, the record company flew us out to LA.

The most entertaining part of our flight to California was that neither Ronnie Brown nor Rodney Davis had ever flown on an airplane of any kind before, much less a big jetliner. Watching the two of them looking out the windows of the plane and chuckling among themselves throughout the flight was the highlight of the trip. These two small-town guitar players from Tuscaloosa were headed to Hollywood and stardom. Hey—so was I.

After a few nights in the hotel, we settled into our temporary homes. Ronnie, Rodney, and I shared a nice house in Hollywood while Johnny and Court stayed in a home in Topanga Canyon, fairly close to us. The new band immediately began getting our act together because we only had a short time to rehearse before our first tour. We had to transition from playing small bars and clubs to playing huge venues in front of thousands of people, so the first few days were mind-boggling.

Another highlight from our first few days in Hollywood was seeing Ronnie and Rodney discover the food-vendor truck that parked right outside our place. They were amazed that they could order breakfast from the front yard of the house. It was like watching two kids in a candy store, even though they were grown men. Every corner that we turned in our new music business was better than going to the circus for the first time!

Our rehearsal room had been rented for us by Elektra to pull our stage performance together, and we shared the room with another group. Wouldn't you know it—the other band was none other than Alice Cooper! Johnny would joke with the practice-room attendants everyday by asking, "Has *she* finished up yet?" (meaning Alice Cooper). This made the attendants so mad; they would always answer Johnny with a snarling, "Alice is not a girl!" This just provoked Johnny to ask the same question in a different kind of ignorant Southern redneck way every day: "Is *she* winding up?" he'd ask, as he continued the charade.

Johnny played this good ole Southern boy part to the hilt everywhere in LA, even though he was extremely smart, wise, well-read, and came from a prominent family in Decatur. He was a trickster who loved a practical joke.

One of Sailcat's first personal appearances was on Dick Clark's *American Bandstand*. For our first song, Johnny requested a large wind machine for the tune "Walking Together Backwards," which Johnny sang. I don't think the Dick Clark production team had ever provided props for the guest act before, but they gave in to his request. The wind blowing our hair and shirts looked great on screen for the song; the television production staff, crew, and even Dick Clark himself loved the effect.

After that first tune, Dick came over to interview the group. Dick asked Johnny to introduce the band first, and then he asked him, "Why does so much great music come out of Muscle Shoals, Alabama?"

Johnny's answer was "'Cause there ain't nothin' else to do there." Dick was so taken aback by Johnny's answer that he stumbled a bit on his next question.

Dick Clark's production system was set up to record three *American Bandstand* shows over the course of one day. Our show wound up being the last one taped, but our tour manager had instructed us to arrive early that morning. This was not a mistake on his part: he had been told to have the band there at 9 A.M., instead of just before we went into makeup at 2 P.M.

The record company and booking agency had lined us up two professional tour assistants for us, and they both had plenty of experience working with top recording acts on the road. Jim Niper, the tour director, was also Van Morrison's tour manager. The tour assistant, Randy, had been working in the same capacity with the group Gypsy, which was a hot West Coast band. Randy was a one-person crew who did the work of a five-person team; he always got the job done and well ahead of schedule.

Jim and Randy consistently had us at the right place at the right time and ready to perform. They were not the type of tour managerial personnel to be argued with. What they said was what you did because they were always right on the money. This was particularly effective when it came to moving Johnny Wyker around. Jim told us that Van Morrison was very difficult to control, and this was also true of Johnny. Jim Niper was just what the doctor ordered for our group—especially Johnny.

At the *American Bandstand* studio, our group found a welcome surprise, as our dressing room was stocked with all kinds of snacks, beer, and hard liquor. We had not expected this sort of treatment on a Dick Clark production. On camera, Dick came across as the clean and well-behaved good guy on the block, so alcohol in the dressing room was startling. We started out the day eating snacks and partaking in a couple of beers. A short time later, the beer was replaced by hard liquor. By the time we were called down, hours later, for the taping of the third show, we were feeling no pain.

The first show taped featured Jim Croce, the second featured the Brady Bunch, and the third was our band. The Brady Bunch performed a dance number for their show. I had a terrific crush on Maureen McCormick (Marsha), so after their performance, I gathered up my courage and Southern charm and went down to introduce myself. The hard liquor helped with my courage and did away with my shyness.

Here I was, face-to-face with my TV girlfriend. We talked and, surprisingly, she laughed at my small-talk jokes. Was she laughing with me or at me, I wondered at first. So, I asked her, and she assured me that it was with me, although she said that maybe my bellying up to the Dick Clark bar did have me a wee bit whimsical.

It wasn't very far into our conversation that I got up the courage to ask her for a date. She was open to the invitation but said her chaperones were very strict. We tried every trick to just go to a movie and dinner, but her chaperones wouldn't budge an inch. She was seventeen at the time, so we talked about what we could do when she turned eighteen. That was an eternity and several thousand miles away for both of us, but becoming an acquaintance of hers and having her call me by name set my heart ablaze—not to mention other parts of my young and anxious body. What healthy young man would not have loved to be one-on-one with Marsha from *The Brady Bunch*?

I also met and struck up a friendship with Maury Muehleisen, Jim Croce's guitar player, on the *American Bandstand* set. Maury and I began to hang out together at the Hollywood clubs and music halls—the Troubadour being one of our favorites. The members of Jim Croce's group were excellent musicians and real gentlemen, as was Jim himself. Not far down the road and a few shows later, we were very saddened to hear about Jim, Maury, and the band losing their lives in a small-plane crash; such a terrible thing.

Many of our great musical artists and musicians were lost in tragic aircraft accidents: Otis Redding, Ricky Nelson, John Denver, Patsy Cline, Stevie Ray Vaughan, Buddy Holly, J. P. Richardson (the Big Bopper), Ritchie Valens, plus Lynyrd Skynyrd's Ronnie

Van Zant and two of other members of the band, Steve Gaines and Cassie Gaines.

The makeup-department dressing room only held two people at a time, so I was the last in Sailcat to get makeup. Much to my surprise, I was paired up with Dick Clark. Mr. Clark—who insisted that I call him Dick—had a million questions about the Muscle Shoals music scene, and I had a multitude of answers for him about what made Muscle Shoals so special.

I explained to Dick that the first hits to come out of Muscle Shoals were made by soul and blues artists. I told him that the first major international and recognizable record to come out of Muscle Shoals was producer Rick Hall's FAME Studios hit "You Better Move On," which was recorded by Arthur Alexander. I pointed out that the hits started coming one after another after that record and included Percy Sledge's smash "When a Man Loves a Woman."

I said, "Black artists are pouring in there to record—Aretha Franklin, Clarence Carter, Wilson Pickett, Otis Redding, Michael Jackson and the Jackson Five, and on and on." I also emphasized that the little town in northwest Alabama soon morphed into a place where white artists began to come to record, too, all hoping for big hits. Acclaimed performing and recording artists like Linda Ronstadt, Leon Russell, Rod Stewart, the Rolling Stones, Boz Scaggs, Bob Seger, Paul Simon, Cher, and Bob Dylan were some the talent who frequented the Muscle Shoals studios. I told Dick, "There was hardly a time that I would walk into a studio and *not* see a popular top band or solo artist."

Clark also found it interesting that the county that Muscle Shoals was located in was "dry." Absolutely *no* alcohol could be purchased there. There were no nightclubs, and there were only a couple of restaurants and motels. Artists came there with only one thought in mind—to make a hit record. He laughed when I told him that the local citizens hardly paid any attention to the stars who might be eating across from them in one of the small, local restaurants. There were positively no distractions in the town of Muscle

Shoals other than an occasional fire truck or police car rushing to an emergency, so the groups could focus solely on the music.

Years later, Gregg told me that Muscle Shoals always meant a great deal to him, and he chose to record his last album, *Southern Blood*, at FAME in in 2017, shortly before he passed. As he said at that time, "Muscle Shoals is a very special place to me. It's where my brother first made his mark, and it has this unbelievable vibe, man."

Hollywood was a whole different animal. Booze, drugs, and groupies were everywhere. It was hard not to get into trouble there, and it was a good thing that our tour began soon because we had to spend most of our days in Hollywood rehearsing.

Imagine how surprised and amazed we were when Sailcat was chosen to open for David Bowie's first US appearance as Ziggy Stardust, which was held at the Santa Monica Civic Center. To this day, I don't know how our booking agency matched up a Southern rock band with Bowie's Ziggy Stardust persona. His act didn't remotely resemble our Sailcat stage show; David came onstage with orange hair, extreme makeup, and provocative attire.

Of course, we went on first, so I roamed around the audience after our set, and I didn't see one individual that was dressed like they came to see a band from the South. The crowd out front was dressed in all sorts of strange garb. They looked like that they were costumed for Halloween, but, surprisingly, they were receptive to our set. This was by far the most interesting show that we ever participated in, and the whole concert went very well.

Bowie kept to himself in his dressing room until it was his showtime. The rest of his band were very cordial, especially his guitar player. I have to say that Ziggy's provocative appearance set the place on fire; Bowie definitely had his act and show down to a science.

Looking back and seeing how David Bowe's career evolved shows just how smart and professional an entertainer he was. I really enjoyed his performance that night—especially how he had the audience in the palm of his hand. To this day, I believe that the Ziggy Stardust image was a stroke of genius.

Jim and Randy, our tour assistants, were remarkably resourceful when it came to loading all our equipment into the belly of the plane for every flight without having any prior baggage approvals—and with no charge. Time after time, and in town after town, they pulled this off. When asked how they were able to do this, the answer was just, "We're good." I think there must have been some "under the table" transactions taking place, but I'll never know for sure.

Back in the early 1970s, there was virtually no airport security—no bag checking, personal-effects monitoring, or body scans. You got your ticket and proceeded to the airplane. A person could be carrying a gun, knife, scissors, razors, bombs, or drugs and not be stopped or detained.

Johnny Wyker loved to smoke his cannabis, maybe as much as Bob Marley loved his. He would try to sit at the back of the plane on every flight if there was space available. If it wasn't possible for him to get a back seat on an assigned-seating flight, he would try desperately to get our tour manager to get him a back seat before boarding.

Johnny had a pot-smoking device that he called a wazoo, which was a one-hit pipe designed not to release any smoke. He would put the airline blanket over his whole body, load up his wazoo, and smoke pot during the whole flight. He would look out from under the blanket every now and then with that big Wyker smile on his face. This high had him enjoying every flight, long or short.

We were in the air, en route to a concert, when our episode of *American Bandstand* aired, but we were able to watch it later at Muscle Shoals Sound Studio. They had one of the first video recorders and had recorded it.

31

Sailcat Takes Flight

We flew all over the United States during that first tour—we called it "leap frogging." After a few shows, going from the plane to a limo, to a hotel, to the venue, back in the limo, and then back on the plane, we literally forgot where we were on any given day. We were coming onstage in Charlotte, North Carolina, one evening when Johnny greeted the crowd by saying, "It great to be here in Newark!" The crowd jeered. Later on, it became very funny, but Johnny didn't make that mistake again.

We had several shows with the Guess Who while on that tour. Burton Cummings, of course, was the lead singer, keyboardist, and songwriter. After a show in Las Vegas, I was relaxing in my hotel room when there was a knock on the door—it was Burton. He said, "Come on, Connell, let's go gamble some."

I was not a gambler. If there was a 50/50 chance, I would lose. He mocked me and said, "OK, you're gonna miss out."

A couple of hours later, there was another knock on the door as I was watching *The Tonight Show*. I opened the door and a hand stuck in the small crack that I had allowed in the door. The hand held $5,000 (that's $50,000 today). It was Burton. He said, "I told you to come along with me." The next day my big thrill was going to see Hoover Dam. Not exactly a $5,000 prize!

We opened for many top acts during our tours, including Bad Company, Deep Purple, Foghat, the Grass Roots, Dan Hicks and the Hot Licks, the Raspberries, and many others.

At the end of the first tour, we flew back to Los Angeles, where I met a quite beautiful lady with long, straight, dark-black hair and a great tan who dressed in clothes that had a Native American vibe. Her face—especially her smile—was radiant. We hit it off and began to see each other frequently. Finally, she stayed in my hotel room with me for a while. One day, while exchanging our histories,

I discovered that she was a full-blooded Sioux princess. It was a relationship I never forgot.

We sometimes unwound in LA by frequenting the popular halls and clubs that featured name acts. At one of these rock arenas, I met a very different girl who turned out to be a couple of years older than me, but that didn't matter. She was a little high, as I was, and she was fun to talk to and be around. As the night progressed, we found our way back to the small place where she was staying. We had many conversations, sharing our memories and experiences. It turned out that she had found her way into the rock business as a music critic. She had majored in journalism and English literature, and, afterwards, had landed a job with *Jazz & Pop* magazine. Strangely, I had been working on a BA degree in broadcasting and film before I started touring with Sailcat. Her name was Patricia Kennealy, and she was very proud that she had become one of the first female rock critics and writers.

Now hold on to your boots: as we began to share more and more of our professional information, all of a sudden Patricia revealed that she was the widow of the late Jim Morrison. Damn, here I was entertaining and being entertained by one of the most notorious ladies in rock and roll history. She didn't cry about Morrison, but really wanted to know more about me. Imagine that. Jim Morrison's widow wanted to know my background! I was so overwhelmed and totally awed by her that I couldn't bring myself to go back to see her again. I wouldn't know where to even start having another conversation with her. I truly felt that I was not worthy to accompany a lady with her history or maybe engage in her grief. One gracious evening with her was more than I deserved. Now I knew why she was way over my head, but it was another evening that I'll never forget. Patricia Kennealy-Morrison—I still can't believe it.

Before the second tour, all five members of Sailcat flew back to Alabama. We had spent a great deal of time in Hollywood and across the United States in the last several months, and we missed—and needed to see—our friends and loved ones.

32

Sailcat's Swan Song

I loved Johnny Wyker. He had the greatest sense of humor, which could sometimes be very dry. You had to pay close attention for the punch line. He also was very reckless, although he had had a well-rounded and disciplined upbringing. His great-great-grandfather operated the first ferry across the Tennessee River at Decatur, but the family money didn't impress him much. Johnny was all out for risky fun.

We had the life of luxury on our first tour of flying to each concert, staying in fine hotels, riding in limos, eating gourmet food backstage, and drinking great beer and top brands of liquor. Our experienced tour assistants guided us every minute of the day to do the right things. All we had to do was walk onstage and play, and playing music was the drug of choice for all of us—except for Johnny's constant pot smoking. Now don't get me wrong; the rest of the band took a hit of weed every now and then, too, and we all drank to a limited capacity, but Johnny's party never stopped.

Johnny had many good qualities, which included his natural charisma, songwriting skill, and performance showmanship. Johnny also liked to be in control. He was an absolute control freak, but frequently his decisions were not thought through very well, as was evident on our next tour.

Johnny decided that he could save a lot of money by firing Jim and Randy, driving on the next tour, and handling all the logistics himself. Horrible mistake! He called Ronnie, Rodney, Court, and me and told us that we were going to do this next tour in his grandmother's Cadillac and pull an equipment trailer. He was replacing Jim and Randy with one new crew person, George Berry, who had zero experience handling a road act. We soon learned that these changes were the result Johnny's increasing drug use, which led to his delusions about driving the entire next tour. He was losing his rationality, which was startling since he came up with the concept leading to a hit song, an album, our performance structure, and the band's song list. His distorted decision-making skills became abundantly clear to the band after we learned that Johnny had added to his marijuana use by acquiring a quart jar full of quaaludes before leaving Alabama. We were all shaken and had no idea of what was to come from his quaalude abuse.

Johnny would now be calling all the shots. He was responsible for taking care of the travel plans, hotel reservations, per diem for food, venue contacts, load-ins, sound checks before the show, performance cues, collecting pay, equipment load-outs, getting us from the venue to motels, paying for motels, and then planning the next day's logistics. This could not possibly be done while using quaaludes.

Our new road crew of one, George Berry, took the wheel of the Cadillac as we drove out of Alabama, heading for our concerts up the East Coast. The other members in the band were beginning to see what a grueling trip this was going to be as we went through the Appalachian Mountains with six grown men riding side by side, and with the lead man very high on drugs. He stumbled out of the car, he stumbled into the hotel, and he stumbled onto the stage. Johnny barely managed to perform during the East Coast gigs, and we constantly worried about his stumbling and slurred speech. The band was particularly concerned about our premier performance at Carnegie Hall in New York City.

When we arrived at Carnegie Hall, our crew person's first dilemma was working with all the union workers. Union rules didn't allow George to touch one piece of equipment from the trailer to the stage. This particular rule came as a real shock to him because on the previous East Coast gigs, he had been responsible for moving our equipment from the trailer to the stage, and then setting it up.

Thankfully, the band was successful in convincing Johnny to stay off the quaaludes for the Carnegie Hall sound check and performance. The show went very well, and the band sounded extremely professional, which was a huge relief. We did an incredible set before Don Hicks and the Hot Licks took the stage, and they were a really smoking group.

Before our set, the New York City record company executives from Elektra were there in the dressing room, including David Geffen, the record company president. All of them had high praise for our accomplishments, the hit single, and the album. Of course, they were seeing dollar signs as they listened to our performance and noted that "Motorcycle Mama" was nearing the Top Ten in all the music magazines.

A hippie girl in Hollywood had embroidered the *Motorcycle Mama* album cover on the back of my blue jeans jacket perfectly; it was an amazing reproduction. Geffen offered me a good sum of money for the jacket, but I turned him down. I should have sold it to him because months later, the jacket was stolen out of my vehicle in Atlanta.

It was very nice to see our old friend Fred Styles backstage. We had played in bands together in the 1960s, and he had promoted shows for the Allman Joys and the Rubber Band. Fred had moved up to New York City from Alabama in the late 1960s to make his way into the television network and film business, and the next day he took the band out and about and photographed Sailcat.

After Carnegie Hall, we drove straight through to Chicago to perform in the prestigious Aragon Ballroom. After ingesting a multitude of quaaludes, Johnny could hardly stand up onstage, play his guitar, or sing. He was swaying and falling so much that the fans in front of the stage were holding their hands up to catch him if he fell into the them; they were fuming and jeering us. Johnny was so delirious during the first song that Court Pickett wisely unplugged his guitar from his amplifier because he couldn't even play it. Before the second song, Ronnie, Rodney, and I made a mad rush out the backstage doors for the limo for fear of being attacked by the crowd. We knew that we were going to get mobbed if we continued to play alongside Johnny.

The next day, the review in the paper read, "Sailcat looked like more of a trapeze act than a band." A record company representative who was at the Aragon performance forwarded the news to the main office in Los Angeles the next day. Johnny was in for a severe tongue-lashing once we arrived back in LA.

After this concert, we drove directly to Los Angeles, with an overnight stay in Vail, Colorado. The six of us in the one Cadillac really took its toll on this final leg; this was way too much stress for all of us—except for Johnny. He just continued to consume more and more quaaludes and smoked pot constantly.

Johnny Wyker's massive use of drugs eventually led to the downfall of Sailcat. The band lost all confidence in him. He wasn't the same Johnny that we had enjoyed traveling and playing with on that first tour.

This last tour was the end of stardom for Sailcat. *Motorcycle Mama* sold pretty well, reaching number thirty-eight on the album chart. Sailcat issued a subsequent non-LP single, "Baby Ruth," but we never made another record, and that was the end of the band. Ronnie, Rodney, and I flew back to Alabama holding on to the multitude of surprises and adventures that we had experienced—the good ones, not the bad.

Sailcat might have had a bright and lasting career. To this day, I don't know if Johnny ever realized the possibilities for the group. We all realized that recording, touring, playing, and performing became just one big party to Johnny, but I'll always love that scoundrel because of his endless friendship and unique creativity. Back in Tuscaloosa, we formed the new Sailcat, without Johnny, and went back to playing those old bars and juke joints that we had played before "Motorcycle Mama" became a hit.

In a way, I related Sailcat's struggle to that of Jerry Lee Lewis. He had to go back to playing all those dives and beer joints when he was banished after marrying his thirteen-year-old cousin; he persevered and did what needed to be done. The four of us who were left in Sailcat had to make a living. Although it was difficult to go back to playing those smaller rooms, we played with dignity, as did Jerry Lee, after his fall from grace.

Johnny Wyker passed away in 2013. Rest in peace, Johnny. You were a one-of-a-kind musician, songwriter, and performer and a kind and loving human being, regardless of your demons.

33

Music Publishing and Recording Again

In 1974, Paul Hornsby called me and said, "Why don't you set up a music publishing company? You already have quite a few up-and-coming songwriters in the bands that you're playing in. Start by auditioning their songs."

So, taking Paul's advice, I began researching, ordering forms, typing the forms on my old manual Underwood typewriter, and mailing out all the necessary paperwork to properly set up a music publishing company. A funny part of filling out all of this paperwork was that I couldn't come up with a name that the performing-rights organization, Broadcast Music, Incorporated (better known as BMI) would approve. Their policy was that they wouldn't approve a name that was like or similar to any of their other represented clients. After submitting scores of names, I finally just had to make one up, and Xaigon Publishing Company was what I came up with. I thought about how I came up with that name a few years later, and then it came to me. I had only been out of the service for a short time, and the Vietnamese city that my squadron was most familiar with—from references to it on radio, television, and in articles—was Saigon. Subconsciously, I had taken the least used letter in the alphabet, "X," and followed it with "aigon." This name was approved, so I went with it, and the publishing company went into business in 1974.

Paul also said, "When I complete my contract with my Capricorn Records, we'll go into the publishing business as partners." Xaigon's first official song release was written by Mike Duke and was included on a Wet Willie album. His composition had a fitting title to kick off the new publishing company: it was called "Trust in the Lord."

Mike Duke was signed to a five-year songwriting contract by Xaigon Publishing Company, and Paul asked me to put together some musicians to record some of his songs at New London Studio in Birmingham. I put together a rhythm section made up of Tuscaloosa musicians, including guitarist Tippy Armstrong, bassist Charlie Hayward (who would later play and record with Charlie Daniels), Mike on keyboards, and me on drums. We recorded demos of some of Mike's strongest compositions. Several of these songs were later recorded by Wet Willie, especially after Mike became a member of the group, since his tunes fit the band perfectly.

Another early Xaigon Publishing Company song was written jointly by Tippy Armstrong and Mike Duke and called "Don't Stop the Honeymoon in My Heart." Kitty Wells later recorded it on one of her albums.

Although Wet Willie recorded a number of exclusive Mike Duke songs, our biggest Top 40 hit with Wet Willie was a tune cowritten by Mike and other members of the group entitled "Street Corner Serenade." It became a hit in 1978 and made it way up the charts.

In 1976, Fred Styles wrote a few songs while in New York that he wanted to record in the South using competent recording musicians; once again, all the musicians were from Tuscaloosa. They included Eddie Hinton (session musician and writer), Tippy Armstrong (session musician and writer), Mike Duke (Wet Willie writer and keyboardist), Joe Rudd (bass player), and me on drums. We called ourselves the Tuscaloosa All-Stars. Of course, I had Tuscaloosa All-Stars T-shirts made for everyone.

Eddie, who had become a terrific writer in Muscle Shoals, turned a few of Fred's country-sounding songs into R & B and blues songs. The transitions were beyond marvelous and a true stroke of genius. We rehearsed in a small studio in Tuscaloosa called Greenwood Studio, which was located in an old, deserted formerly black church that was surrounded by a large lot full of wrecked cars. It was definitely in the boonies just outside of town. My buddy Mark Harrelson was the audio engineer. As we were rehearsing for our upcoming recording session in Birmingham, he recorded us on a four-track machine. The songs had an incredible amount of fire, and Mark did an outstanding job capturing that. Fred Styles recently released a few of them on two discs entitled *Bandcestors* and *Bandcestors Too*, which contain several live recordings of the rock and roll hits of the late 1950s and early 1960s that we were performing, well ahead of the British Invasion.

It had been several years since I had last played with Eddie Hinton, who had been my drumming mentor when I was playing with the Men-its in 1965 and 1966. After the initial run-through of the first song in rehearsal, Eddie turned to me and said, "Damn, Connell! You've finally grasped the concept of rhythm." I was never so thrilled and proud in my life as I was on that day. That was the most outstanding compliment that I had ever received—and still is.

The master session was recorded at New London Studio in Birmingham, again with Paul Hornsby as producer. At the time, Paul had been staying busy producing the Marshal Tucker Band, Charlie Daniels, and Wet Willie at Capricorn Studios in Macon.

Eddie, Tippy, and Joe have passed on, but all are immortalized on the numerous recordings that they played on. Eddie always stressed to me the importance of recording every chance that I got to make myself immortal. All of us have done just that, and some of us continue to do it. Paul has always been one of my greatest champions, and he never failed to get in touch if he saw an opportunity that needed me and that I needed as well—he'd make it happen.

34

The Winters Brothers and Tommy Stuart

In 1975, Paul was hired to produce a group from Nashville called the Winters Brothers Band, headed up by Dennis and Donnie Winter. The problem was that they had fired their drummer and needed one for the sessions. Paul asked if I would rehearse with them and record the album. The session pay was going to be significant, so I accepted the job.

I traveled up to Dennis and Donnie's home, which was located a few miles south of Nashville, in the community of Franklin, Tennessee. They came and met me at a country store, and I followed them to their home. We started by having a "get to know you" conversation, and to my amazement, they said that their father had played in Marty Robbins's band. Due to their father's influence, the two sons took up playing guitars, which eventually led them to writing songs and forming a band. This story seemed eerily similar to how my family's musical background had influenced me. I really enjoyed learning their songs and looked forward to recording with them at Capricorn Studios, with Paul producing it. The rehearsals lasted from the time that we woke up until the time we went to bed, day after day. Dennis and Donnie were dedicated musicians who wanted to record a great album. The arrangements were not easy, but after hours of rehearsal, I soon got the hang of them. The arrangements had many stops, kicks, and accents, which gave me a hard time in the beginning.

We traveled to Macon and to Capricorn Studios, staying in a low-rent motel, but I had stayed in worst. The motel didn't matter because most all of our waking time was spent recording. After we finished the basic tracks, extraordinary side musicians were brought in to add to the tracks. Adding to our recorded tracks were Charlie Daniels, Toy Caldwell, guitarists for the Marshall Tucker Band, and Mr. Marty Robbins himself. It was a true honor to meet Marty, who was much shorter than I had envisioned him to be. He was so gracious, and a good musician as well. I had heard his name all of my life, and meeting him was almost as overwhelming as when I first met Chet Atkins.

The recording sessions came off very well in the studio, but we also recorded a few live performances in Atlanta. In my opinion, those recordings were even better than the studio recordings. I'll never forget one of the live tunes, "Home Grown Shit." The first line of the lyrics went, "We've got some home grown shit in the back of our truck, and two tokes will get you fucked up." It went on and on about reefer. It was something I wouldn't want my mother to hear, but the crowd loved it. This was the first song that I had recorded or played that had any cuss words in it.

We thought that we had a great product, but because Capricorn Records was beginning to have financial troubles at this time, the album was not released after we finished it. I later saw that the album was being offered for sale online by another record label, and I was glad to see that it was finally available.

The Winters Brothers always dressed in a cowboy motif, not only around the house, but onstage as well, but I was a far cry from being a cowboy person. After a few gigs, the band decided that although I played well, I just didn't fit in with their persona, so I was let go, but the experience was a lot of fun and rewarding since I was immortalizing myself on recordings, as Eddie Hinton had instructed.

A little while later, Birmingham's New London Studio was the setting for recording several new tunes by an old friend, Tommy Stuart (one of the Rubber Band's sax players). Because I was going to publish the tunes, it was necessary for me to set up a second publishing company because Tommy wasn't a Broadcast Music, Inc. (BMI) writer. He had signed his performing rights with a rival organization, ASCAP, the American Society of Composers, Authors, and Publishers. My publishing company was affiliated with BMI. I had to set up a second publishing company with ASCAP that I called Fancy That Music, and it was a pleasant surprise when this name was approved instantly by ASCAP.

Tommy Stuart is a multifaceted musician and songwriter. He was a long-time friend and schoolmate of mine from the first grade through the twelfth grade, and then later at Livingston State college. Tommy recorded the tunes that he had selected solo, just him playing piano and singing without any accompanying musicians. When we got to the conclusion of the recording session with the songs that he wanted to play and record for me, he said, "I've got one more song, but it isn't that good."

I said, "Play it."

He said, "I really don't want to, but if you insist, I will."

It began with a catchy intro, and as the melody and lyrics continued, the composition kept getting better and better. Halfway through the song, I was almost in tears. He really hated to lay this tune down on his demo tape, but it ended up being the most terrific and timeless tune that Tommy and I would ever record. The song was entitled "Hound Dog Man" and was a tribute to Elvis Presley. We later made a recording of it with a rhythm section, and he added it to an album that he was self-producing. The story of that song got even better when it was recorded by Roy Orbison, Glen Campbell, Lenny LeBlanc, and Sailcat. President Jimmy Carter was even captured on television singing it along with Glen Campbell when Glen performed at the White House. Yeah, Jimmy Carter knew the lyrics. I had a big grin on my face as I watched the president of the United States singing the song that Tommy had said wasn't a very good song. Tommy had actually written "Hound Dog Man" as a tribute to Elvis Presley a few years before he passed away, so it was written as a living tribute to Elvis, not as a memorial song.

Today, Tommy Stuart has several albums that can be acquired via iTunes. Tippy Armstrong and I played on quite a few of the songs on those albums. Tommy is one of the most prolific songwriters and well-rounded musicians I know. He received a degree in music and can play most any instrument. It's equally nice to see that the three recordings of "Hound Dog Man" by Roy Orbison, Glen Campbell, and the Rubber Band can be found online.

35

The Bobby Whitlock Band

In the winter of 1977, Paul Hornsby once again called me with a job offer. Bobby Whitlock was forming his own band. Bobby caught my attention when he played with Eric Clapton on the Derek and the Dominos album *Layla and Other Assorted Love Songs*. Duane had played a crucial role on this album, and he became good friends with Bobby. Duane had told me he would find me a job after I left the navy, and after Paul's phone call, I was wondering if this might be the one. So, it was off to Macon, Georgia, again.

The large rehearsal hall I walked into was located in a deserted building with a big echo. That didn't much matter because I was beginning to rehearse with Bobby Whitlock, an absolutely amazing Hammond B-3 organ player and singer. I had never heard a B-3 sound like his—Bobby could play the shit out of it. He seemed to have total control of not only the organ stops and sliders located above his keyboard, which changed the organ's sounds, but he also used his knee to control the speed of his Leslie. The Leslie was located in a cabinet that housed two speakers revolving at different speeds to give the desired effects. I later learned that he had designed changes to the organ's internal components to give his B-3 even more dynamics. I had heard him play on recordings before, but playing across from him live was almost a spiritual experience. My drumming expertise seemed to excel when playing with another master of craft—like when I played with Duane. The B-3 was Paul's main instrument, but I later learned that he also played guitar well, too. Then there was his superior vocal ability. I had no doubt that Bobby could carry a band. He and I hit it off during the audition, and I immediately joined the Bobby Whitlock Band.

After receiving royalties from some of his previous recordings, Bobby purchased a 1957 two-door Chevy with a V-8 engine. It was a real beauty and in mint condition. Riding around Macon in this short gave me a sense of pride like I had when I was driving my 1950 Studebaker Champion back in Tuscaloosa.

We began playing at local clubs in Macon and in Tuscaloosa as well. The band was made up of Bobby on vocals and B-3, Billy Crain on guitar, Steve Hinson on guitar and pedal steel, me on drums, and a talented bass player with a secret problem. After getting the group broken in, I booked us a small Florida tour, which included some of the same venues I had played earlier with the Allman Joys and Buttermilk. I rode with Bobby as we hit the road to Florida in the 1957 Chevy, and, boy, what looks we got!

During our first gig, we noticed that our bassist was very sick and had a difficult time playing. He had become too involved with hard drugs back in Macon and was suffering through heroin withdrawal. Bobby said the guy had to go, so I volunteered to call my old friend and great bass player Tommy Gardner to replace him. Bobby said, "Get Tommy down here."

Tommy caught a bus from Tuscaloosa and met us in West Palm Beach, but he started with us on guitar, not bass, because we needed our troubled bass player until Tommy learned the songs. After that, he was given his notice. Tommy's addition on bass was only one of his talents; he also gave the band a good R & B backing vocalist, which enhanced the group's dynamics.

The most grueling gig we played had us traveling straight through, from Memphis to Texas, with five musicians riding in one car. The morning after our arrival in Austin, we found a superior Tex-Mex restaurant. Their mouthwatering huevos rancheros brought us back to life. The large club's backstage catering could spoil any band, and the variety of Tex-Mex food available to us was impressive. The menu was topped off by an unlimited supply of Lone Star Beer. To our disappointment, there wasn't a large crowd at the hall for our performances. This wasn't what we had anticipated when we first got notice of the gig in Austin.

Soon after the Texas gig, the Bobby Whitlock Band was booked into one of the most popular music halls in Nashville. The dressing room was in a separate building, which was a short walk from the club. The first night, the walkway from the dressing room to the stage was lined with a large group of people encouraging us on, shaking our hands, and sometimes hugging us. Walking in front of me was Linda Whitlock, Bobby wife. She had been partying with the band and was delightfully tipsy and giggly. She stopped in front of this one guy who was standing along the walkway with all the others who were cheering us on and touched his hair, stepped back, and laughed, saying, "You've got that long straight greasy hair, just like Neil Young." It was more than hilarious because the guy *was* Neil Young! We all had a good laugh, including Neil!

After the show, I wandered over to a bar across the street to have a drink, and sitting there all alone was Neil. I had met him in Hollywood a few years earlier when I was with Duane and Gregg Allman, so I went over and sat down next to him. We exchanged introductions again, and Neil complimented me on my drumming. We sat there drinking and talking until last call was given. Suddenly, I received a spectacular compliment: Neil asked, "Why don't you get on my bus and leave Nashville with us." In other words, he was offering me a job drumming with his band. I guess he was thinking about letting his current drummer go. "What?" I asked, and he repeated the offer. I thought for a second and told him that I was pretty much dedicated to working with the Bobby Whitlock Band and seeing that the group reached its goals. Later on, I asked myself, "Is this a decision that I'm going to regret?"

Shortly after the Nashville gig, we went into Ardent Studios in Memphis to record some of Bobby's new songs. The sessions went well, and we were all pleased with the product. Our plan was to come back at a later date to complete enough tunes for an album.

In mid-August of 1977, the Bobby Whitlock Band played a two-night engagement—along with the fabulous Albert King—at the Ritz Theatre in Memphis. The first night was a wonderful show. Albert King's guitar playing was more than smoking—it was on *fire*!

The morning after our first night playing in Memphis, Tommy Gardner and I went downstairs to the hotel's restaurant for breakfast. A surreal feeling came over me that everyone in the restaurant seemed to share. When the waitress walked up, we asked her why all the patrons seemed to be in some sort of trance and talking quietly among themselves. She said, "You haven't heard? Elvis Presley passed away last night."

I don't know how to express the shock that went through both Tommy and me. Without a word, we just stared at each other—we were in disbelief. Now we understood why everyone there was in the doldrums. The extreme sadness was imprinted on everyone's faces, and then we turned our attention to the television across the way. Plastered on the screen was the news: the King was gone. What could we say to each other? We just sat there speechless and motionless.

Bobby had told us the night before that he had received a message that Elvis had heard about our band and wanted us to come out to Graceland the next day to play him some tunes. The excitement of that once-in-a-lifetime experience quickly turned into our silent mourning—not for missing the chance to share music with Elvis, but that he had passed away. How could that happen?

Our band just knew that we wouldn't go on for the second show that night. We forced down breakfast and returned to our room, where the TV programming was a constant newscast of the tragedy. Although it seemed obvious to us that we wouldn't be performing that night, we proceeded to the Ritz to at least show up and fulfill our contract. To our amazement, the hall was packed. The management said that, in fact, the show was going on. The curtains opened and everyone was holding up lighters and candles. I guess the city of Memphis needed an outlet for their grief, so they had come to hear the blues. Both the Bobby Whitlock Band and Albert King and his group played the blues with more intensity that night than any other time during our long jaunts on the road.

When I was led to my drum set seat by a crewperson with a flashlight, there was a black T-shirt pined to my seat with Elvis's picture on it and a note. The note said, "This Is the Only One." My heart dropped and my eyes swelled with tears. During the first tune,

I couldn't see the other guys through my blurred eyes. The total pain of rock and roll's terrific loss and our actually being in Memphis on this extremely sad day will always lay heavy on my heart and my soul. It got even more depressing when I heard Glen Campbell's recording of my song, "Hound Dog Man," on the radio the next day.

Leading up to those Memphis gigs, I had been tossing around the idea of getting off the road and concentrating on recording and publishing. After I played my heart out that night, I turned in my notice. After I returned home, I finished my degree from the University of Alabama in broadcasting and film using the GI Bill, played with other artists occasionally, and recorded with new, up-and-coming artists with original songs whenever and wherever the opportunity arose.

36

Off the Road and Back in the Studio

The first gig that I landed back home was at a club across the Black Warrior River from Tuscaloosa in Northport, Alabama, called the Red Ox, which was a notorious after-hours club that filled up when all the other bars and clubs closed in Tuscaloosa. Being an after-hours club, we played from 9:00 P.M. to 4:00 A.M. every night but Sunday. That added up to seven sets a night plus rehearsals on Sunday afternoons. Thanks to all that playing, my drumming proficiency went through the roof.

Staying open so late led to wild drunks and fights, which broke out frequently. The bouncers were as tough as any guys around, so scuffles were usually broken up quickly. Occasionally, the fights might involve several men who would begin busting up a part of the club as everyone ran for cover because no one knew who might have a gun. Yep, there were gun-carrying patrons entering the club every night—men and women alike.

While I was playing across the river in 1980, my mom went into the hospital with complications associated with a faulty heart valve caused by a childhood bout with rheumatic fever. To overcome the valve inefficiency, her heart enlarged through time to the point where it could no longer deliver sufficient blood. Essentially, my mother died of heart failure that had been complicated by a serum hepatitis infection she most likely contracted in the hospital from an incorrectly sterilized medical device. As she became worse, my brother, my dad, my first cousin Beth, and I sat for eight-hour intervals with her. I would play seven hours, sit with Mom for eight hours, and then sleep at the hospital for a few hours in the basement room my father acquired for us. One night while I was playing, my dad called the club and spoke to the manager. The manager stopped the band and I went to the phone. Dad delivered the news that my mother had passed away; she was only fifty years old. It wasn't long after her death that I left the Red Ox.

Later, while I was doing some publishing research, I came across a tape by a Birmingham band called Dogwood that I remembered hearing in the early '70s. Their most prolific writer was one of the guitar players, Don Tinsley. I called Don, who was living in Montevallo, Alabama, which is just below Birmingham. We decided to work up some of his tunes at my house and record them as demos at New London Studio.

Knowing that our loud music would disturb my neighbors, I lined the living room walls all the way around with blankets. Don and I practiced his songs day and night for days, and then went to his house in Montevallo and did the same thing. After we were confident about several tunes, we went into New London.

Man, the magic happened! There was only Don and me on the session; he played the main rhythm guitar part and sang as I laid down the drums. Then Don would overdub the other guitar parts, put on a better lead vocal, and sing the harmonies. The first tune that we laid down was "Hey Anna," and I mean, the track was right on the money. The unusual drum part I came up with fit the song perfectly. Although we recorded several more tunes, "Hey Anna" was the one that got us to the new Muscle Shoals Sound Studios.

I had known the studio's session musicians—the Muscle Shoals Sound Rhythm Section—since the '60s, so I took our demos up to the Shoals and played them first for Jimmy Johnson, who then relayed them to David Hood, Roger Hawkins, and Barry Beckett. David Hood and Roger Hawkins immediately offered to produce us, shop the songs around, and introduce the two of us as a band. If we were picked up by a record company, we would then put a full band together.

Muscle Shoals Sound provided us with motel rooms and free session time. I kinda thought Roger would be playing drums on Don's tunes because he had played on so many hits, but when he heard the unusual drum part that I played on the demo of "Hey Anna," he said he wasn't the drummer for the job—I was. He also wanted to know how I had become so good! What a compliment that was. I told him about how I'd recently been playing seven hours a night and rehearsing on Sundays every week. "That'll do it," he said.

Don and I laid down the basic tracks on three additional tunes, and afterwards, under the direction of David and Roger, several Muscle Shoals musicians added parts to the tracks, including guitarist Duncan Cameron of the Amazing Rhythm Aces.

Don and I anticipated getting a record deal, but after David and Roger shopped the tracks for a period of time, there were no bites. To this day, I don't know why a record company didn't pick us up—those were great songs and superb tracks.

I still wanted to continue playing live, so I got together with bassist Tommy Gardner from the Bobby Whitlock Band, Barry Anderson from the Red Ox, and local guitarist Roy Potter to form the Lifters.

We had heard of a new club being opened in town at the old downtown train station, but the building had to be gutted and renovated. Needing immediate income, Barry and I signed on for construction work, which turned out to be a good thing. While working, we would talk to the owner and manager about our new band and how we were ready to open their club. We could audition for the job, but there was a catch. It was 1980 and a big Texas music and fashion fad had just taken hold. The club was going to be called J. R.'s Crystal Palace, with a Texas theme, including a mechanical bucking-bull machine right inside. They wanted Texas and country music, and we had been rehearsing rock, R & B, and blues. We got to work learning Texas and country music, auditioned, and got the job playing four sets a night, Wednesday through Saturday. J. R.'s soon became the most popular club in town and was packed nightly. A couple of weekends during the fall I helped them to get in Delbert McClinton to play alternating sets with us.

It didn't take long for the Texas fad to die, and so did the club. The Lifters would have to hit the road, playing locally when possible, but I wasn't keen on going on the road again. One night while playing in Tuscaloosa at a popular bikers' club called the Chukker, a local guitarist named Joe Terry sat in with us. I knew his name from his connection to Alabama Public Television, and after the gig, I asked him about work with their production facility on the University of Alabama campus.

It was 1981, and I decided that I needed to put my diploma to use and get a real job with benefits and a retirement plan. I had used the G.I. Bill to earn my BA degree in broadcasting and film between tours with all those bands. Joe was kind enough to refer me to the appropriate people at the production facility.

After talking to the production director, I was offered a job with Alabama Public Television as an assistant crew supervisor. I steadily made my way up the ranks to crew supervisor, assistant operations technician, and finally producer and director, but my love for music didn't stop there. The first show I produced was on Delbert McClinton, and the second was produced with Joe Terry on the history of Muscle Shoals Music.

My love for playing music didn't stop, either. Not long after being employed at APT, Joe Terry and I put a band together and began playing at a new club in town called Two Ladies. We played Wednesday through Saturday, four or five sets a night. Getting off at 2 or 3 A.M., I would get a few hours of sleep until 6:45 and be at work by 8:00 in the morning. I would come back home at 5:30, nap until 7:30, and be back playing at 9:00. This went on for a year and a half. It was grueling, but the money from both jobs was great.

After this gig played itself out, Joe and I continued playing with various musicians. We called ourselves the Lifters, even though I was the only original member left. My dentist, Rush Smith, who was a good guitarist, played with us. It was Rush's first band, and he was so excited about playing live. We played many venues until Rush had to leave due to his dental practice responsibilities, and then Joe and I quit playing music for a while.

That lasted until the night Joe wandered into a bowling alley bar and heard a local band with two outstanding horn players, Mark Jackson and Ben McCoy, and a fabulous bass player, Milton Davis.

The next day, Joe told me about these guys and said, "Why don't we steal them?" And that's what we did. A new and unusual group was formed with a guitarist, bass player, and drummer plus a sax and trombone horn section. We called ourselves Apollo and the Death Horns, and this was one of the most blasting five-piece groups I had ever played with. Every rehearsal and gig was an absolute pleasure. Apollo and the Death Horns ceased to exist when three of the members accepted jobs in their chosen professions in other cities...everyone but Joe and me. We stayed on as a producers and directors at the Center for Public Television.

In 1987, I married a lady from Tuscaloosa, Katherine Anne Finlay, and in June of 1988, she and I became parents when our first son, Braxton, was born. Two years later, in November 1990, our second son, Nathan, came into the world. I hung up playing honkytonks and set out to raise my two boys, but I continued to play on several of my old friends' recording sessions.

As Dr. Jim Salem once told me, "Have your bags packed and be on the right street corner at the right time when the right bus comes along." Unexpectedly, that bus was going to come around again one more time for me—and what an unexpected and phenomenal ride it turned out to be.

37

Back with Brother Gregg

It was early fall of 2014, and March McCrory, my long-time great friend, told me that the Allman Brothers Band was scheduled to play their final concert in New York City in October. Her proposal was that if I secured backstage passes, then she would foot the bill for our excursion, and I took her up on it.

I contacted Michael Lehman, Gregg's manager, and told him of our plans to surprise Gregg at the last ABB performance and asked for the appropriate backstage passes. Michael made the arrangements, and we were ready to proceed with our plans. March and I left Tuscaloosa for New York in the very early morning of the day before the concert—the surprise was on!

I hadn't been to NYC in years. In fact, the last time I was there was when Sailcat played Carnegie Hall. The taxi driver spoke broken English and charged us an arm and a leg for the hectic ride from LaGuardia to our hotel, but we were there! After walking blocks and blocks to find a reasonably priced dinner, March ended up spending a fortune for our first simple meal. The nightly expense for a closet-sized hotel room was also through the roof. The cost, confusion, and misery of big city life hadn't changed.

I was beginning to think March had negotiated a bad deal by exchanging backstage passes for the cost of the trip (and we were going to be here for four days), but she was still ecstatic that she was finally going to meet Gregg *and* attend the Allman Brothers Band's last show, so that was OK. We turned in early so we would be fresh for the next day's concert.

It doesn't matter how many times you are rewarded with backstage passes, it's always a hassle getting through the huge crowd outside, locating the correct backstage door, and connecting with the right person who's holding your legitimate credentials. Even with backstage passes, there still remained the rigorous process of getting to Gregg's dressing room, which proved to be more difficult than getting into the Oval Office to meet the president! March and I were finally directed to an old, small theater elevator which would take us up to another level. When I exited the elevator door, Gregg and I were staring at each other face-to-face. He quickly broke into a wide grin, and I knew that the surprise had been pulled off!

We hugged and couldn't stop laughing about the surprise. Gregg's fiancée, Shannon, and his daughter Layla were also in the dressing room. Gregg and I soon began to recall all the mischief that we had been involved in back in the Greenwich Village days of the Allman Joys. He was very animated as he told Shannon and Layla about the Allman Joys and the Blues Magoos making smoke bombs at the Albert Hotel. His laughter was so loud that it must have carried all through the back of the theater.

At one point during our conversation, I told him that I had started writing about my time with the Allman Joys. Gregg's interest and fascination about the stories I had written grew as I reminded him of our early escapades. He didn't remember some of our adventures at first, but as I elaborated, he began to recall them, and he would let out a huge laugh!

Gregg suddenly said, "Hey, Billy! Why don't we write a book about the early Allmans?" That was the concept or title that he kept calling the proposed project—the "early Allmans," not the Allman Joys. His autobiography, *My Cross to Bear*, had been published a few years earlier and was a best seller. He said his publisher would love to have another Allman history book, especially one with behind-the-scenes stories and escapades with Duane during the early days. I added that I also had some rare photos as well.

Afterwards, while Gregg was touring with the Gregg Allman Band, my youngest son, Nathan, and I kept polishing up my manuscript about the Allman Joys. After we had a fairly well-edited version, Nathan had two copies printed and nicely bound: one for Gregg and one for us.

In June 2015, Gregg invited me over to his place in Savannah, which I presumed was going to be a book-writing visit. I was temporarily without wheels because my oldest son, Braxton, had accidentally totaled my car, so up stepped Nathan, who offered to ferry me over to Savannah in his nice, comfortable GMC truck.

I guess Gregg was anxious about our visit because he kept sending texts while we were traveling, inquiring about where we were and figuring the time of our arrival. We finally reached the security gate at the entrance to his expansive neighborhood and entered the code Gregg provided. We pulled up to the next gate, which was the entrance to the long and winding driveway to his home. The driveway was lined with beautiful native palms and dense, manicured tropical foliage that hid his home from the road. We drove up to the front door, and Gregg and Shannon greeted us with hugs and smiles. I immediately presented him with one of the binders that contained my manuscript on the Allman Joys.

The first night, Nathan and I were treated to a wonderful steak dinner, and every day we were fed like royalty. We each had our own bedroom upstairs. My room featured pictures of Duane and Gregg when they were very young along with pictures of Ms. Allman, who was affectionately called Jerry by family and friends. Jerry had recently passed away, which was one more tragic event in Gregg's life. She had been so supportive of Duane's and Gregg's musical career.

Nothing was mentioned about writing the first evening. Nothing was mentioned the next morning either, as Gregg proudly showed us his custom cars and bikes. He took us on a golf cart ride to view the neighborhood and the water around his home, which also had a very impressive pier and boathouse. On day three, I brought up the subject of writing again, so Gregg got out a recording device and the two of us began telling stories which I had already written about. After that short writing/recording session, we used up the day as usual, hanging around his home and listening to music. The visit was nice for spending quality time together, and the food was fantastic, but we had put only an hour into recalling a couple of the Allman Joys' adventures. I was a bit disappointed because when we had spoken on the phone, I got the impression that most of this trip would be taken up with organizing and writing some of the proposed book, but that didn't happen.

During the visit, I failed to notice that Gregg might already be suffering some side effects from an illness I wasn't yet aware of. I also didn't recognize that his enjoyment of spending more time than usual with a long-time friend was vastly more important than my selfish objective of writing a book because Gregg knew something that I didn't.

Before we left, Gregg sincerely asked, "Billy, how are things really going for you?"

I replied, "Gregg, everything's fine, but I've been kind of lonely. I live alone and don't have any visitors, except occasionally from my sons. This visit with you and Shannon, and also having Nathan around, has really brought me out of my doldrums."

Gregg then said, "You need to come out on tour with me. You won't be lonely out there. There are more beautiful ladies than you can shake a stick at."

I came back, "Are you serious?"

Gregg replied, "Yeah—you can sleep right in front of my compartment on the tour bus. I don't have a spot in the band for you right now, but I really want you back out on the road. Think about it."

With my head spinning, I told my friend that I certainly would.

As Nathan and I were getting in the truck to leave, Gregg came running out and handed me a big plastic bag of the incredible pot that we all had been smoking. Nathan and I just looked at each other stunned. I asked, "What do we owe you for this?"

Gregg simply smiled and said, "Aww, man, you don't owe me anything. People are always giving me tons of this stuff free. I don't drink anymore, dare not do hard drugs, and don't smoke cigarettes, but I will take a toke of this occasionally. Hell, we'll be touring states where it's legal now."

With his generous goodbye, we drove off, wordless and lost in thought.

38

On Tour with the Gregg Allman Band

Once back home, Gregg and I talked frequently on the phone over the next few months. Then one day he called and said, "Hey, Novice. My tour manager is lining up plane tickets for you to join the tour in Portland, Maine, on August 17th. You still wanna come out with me?"

I was blown away, just like I was when Duane and Gregg first asked me to play in the Allman Joys almost fifty years earlier. I instantly replied, "Are you kidding? I'd love to come out with you!"

Five decades after first being on the road with Duane and Gregg Allman, I was on tour with Gregg again. As Gregg had indicated on the phone, his tour manager provided me with the flight information, and I was told tickets would be waiting for me at the Birmingham Airport Terminal. Hey, that sounded like a replay of what Gregg and Duane had done for me all those years before.

My son Nathan gave me a ride up to the Birmingham airport, which is sixty miles from Tuscaloosa. My flight left very early in the morning, so I had decided to stay overnight at a motel next to the airport. That way I wouldn't miss my flight and Nathan wouldn't have to get up to drive me to Birmingham.

Well, I turned in early since I was getting up at the crack of dawn. I called the front desk for a wake-up call that would give me time for a shower and a cup of coffee. I don't know who dropped the ball, but I woke up at what I thought was the middle of the night, but when I looked over at the clock, the numbers jumped right out: 5:00 A.M. My plane left in 45 minutes. Damn! No time to jump in the shower or have a cup of coffee. I barely had time to put on the clothes I'd been wearing the day before and get downstairs. The desk clerk made a call, and a van appeared which took me to my airline's drop-off and ticket counter. It must have been my guardian angel who woke me in time to barely catch my flight. I looked like a ragamuffin standing at the ticket counter. I had tied my hair back to help cover up the fact that it hadn't been washed. This was the extent of my grooming for my flight. I was flying to Detroit to make a connection to Maine.

Once I arrived in Detroit, I noticed signs welcoming and directing service members, service retirees, and veterans to a private lounge, so I headed straight for it. The lounge had many comfortable chairs and couches on which a few active members of the armed forces were getting some well-deserved rest. It took me back to when I traveled home on leave when I was in the navy. The lounge had lots of free food, nonalcoholic drinks, free toiletries and washcloths and towels in addition to some very kind attendants. I met several friendly members of the armed forces who were on active duty and veterans like myself who were also taking advantage of this special lounge. It was definitely a five-star waiting area compared to the civilian waiting areas out front, which had none of the amenities provided in the Armed Forces Lounge.

I gave myself a spit bath, put on deodorant and a fresh shirt, and brushed my teeth. I also brushed my hair and tied it back again to try to hide its greasiness because it just wasn't possible to wash my longer hair in a small sink. I had been letting it grow out a little so I would look more like what I thought a Gregg Allman band member might look like. Once I met the band, I saw that I had made a miscalculation. Gregg's band and crew, other than a couple of members, were sporting short hair. Anyway, after sprucing up a little in Detroit, I now felt more like a human being again; at least I didn't stink. The lounge was so comfortable that I felt like I could have made myself right at home and stayed for a few days, but it wasn't comfortable enough to take away from the grand adventure that was waiting for me.

A short time later, I boarded the plane for Portland. When the flight landed, I went to the baggage area, grabbed my luggage, and flagged down a taxi to take me to the hotel.

In all my travels, I had never made it to New England, so the taxi ride was like being on a vacationers' riding tour. Portland had several quaint areas of homes and shops plus a scenic port as well. When I walked into the hotel lobby, I was astounded by what a fine place Gregg was staying in. When I entered my room, I opened the door, and *wow*! It wasn't a room at all! It was a classy suite, not anything like I was expecting. Gregg had told me to call him as soon as I settled in, which I did. He answered, "Welcome to Portland and the tour, Billy."

I gave him a big thank you but followed up with, "Gregg, you didn't have to put me up in such a swanky suite."

Gregg replied, "Yeah, this is a far cry from when we were living at the Albert in the Village way back when, huh? Don't fret, this is no special treatment. The whole band and crew are staying in rooms just as nice. I've come a long way from staying in dumps when the Allman Joys were on the road. So, it sounds like you're pleased with your accommodations?"

I came back with, "How could I not be?!"

Gregg then said, "Well, get your ass on over to my room."

I came back with, "OK, be right there."

I located Gregg's room and knocked, and the door was opened by Gregg's close friend Chank Middleton, who was wearing his long-time dreadlocks and his traditional Bob Marley T-shirt. Chank welcomed me with a big smile and said, "Come on in, Billy."

"Billy" was what both Duane and Gregg had always called me instead of Bill, so I knew that I must be at the right room. Make that the right gigantic suite. Chank opened the door wide, and there was Gregg, sitting on a nice sofa and looking at me with a big smile, too.

He said, "Yeah, Billy—come on in. Glad you made it safely."

Chank and I laughed at the fact that I had been touring with Duane and Gregg two years before he met them in Macon, while I was in the service. Gregg told me that I was the oldest member in the band and crew except for him. I felt that we were real partners after that revelation. We could talk about subjects that were beyond the scope of the younger guys. I immediately thanked Gregg for the plane ticket, the incredible room, and this opportunity to tour with him. Gregg simply said, "Aww, Billy, don't sweat the small stuff."

After chatting for a while, Chank handed me a Gregg Allman Band August and September 2015 tour guide, which contained everything the band and crew would need to know. I took a quick look at the itinerary.

Thursday, August 13th: Band and Crew fly into Scranton, PA

Friday, August 14th: Constellation Brands P.A.C., Scranton, PA

August 15th–17th: Off. Portland, ME

Tuesday, August 18th: Maine State Pier, Portland, ME

Wednesday, August 19th: Blue Hills Bank Pavilion, Boston, MA

Thursday, August 20th: Off. Rochester, NY

Friday, August 21st: Constellation Brands P.A.C., Canandaigua, NY

Saturday, August 22nd: Bank of N.H. Pavilion/Meadowbrook, Gilford, NH

August 23rd–24th: Off. Alexandria, VA

Tuesday, August 25th: The Birchmere, Alexandria, VA

Wednesday, August 26th: The Birchmere, Alexandria, VA

Thursday, August 27th: Off. Holmdel, NJ

Friday, August 28th: PNC Bank Arts Center, Holmdel, NJ

Saturday, August 29th: Nikon at Jones Beach, Wantagh, NY

Sunday, August 30th: The Borgata, Atlantic City, NJ

Monday, August 31st: Off. Cary, NC

Tuesday, September 1st: Koko Booth Amphitheatre, Cary, NC

Wednesday, September 2nd: Pier Six Pavilion, Baltimore, MD

Thursday, September 3rd: Off. Albany, NY

Friday, September 4th: Saratoga P.A.C, Saratoga, NY

Saturday, September 5th: Hershey Stadium, Hershey, PA

Sunday, September 6th: Band and Crew Fly Home

After we reminisced for a bit longer, talking and laughing until we hurt, I told them about almost missing my plane in Birmingham without a shower and that I really needed to get cleaned up.

Gregg asked, "Hey, can you meet Chank and me for dinner downstairs in the restaurant in an hour?" I accepted his offer and then returned to my room to shower and change clothes. I met them on time at the hotel's swanky restaurant. The items on the menu were all five-star dishes with five-star prices. Gregg told me, "Listen, Billy, I want you to get anything that your heart desires."

My eyes quickly turned to the Maine lobster. I hesitantly asked, "Can I have the lobster?" I'd never been to Maine before and had always wanted to eat a truly fresh Maine lobster. I told Gregg that I would be paying for it.

"Go for it, Billy, and I won't hear any more nonsense about you paying for anything. You're my guest. I don't think I'm gonna go broke over one little ole lobster. Get two of them if you want." The next thing Gregg said really threw me for a loop: "Billy, I wish we could have hired you when you got out of the service. Your playing was so right for Duane and me."

I just sat there in a daze, totally speechless. There was nothing I could think of to say. What a compliment, half a century later.

When the food was brought out, my eyes must have bugged out a foot. I had never seen such a huge, beautiful lobster in my life; it actually filled a very large platter. No one in the restaurant seemed to recognize Gregg, but the waitress must have and then passed it on to the chef. We tried to talk while making our way through these huge, incredible dinners. After the three of us had finished, we said our goodnights and headed back to our sleeping quarters because all we were going to be able to do for the rest of the night was lie down.

The next day, the tour manager, David "Vid" Sutherland, introduced me to the two tour buses that the Gregg Allman Band and crew traveled in, with one bus for the band and one for the crew. Everyone had flown to the location of the first show, and each was scheduled to fly back home after the last performance of the tour. But in between, all personnel moved on the tour buses. Vid

Sutherland pointed out my sleeping area on the band bus along with the amenities, which included a kitchen with a refrigerator and microwave, a lounging area with televisions where the band hung out when not sleeping, and, of course, the bathroom. It was emphasized that there was no pooping in the bus toilets, and that worried me a little. What if there was an unplanned emergency? All our luggage was stored in compartments under the bus.

Since we were off for two days before the concert, I had plenty of time to walk around Portland, eat some more Maine seafood, and shop. This was September, and it was very warm. I couldn't imagine what this place looked like in January. Brrrrrrrr!

THE BAND
Gregg Allman: Hammond B-3, Lead Vocals/Guitar
Scott Sharrard: Guitar
Steve Potts: Drums
Marc Quinones: Percussion
Ron Johnson: Bass
Peter Levin: Keys
Jay Collins: Sax (Tenor/Bari)
Art Edmaiston: Sax (Tenor/Bari)
Marc Franklin: Trumpet

THE CREW
David Sutherland: Tour Manager
Earl McCoy: Production Manager/F.O.H Sound
Earl Francis: Lighting Director
Rachel Turner: Stage Technician
Martin Gelharr: Stage Technician
Josh Bennett: Stage Technician
Chank Middleton: P.A., Gregg Allman
Michael Gallun: Monitor Engineer
Chris Samardizch: Projection
Bo Ives: Merchandising
Jeff Duncan: Truck Driver

Chris Chester: Bus Driver
Jim Lee: Bus Driver

The night of the concert, Gregg first took the stage alone and walked to center stage. He put his hands together in a prayer position and bowed numerous times to a wild, screaming audience. Then he walked over to the B-3 organ as the rest of the band came on, again to a loud applause.

Gregg counted the first song off, and they all took off with the Allman Brothers Band's signature first tune, "Statesboro Blues," during which the crowd's yelling, screaming, and applauding sounded like it was going to take the roof off the hall. They continued through the show with both new Gregg Allman songs that had been on his solo albums mixed with some of the Allman Brothers Band's popular tunes, with each selection receiving a huge ovation. Of course, after the last tune, Gregg bowed and the band left the stage, only to be called back for encores. It was a very successful show.

At the end of the show, we all loaded onto the buses. Gregg introduced me to the band as we all were lounging in the TV area. After a bit, I heard a voice from Gregg's compartment yell, "Hey, Billy, come on back here with me." I went back to his private room. Instead of a private bunk, Gregg had a living compartment in the rear of the bus equipped with a double bed, a dining booth which would seat three people, his own built-in cooler, and plenty of cabinets for storing his clothes and other various items. His cooler was filled with Fiji bottled water...that's it. Gregg didn't drink alcohol or sodas, and hadn't for years, ever since his last seventy-nine-day stay in rehab. I think he needed a friend of his age to talk to. Being so famous and older than his band and crew, it seemed like no one felt comfortable talking with him but me, his old buddy, the "Novice." I witnessed that night that the old saying "It's lonely at the top" was very true. After we were completely worn out from hysterically laughing at all the old stories, musician friends, and adventures, I had to hit my rack. I know that our time together was good medicine for both of us.

During the night, I had to take a leak and noticed Gregg's lights were still on. I didn't think much about it at the time, but the same scene repeated itself the next night, so I stuck my head in and asked him why he wasn't getting some shut-eye. He pointed at the floor. After a short delay, I asked, "What?"

"Novice, listen to that engine."

The expression on my face must have been asking again, "What do you mean?"

Gregg replied, "Isn't that engine loud to you? Shit, I can't sleep while lying in bed over this loud diesel engine. The compartment back here is nice and private, but I wish it was not directly over this god-awful engine."

I reminded him, "When all of us in the Allman Joys had to sleep while sitting up as we traveled at night in the Chevy wagon, you had no problem sleeping."

Gregg replied, "That's because the Chevy's engine was way up front from the back seat and not right under me. The Chevy wagon's engine was nowhere as loud as this fuckin' bus engine. Besides this diesel engine being so loud under me, there's the damn shifting of a hundred gears, too. Combine both, and you have me wide awake every night."

For this entire tour, Gregg stayed awake in his private compartment while the rest of us slept soundly in our bunks. He caught up on his sleep during the day once we arrived at our next hotel. No wonder he looked so tired when we would get off the bus at our hotel every day.

I slept very well while riding down the highway in the tour bus. The minor "rocking and rolling" of the bus as we traveled had the opposite effect on me. I slept like a baby, but then I didn't have to sleep over the engine. Also, I had been lonely from time to time back home in my small apartment because I never had any company. All my good friends lived in another town or city, so traveling with Gregg, my new musician friends, the tour manager, and bus driver made it possible for me to have "stay over" company every night. Although, if I had to stay with this "overnight company" on a permanent basis, I'm sure that I would get tired of being on this tour bus with ten other guys, and the bus would keep getting smaller and smaller.

Gregg had invited the Doobie Brothers to play on most of the tour: the Gregg Allman Band and the Doobie Brothers—a strong double bill indeed!

39

The Road Goes On...

The previous spring, I had attended a concert in Dothan, Alabama, featuring a band headed up by my old friend Paul Hornsby. A reception had been held in Macon the night before the concert, and there I met a nice young lady named Angie. After the reception, Angie invited me to go to a party featuring several local bands, and I accepted. As the night went by, I discovered we had very similar tastes in music. During the party, this new friendship evolved to where it was like we had been friends for years instead of hours. I had to leave the party early because my friends had me on a rigid, two-day schedule, so I flagged a taxi while thinking about the nice memory I had just made. But it turned into more than that. Angie and I continued to text each other occasionally, and in one exchange, I mentioned that I was going on tour to hang with Gregg and his band. She asked about our schedule and was fascinated by all the cities and venues that we would be working.

A few hours before the Boston concert, my hotel room phone rang. Who would have ever thought? It was Angie on the phone. What an unexpected surprise! I asked her how it was going down in Georgia, and then came a bigger surprise: she was checking in downstairs at the same hotel where we were staying. Holy moly! Next, I stupidly asked how she had found us. Laughing, she told me that our touring schedule, complete with hotels, was easy to look up online. Duh...double stupid me. Nevertheless, I was thrilled that she was here.

After a brief pause on my end as I was processing what to say next, she broke the silence and asked, with a little tongue-in-cheek sarcasm, "Well, are you going to take me to lunch or what? Why don't we go down to Boston Harbor? I hear that they might have a Long John Silver's down there." Then we both started insanely laughing at each other, and the Boston Seafood quest was on.

After a scavenger hunt, we agreed on a very nice place over-looking the harbor. Later, we rode with Gregg in his limo to the concert venue. Just as she and I had connected that night back in Macon, she and Gregg hit it off as if they had known each other forever. Angie had the unique ability to fit in wherever she went and with whomever she was around, and I think Gregg admired her for not being starstruck around him. A good time was had in Boston, and it was a shame we had to leave town right after the concert. Angie and I said our goodbyes, and the tour buses set off down the road. After the band wound down with some laughs in the living room area of the bus, we all slipped into our bunks.

The next big surprise would be mine, for my brother, Dr. Terry Connell. Terry called me and asked if I was still in touch with Gregg. If so, he wondered if I could possibly do him a favor by con-tacting him and asking if he could arrange passes or tickets for Terry and his wife to see the Gregg Allman Band's concert in Buffalo. I didn't let on to how close Gregg and I had remained over the years, and I didn't dare tell him that I would be accompanying Gregg on this tour; I just told him that I would look into it.

It would be a couple of weeks before Gregg would be perform-ing in Canandaigua, New York, which was next door to Terry's home in Buffalo. Terry hadn't seen Gregg since Duane, Gregg, and the Allman Joys crashed at my parents' home when Terry was just ten or eleven years old.

After not hearing from me for a few days, Terry called back to say that he had bought regular seats because the show was selling out, and he didn't want to miss the show. I still didn't tell him that I was going to be there. I hadn't seen my brother in ten years. Man, this was going to be the ultimate setup and surprise for him.

When we got to the amphitheater where the concert was being held, Vid told me that he had located Terry and his wife's assigned seats. Before Gregg was to come on, I took his backstage passes and made my way up to their seats. I walked around behind them, leaned over, and right in his ear asked, in a disguised voice, "Aren't you Dr. Terry Connell?"

My hair was much longer and much grayer than when he had last seen me a decade earlier. He turned around and said, "Yes, sir, I am."

I just stared at him until this strange look came over his face. Momentarily, he asked, "Bill?"

I replied, "You got it, bro."

He was blown away! I'll never forget the look on his face. I was supposed to be more than a thousand miles away, and suddenly, here we were, face-to-face.

I took them backstage, where Gregg spoke with us for a good while before going onstage. They had pictures made together, and it was the spectacular surprise that I had envisioned.

We left immediately after the concert and traveled to Gilford, New Hampshire. The backstage food provided at this site would not be upstaged by any of the other venues that we would hit on this New England tour. Upon entering the food tent, one was first presented with an old antique boat filled to the brim with a huge variety of fresh, iced-down shellfish. Next, there were several locations featuring renowned chefs preparing an unbelievable variety of fresh, hot seafood dishes as you watched. All afternoon attendants kept serving up a bounty of shelled lobster tails which I would snack on. The food court stayed open all afternoon and night as chefs continuously cooked. For me, they could have had only one dish: lobster, lobster, and more lobster. The food under this tent was unbelievable!

While on this East Coast tour, I decided to get in touch with my old bandmate and lifelong friend Fred Styles. I knew that he would love seeing both Gregg and me together again since Fred had promoted and booked beaucoup gigs for the Allman Joys.

Fred and I had stayed in touch through the years even though for forty years we were more than a thousand miles apart. He and his wife had recently moved from the hectic daily life of New York City to Roanoke, Virginia. I called him a few days before Gregg's band would be performing in nearby Alexandria, Virginia, and when he heard that we'd be in the area, neither wild horses, a record-breaking blizzard, or the Plague could have kept him away. The band was going to have two days off in Alexandria, so that would give us time to catch up and reminisce about the old days.

On our first day in Alexandria, Gregg had to find a Western Union location to wire some money. The driver showed up in a nice Cadillac SUV limo. I'd never seen one of these models before, but it was swank all the way. Gregg told the driver to take us to a Western Union. Well, the unfortunate driver drove to a half dozen places that didn't have a Western Union, and finally Gregg went ballistic.

"Man, I thought you were a professional driver. Why don't you know where a simple Western Union is?" I got on my phone and instantly found a map to get us to the closest one. I then guided the driver to the location. Gregg looked at me and rolled his eyes.

After Gregg made his transaction and got back in the limo, I began to humorously mention that my pants were falling down because I had lost some weight. As we passed a large Target store, Gregg commanded the driver to pull in. Gregg said, "We gonna get you a belt, Novice."

We walked through the doors, and in an instant I realized how fearful Gregg was of being recognized in public. He was always just plain old Gregg to me. I had visited Gregg at his home and in entertainment venues, but this was the first time that I had been with him when he was in the general public. His next statement drove the point home when he said, "Novice, I've never been in a Target before."

Wow! I was suddenly walking in his shoes and realized that he might not have been out of his own bubble for years. He just lived life at his fabulous home in Savannah, at recording studios, in his hotel room, onstage, or sneaking into a back table at a hotel restaurant when on tour. Now I better understood why I saw new jeans being delivered to his home rather than purchased in department stores.

Funny thing was that upon entering Target, he was like a kid in a candy store. He began shopping and loved it! His first stop was the men's lounging-pants section, but he was only window shopping.

It was ironic, and maybe a revelation for him, that not a single soul recognized him in Target. During this outing, his fear of being among the public might have lessened and opened up everyday human activities for him—and only because he wanted to buy me a belt.

It was time to check out, and still nobody had recognized him. Gregg fiddled with his phone while in line and didn't notice that it was his turn to check out at the register. Damn, how long had it been since he stood in a department store line? I just kept laughing, but under my breath. The whole Target experience was like going to the circus with Gregg; the crowd behind him was getting a little annoyed at his check out incompetence. Hey, guys, don't you recognize who this fumbling dude is? Nope. They still didn't recognize him.

When I went to pay for my belt, Gregg grabbed it and said, "Don't sweat the small stuff, Novice. I got it." Then Gregg looked me straight in the face, and he raised his voice, but in a humorous way, and said, "Novice, this belt isn't even real leather!"

This almost brought the crowd behind us into a full-blown rage. He simply ignored the anger of the people behind us in line and ordered me to "go get you a real leather belt, Novice."

Once in the belt department, which was at the back of the store, I rushed, rushed, and rushed, violently searching for a real leather belt. At this point, I was sure those John Q. Public people in line wanted Gregg hung up in the meat department.

Wouldn't you know it: Target didn't have one single real leather belt. I ran to the register and screamed, "Gregg, they don't have any real leather belts!" As the boiling gang behind us released steam out their ears, he reluctantly bought the original belt for me anyway, saying, "Novice, we still gotta find you a real leather belt." Sometime later, I threw the "not a real leather belt" to a guy in a back alley behind a concert hall. He yelled back, "Thanks for the leather belt!"

We got back to the hotel, and as Gregg and I were waiting for an elevator, guess who walked up? It was Angie! Gregg and I both stared at each other as if asking the same question: "What? Again?!"

Angie broke the silence saying that she had enjoyed being with us in Boston so much that she decided to join us again in Alexandria. Of course, she had booked a room at the hotel where we were staying, which was good news. She stayed with us for the three days we were there, and, again, her company was a welcomed surprise. She was a home gal, a true Georgia lady who was a pleasure to spend time with. We took a historical tour of old town Alexandria with Fred Styles and his wife, Peggy. Gregg asked me if we were romancing; he was back asking the same type of questions he'd have asked in the old days. Gregg was "old-school" meddling. I just left him wondering, but he kept on because it killed him not to know. Gregg was like, "C'mon, son, go for it. She's very attractive, and what about that caboose? She ain't following you around the country for a free burger."

One thing I found out a few years later was that Gregg and Fred had spent some time together, just hanging and talking like old friends do. At one point, a very upbeat Gregg had said to him, "Fred, I've finally got the band I've always wanted. I love it, man. I've even got a horn section!" Then Gregg said this: "You know, Fred, I'm hoping that at some point Bill can come back as my drummer. He'd be perfect for this band."

I was absolutely floored when Fred told me this. Gregg had never said a word to me about it before he died. Hearing those words—even after the fact—meant the world to me, and it's something I'll never forget.

Traveling to dozens of different venues, cities, and states and spending time with Gregg and his band was the most exciting and fulfilling thing that had happened to me in years. Back while my youngest son, Nathan, and I were visiting him in Savannah, Gregg had asked me how I was doing, and I always answered, "OK." Later, he took me aside and stared me down until I knew he was very serious and demanding the truth.

"How are you really doing, Billy?" This was my old friend asking. I couldn't escape his true concern. There was no stumping a Road Scholar like Gregg. He got the answer he expected: "Lonely."

My experience of being on tour with Gregg and not being lonely was nearing an end; I couldn't stop thinking about being a bored homeboy again. I knew that he knew that he had given me life again, but in a few days, I would awaken from this beautiful dream.

While freshening up for the show in Alexandria, I had an epiphany. Instantly, and without reluctance, I called Gregg's room. When he answered, I jumped in before he could even say hello with my big idea.

"Gregg, is there a chance in hell that you could find a job for me with your touring company? It doesn't matter what—I just want to stay out here working with you, the band, and crew. This is what I've always wanted to do for years. You know that's true by seeing the happiness on my face. You won't find me frowning while working with my old pal out here. The impression that you and Duane left me with so many years ago, beginning when we were so young, will never diminish."

Gregg briefly interrupted: "Billy, there haven't been many musician friends that Duane and I would rather have been playing with than you. You have always been our favorite pick for the drummer who best fit our kind of music, and you and I were both frantically running from the draft demon together. We thought all along that it should have been you who would be playing drums with us forever. When you got drafted it broke our hearts."

I came in, "Buddy, it's so obvious that all of you are having such a great time entertaining your audience while playing such a demanding schedule with purpose. They really love you and your tunes. You and your bands' combined positive attitude and musicianship not only sticks with your audience, but it has also rubbed off on me; it's like tar that won't ever wear off. I've only been traveling on your tour for a few days, but the bonds of the Gregg Allman Band will never wear off my mind and body. I'm so glad that you have finally found your perfect solo band. Can you find me a seat on this train? I'll give 110 percent."

Gregg replied, "Well, let me see what I can do. I like having my old friend around, too."

A couple of hours later, Gregg called my room and said, "I've talked to Vid Sutherland, and he wants to interview you in about an hour. He'll see what can be arranged."

My heart went to my throat when I heard that they were actually considering a spot for me; just their consideration gave my heart a boost. After the longest hour of my life, I met with Vid. He asked me a lot of questions and finally said, "Gregg and I will find something for you to do if you're really serious about this, but I'm not gonna have you pulling heavy cables."

I found myself both glad that I had made the call to Gregg and excited to rejoin the music business with my main man, Gregg, five decades after I first worked with him and Duane. I went on a long walk around Alexandria to process what just happened. It felt like I just might—and I say might—be starting one of the most exciting parts of my life.

A couple of hours later, Vid called to say that I was going to be working with the band as his new assistant and that in the morning he would fill me in on my duties. Hot damn and slap me silly!

The next morning, Vid and I got together, and he began giving me assignments that I'd be responsible for. My photo ID stated "Bill Connell, Gregg Allman Band Assistant." So now it was not just a short visit, but a full-time job. It was more than a dream come true because I had never imagined that I would fall into a job again with Gregg. Las Vegas couldn't have predicted that! Goodness gracious and holy shit—I was now working for the Gregg Allman Band!

Here's how twenty-four hours in my typical day would go: the buses and eighteen-wheelers carrying the equipment would arrive in the early morning (still dark or sunrise) at the location of the concert. Hotel keys would be laid out on the buses' galley/kitchen tables with our individual names on them. Each of us had a private room at the location of each show, and I might be in my room from two to six hours, unless it was an off day. I remember staying in one room for just two hours that was advertised for $900 a night. That was $450 an hour for my shower, shave, and coffee.

After all the equipment was unloaded, I would set up the tour manager's computer, printer, and other equipment and supplies, which he used to organize and document the show activities. Then I would help the graphics personnel set up their equipment, projectors, and computers, including the suspension of the huge screen behind the band used to display videos and still photos during the concert.

At each venue, I was responsible for determining the most efficient routes to guide everyone to their designated areas, and I'd placed signs throughout the maze of hallways to direct them accordingly. The routes at each venue changed nightly, and these concert halls were enormous. One might wander around for quite some time to get to their appropriate areas if these signs weren't easy to follow.

I can't help but think about that scene in the movie *This Is Spinal Tap* when the band was at a venue with no signs, so they just kept going from dead end to dead end and in circles in the auditorium's basement trying to find the stage entrance, all while screaming loudly, "Rock and roll, rock and roll!" Too funny! If you haven't seen Rob Reiner's *Spinal Tap*, pick it up, and grab tissues—a lot of tissues—because you'll need them for laughing yourself to tears.

I had to inventory all the food and drinks, nonalcoholic and alcoholic, and other required material that was written into the artists' rider contract. Concert promoters were required to provide each item on the contract, and here's a small example of what might be required in the dressing rooms and on the buses for travel between venues:

* various sliced lunch meats
* condiments (sliced tomatoes, various sliced cheeses, lettuce, mayo, mustard)
* various sliced bread and crackers
* assorted fresh fruit

* salsas, humus, guacamole
* various chips and tortillas and Doritos chips
* various nuts
* various selections of beer in cases
* white and red wines
* cases upon cases of Fiji Water (Gregg's only beverage)

Everything not consumed backstage, I carried to the two buses and truck. In addition, the rider required that a hot meal be served to everyone in our caravan a couple of hours before the concert. This would be made up of several entrees and sides with all the trimmings.

No one went hungry except me. After seeing a photo of Gregg and a big fat me, I started a Paleo diet at the beginning of the first tour and lost thirty-one pounds in six months. I ate meats, vegetables, and fruits and no sugar, alcohol, starches, grains, fast food, or processed food. I also walked when I had a chance. I wore a distance-tracking bracelet that my buddy Fred Styles mailed to me after hearing of my weight-loss crusade, and it turned out that daily I walked six or seven miles just doing my job at each venue. The weight fell off, but, man, those caterers had some magnificent deserts...Damn!

I made sure the buses got loaded with a sufficient amount of ice in their various built-in coolers for the trip to the next venue. The bus refrigerators were filled with food, so all drinks had to be iced down in the coolers in the front and back of each bus.

We had a performance in Cary, North Carolina, and several of the guys in the band heard about a fantastic barbecue place in town. We called an Uber driver and headed to the restaurant, and as we drove up, we could see that was just a hole-in-the-wall. Not to be deterred, we entered the establishment, and it smelled of the greatest barbecue ever. Much to our surprise, there at a back table was Gregg, sitting with Marc Quinones, the group's percussionist. The four of us joined them just as the waiter, who was also the owner, came out with a large platter of different-flavored wings. Gregg then began ordering platters of everything the cook had. We ate and ate and still had doggie bags to go. One wall of the restaurant was lined with bottles of every barbecue sauce imaginable. I bought the in-house sauce, and it turned out to be superior. So good, but for the life of me, I just can't recall the name of the place!

After Cary, we headed up to Baltimore. I used a couple of my off hours to tour the harbor, which was lined with old ships from the 1700s to the 1900s as well as a submarine from World War II. Baltimore had made a beautiful walk around the harbor and piers, and the concert was held at the impressive Pier Six Pavilion.

We hit a couple of New York State's venues—Albany and Saratoga Springs—before heading to our last concert in Hershey, Pennsylvania. At this concert, the Zac Brown Band was the headliner ahead of the Gregg Allman Band, and it seemed like Zac Brown's recent popularity had gone to his head. He had more tour buses than I could count and a crew of 110. We had twenty-two, including the band. Not long before this time, Gregg had been the headliner and Zac Brown the warm-up act, but the music business is a fickle one. While the Gregg Allman Band was performing, Zac's crew began setting up his stage. This was infuriating and insulting, but we all kept their cool. Zac's crew was beyond rude.

This was the last concert on the New England run, so the next morning, at the Hershey airport, as the band and crew were waiting to board their planes to go back to their respective homes, Gregg corralled me.

"It's nice to be back home touring with me, huh, Billy? See you on the West Coast leg."

A real feeling of belonging came over me, and I certainly was glad to be back touring with my lifelong friend again.

When it was time to tour again, my oldest son, Braxton, took me to Birmingham this time to catch my flight to Reno, Nevada, to meet up with the other Gregg Allman Band members and crew. When I arrived, I found that I would be sharing a limousine with Vid Sutherland and one other crew member. We drove up to Lake Tahoe, which was just up the highway, to meet the rest of the group to start our West Coast tour.

As with many shows, Gregg arranged for a few lucky fans to come backstage and have their photos made with him. All the girls wanted to kiss him, and all the men wanted to shake his hand or hug him. This was highly discouraged by Vid, who was directing the photo shoot.

Gregg changed the order of the songs in every show that we did, but he always started with "Statesboro Blues." That gave the audience an instant connection with Gregg, as this was the song that the Allman Brothers Band always kicked off their shows with. It was also the opening track on the 1971 *At Fillmore East* album, which was the game changer for the group.

The band and crew were made up of the same personnel who were on the New England tour. If it ain't broke, don't fix it.

The venues of the 2015 West Coast and Midwest tour were:

Saturday, October 3rd: Harrah's Lake Tahoe, Lake Tahoe, NV

Sunday, October 4th: Field of Dreams, Sonoma, CA

Monday, October 5th: OFF

Tuesday, October 6th: Belly Up Tavern, Solana Beach, CA

Wednesday, October 7th: Belly Up Tavern, Solana Beach, CA

Thursday, October 8th: OFF

Friday, October 9th: Palms Casino Resort, Las Vegas, NV

Saturday, Sunday, and Monday, October 10th, 11th, 12th: OFF

Tuesday, October 13th: Boulder Theater, Boulder, CO

Wednesday, October 14th: Boulder Theater, Boulder, CO

Thursday, October 15th: OFF

Friday, October 16th: Stiefel Theatre, Salina, KS

Saturday, October 17th: Ameristar Casino, Kansas City, KS

Sunday, October 18th: River City Casino, St. Louis, MO

Monday, October 19th: Band and crew fly home

When I saw that we had several days off before the Boulder performances, I thought it would be a nice gesture to invite March McCrory, the lady who had paid my way to see the Allman Brothers Band's last performance at the Beacon Theatre in 2014, to come spend some time with me in Boulder. She accepted my invite, and we had a grand time touring Boulder, shopping, going out to eat, and, of course, visiting the legal pot shops. Those blew us away and shivered our timbers, and unless you've visited one, it's all too much to describe. We were assigned our own guide and connoisseur who described the hundreds of different selections of pot and edibles (candy and cookies containing marijuana). I told him that pot made me paranoid, and he replied that he had a selection made just for customers like me, so...

The tour was going unbelievably well, and I didn't think anything could stop this train we were on. That is until one night, when Gregg and a few of us went out to dinner after the show and I noticed he just wasn't looking right.

He seemed kind of sickly to me, and I couldn't catch his eye. A little while later, I glanced back over and Gregg was sound asleep. I began to worry when, during the next performance, I noticed that his knees were really swollen. Something clearly wasn't right.

When we had a moment alone the next day, I asked Gregg if everything was OK. He admitted that it wasn't.

"I gotta go to the Mayo Clinic right after the last show," he said, and I really began to worry. I flew out of St. Louis about 5:00 A.M. the next day before I got to see Gregg again. It struck me that St. Louis was where, fifty years earlier, the Allman Joys had been so popular; it truly was a full-circle moment for me.

40

Forever Comes to an End

After Gregg's stay at the Mayo Clinic, we talked and texted back and forth constantly, and he appeared to be getting better. In the spring of 2017, my son Nathan and I went to Savannah and brought Gregg the Allman Joys manuscript. When I got back home, he continued to encourage me to complete my work because he and Duane had loved our time in the Allman Joys.

Then, I received this startling text from Gregg: "Billy, my cancer has gone crazy. Hospice keeps a nurse with me 24/7. I don't know what you want to do with these manuscripts, but me...I'm hanging on to every day I have left with tooth and nail. I guess you just never know when your last day is coming. Love ya, Novice."

A few days later, I was sitting on my couch with my oldest son, Braxton, when the phone rang. I answered, and my doctor and close friend said, "I thought I would call and see how you were doing after receiving the news."

I asked, "What news?"

He said, "Well, I'm sorry to have to tell you, but Gregg has just passed away."

I gave the phone to Braxton because all I could do was lie down and weep.

The next day, Paul Hornsby called from Macon and said that I had a seat reserved in the chapel that Gregg's funeral was being held in. It was the same chapel where I had attended Duane's funeral in 1971. My wonderful friend, March McCrory, offered to drive me over to Georgia. I occasionally wept during the trip, thinking about all the great times that we had together. The funeral was very hard on so many people, including his children, his wife, fellow musicians, and close friends.

That night, there was a gathering at the ABB's old communal home, the Big House, which had been turned into a museum for memorabilia from the Allman Brothers Band, Hour Glass, and the Allman Joys as well as items from Gregg and the other individual members of the group.

There was an open bar, and I got lit. While I was talking to an old buddy from New York City, a lady kept grabbing my hand tightly, but I didn't turn to see who it was, thinking it was another friend. When I finished my conversation, I turned and saw a black-haired woman. I didn't immediately recognize her, so I asked, "And you are...?" She simply answered, "Cher."

I have no idea what was said after that. During my moment of weakness, I picked up that first shot...then another and another; I was shamelessly out of control. An alcoholic can always find a reason to pick up that shot. I was weak, but the hurt afterwards was that Gregg had had the courage to remain sober for years until his death.

I had seen a woman dressed in all black and wearing a large black hat at the funeral, and I knew it must be Cher, even though I couldn't see her face. I had never met Cher, but she must have heard about me. I thought a lot of her at that moment for attending her ex-husband's funeral. That whole day seems like a distant dream now, and I would like to take this opportunity to say, "I'm sorry, Cher, for my behavior on that terribly sad occasion. Please forgive me."

And to my dear brothers in music and life: Gregg and Duane, I truly miss you here on earth, but I'll see you on the other side. Your friend forever...Billy, or "Novice."

I have enjoyed such a fortunate, rewarding, and blessed life. When I first began this journey at the age of twelve, I never imagined that it would lead to so many lasting friendships and extraordinary experiences in the music and entertainment industries and in life itself. Here's what I've learned: Never quit believing in yourself. Never give up. Never underestimate your potential. And never forget...always have your bags packed and be on the right street corner at the right time when the right bus comes along!

Bill Connell
A Discography.

The Allman Joys—*Early Allman*, 1966, 1973.

Sailcat—*Motorcycle Mama,* 1973.

Tommy Stuart—*The Rubberband,* 1975, 1977.

Jim Coker—*Jim Coker*, 1975.

Tommy Stuart—*The Employees*, 1976.

Winter Brothers Band—*The Lost Album*, 1978.

Fred Styles—*Bandcestors*, 2012.

Duane Allman—*Skydog*, 2013.

The Mike Duke Project—*…Took a While*, 2019.

Bill Connell
Publishing Credits.

Wet Willie—"Trust in the Lord," 1974.

Lenny Le Blanc—"Hound Dog Man," 1976.

Wet Willie—"Street Corner Serenade," "One Track Man," "How 'Bout You," "Baby Fat," 1977.

Glen Campbell—"Hound Dog Man," 1978.

Roy Orbison—"Hound Dog Man," 1979.

John Goldsmith—"Doin' the Wrong Thing Right," 1982.

Alien—"Don't Turn Me Away," 1990.

Roy Potter—"Running with a Bad Crowd," Call the Doctor," "She's Just a Dream," 2008.

Special Thanks

Chuck Leavell
John Lynskey
Mark Harrelson
Fred Styles
Jack Leigh
David Hood
Paul Hornsby
Linda Whitlock Dennington
Robbie and Dr. Bony Barrineau
Diane and Dr. Rush Smith
Mabry Smith
Don Tinsley
"Tiger Jack" Garretson
Matt Jaffe
Kris Hughes-Craig
Jackie Sullivan
March McCory
Kirk West
The Allman Brothers Band Museum at the Big House

MUSIC AND THE AMERICAN SOUTH

Michael Buffalo Smith,† *The Road Goes on Forever: Fifty Years of The All-man Brothers Band Music (1969–2019)*, with a Foreword Chuck Leavell

Doug Kershaw, *The Ragin' Cajun: Memoir of a Louisiana Man*, with Cathie Pelletier

Don Reid, *The Music of The Statler Brothers: An Anthology*, with a Fore-word by Bill and Gloria Gaither

Paul Hornsby, *Fix it in the Mix: A Memoir*, with Michael Buffalo Smith†

Ben Wynne, *Something in the Water: A History of Music in Macon, Georgia, 1823-1980*

Willie Perkins, *Diary of a Rock-N-Roll Tour Manager: 2,190 Days and Nights with the South's Premier Rock Band*

Bill Thames, *Paper, Scissors, Rock-N-Roll: Ringo, Duane, & Me*

Bill Connell, *Allman Joy: Keeping the Beat with Duane and Greg Allman*